HYPERION: ON THE FUTURE OF AESTHETICS

VOL. XV, NO. I (WINTER 2022)

WITH A SPECIAL FEATURE ON CATALAN LITERATURE

HYPERION *On the Future of Æsthetics*

Publisher: Contra Mundum Press
Location: New York, London, Melbourne
Editors: Rainer J. Hanshe, Erika Mihálycsa
Design & Layout: Giuseppe Bertolini
Logo: Alessandro Segalini

ISBN 978-1-940625-59-1

CONTRA MUNDUM PRESS gratefully acknowledges the financial support received from institute ramon llull for this issue of *Hyperion: On the Future of Aesthetics*.

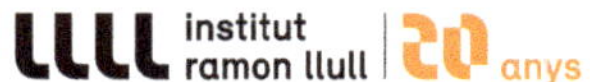

TABLE OF CONTENTS

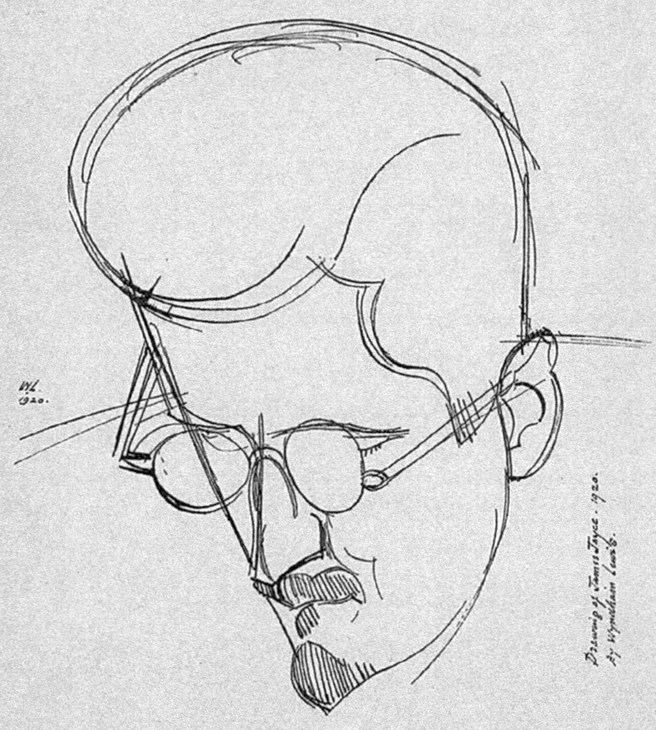

Wyndham Lewis

Ulysses One Hundred Years

FRITZ SENN

All books have their birthdays, even if most of them go unnoticed, except possibly by their authors. Again, Joyce's *Ulysses*, a long narrative in prose, stands out with strident defiance and waywardness. It bestrode the literary scene with spite and presumption and – its price notwithstanding – became notorious overnight. It was instantly banned in English speaking countries until 1933 when an American Judge, Woolsey, cleared it of the charge of obscenity: emetic, it may be, yes, in his pronouncement, but in no way aphrodisiac. Its partial prepublication had a criminal record when a court decision stopped the *Little Review* in 1921.

Within a century, *Ulysses* has become domesticated as a classic, some of its harm taken out. Yet more than every other book it is connected with, of all things! reading: "Have you read it?" has become a standard, inept question. It is still surrounded by an aura.

School requirements apart, nobody *has* to read it. It should be marketed, not as an obligation, but an opportunity, an adventure. After a century, we can probably no longer recapture its impact of 1922. A stab is made here at its pristine elusive whatness, with the handicap of hindsight. At its time, readers compared it to a thunderstorm, so at least I was told by Carola Giedion-Welcker, who first encountered it in 1928, and it changed her life. For many, the book was an outrage or a cultural challenge. In 1969, the first Dutch translation by John Vandenbergh was accompanied with a bumper sticker in the same dark blue as the book's cover: "*Ik heb Ulysses helemaal gelezen*": I have read it in its entirety," an accolade: I have made the pilgrimage and joined the élite, as the world deserves to be informed.

A novel that is no novel, *Ulysses* shrinks its scope to less than a full day and expands language to become encyclopaedic. In his nicely polished looking glass Joyce invented what fiction never did before, a date on the calendar, in fact an annual feast. "*Weltalltag der Epoche*" it was called by Hermann Broch, in an ingenious fusion of "*Alltag*" (an ordinary day, quotidian) and "*Weltall*" (Cosmos).

At present, the 16th of June 1904 (along with the 17th) is 118 years back. The same stretch of time would bring us to 1786 – before the French Revolution. And yet *Ulysses*, with its horse-drawn vehicles, long skirts, obligatory hats or waistcoats, has not become the historical novel as which it could qualify; compare its contemporaries, Samuel Butler's *The Way of All Flesh* or George Gissing's *The Private Papers of Henry Ryecroft*. It feels as fresh as on the first day, in a perpetual Now.

Except that nowadays many actions of 1904 would no longer require physical presence. Bloom would not have to show up in a newspaper office, nor the library, in person, a phone call to the hospital would make a personal visit superfluous, email might convey insurance details to the Dignam family wherever they live. Of course, the funeral and the pubs would still have to be attended. Boylan's visit for one, though not its announcement, needed his physical presence to be successful.

First readers must have been confused essentially much more than nowadays when the book's notoriety has been replaced by a lingering awe. But even today, it calls out for guidance and annotation. It still takes some time to determine where exactly we are, unaided by notes or by maps. The most up-to-date Annotation, by Sam Slote, comprises 1367 pages. Guidance is useful. It is only after a few beats that we find that we are on top of a tower, and what kind of a tower it is will be revealed simply because a foreigner, Haines, explicitly raises the question. Nowadays some editions have the particular tower right on the cover, in spoil-sport narrative anticipation.

First reactions can be gleaned from the virulence of indignation of early reviewers. The book was "a libel on humanity." "It is partly a perfectly cynical appeal to sheer indecency ... *Ulysses* is an anarchical production, infamous in taste, in style, in everything," so Edmond Gosse, a former supporter of Joyce.

Aldous Huxley publicly despised it: "In spite of its very numerous qualities – it is, among other things, a kind of technical handbook, in which the young novelist can study all the possible and many of the quite impossible ways of telling a story – *Ulysses* is one of the dullest books ever written, and one of the least significant. This is due to the total absence from the book of any sort of conflict." The psychologist C.G. Jung failed to appreciate it almost completely: "You read and read and read and you pretend to understand what you read. Occasionally you drop through an air pocket into another sentence, but when once the proper degree of resignation has been reached you accustom yourself to anything. So I, too, read to page 135 with despair in my heart, falling asleep twice on the way."

As late as 2021 we can still learn that "*Ulysses* is an overwrought, overwritten epic of gratingly obvious, self-congratulatory, show-off erudition that, with its overstuffed symbolism and leaden attempts at humour, is bearable only by terminal graduate students who demand to validate the time they've wasted reading it. ... *Ulysses* is best looked upon as a grab bag of great riffs and long stretches of tedious pretentiousness." Contemporary Irish writer Roddy Doyle put in a *caveat*: "*Ulysses* could have done with a good editor .... People are always putting *Ulysses* in the top 10 books ever written, but I doubt that any of those people were really moved by it. ... If you're a writer in Dublin and you write a snatch of dialogue, everyone thinks you lifted it from Joyce. The whole idea that he owns language as it is spoken in Dublin is a nonsense. He didn't invent the Dublin accent. ... It gets on my nerves."

Ulysses does get on nerves; it has a violent effect of one kind or another. Which keeps it alive. The book audaciously did not comply with the rules, especially those concerning propriety and some ingrained taboos. In Joyce's schemata we find, next to heart or eyes, such organs as kidneys, lungs, locomotor apparatus, the skeleton or the oesophagus;

lots of these organs lie around in cemeteries: "lungs, hearts, livers" (6.675).[1]

Readers were not accustomed to the body sending unliterary signals: "His heart quopped softly" (8.1170); "A warm shock of air heat of mustard hanched on Mr Bloom's heart" (8.789). "A soft qualm, regret, flowed down his backbone, increasing ... He felt the soft qualm spread over him ... He felt heavy, full: then a gentle loosening of his bowels" (4.445–60). Ingestion is matched by evacuation, which caused non-squeamish Ezra Pound to delete some sentences from the (unusual) scene where Bloom relieves himself:

> Midway, his last resistance yielding, he allowed his bowels to ease themselves quietly as he read, reading still patiently, that slight constipation of yesterday quite gone. Hope it's not too big bring on piles again. No, just right. ... It did not move or touch him but it was something quick and neat. Print anything now. Silly season. He read on, seated calm above his own rising smell. (4.507)

The non-romantic body frequently intrudes: "Seems to a secret touch telling me memory. Touched his sense moistened remembered" (8.898). An observation, "Dribbling a quiet message from his bladder came to go to do not to do there to do" (8.933), must have seemed unconventional, and even more so when it is realised just what Bloom is considering doing, or not doing. The Old Testament had no qualms referring to the insides, as echoed in a passage in Oxen of the Sun: "Sad was the man that word to hear that him so heavied in bowels ruthful" (14.97).

Death can be starkly unrefined in Joyce's dauntless prospective: "A bowl of white china had stood beside her deathbed holding the green sluggish bile which she had torn up from her rotting liver by fits of loud groaning vomiting" (1.108). The crescendo "loud groaning vomiting" of one – two – three syllables, has an almost physical impact. Crass sexuality comes to a head in Circe, and not every reader would have been ap-

---

[1] James Joyce, *Ulysses*, ed. by Hans Walter Gabler with Wolfhard Steppe and Claus Melchior, with an Afterword by Michael Groden (New York: Random House, 1986).

peased by a whore-mistress whose "*sowcunt* barks" — not excessively aphrodisiac (15.3489).

In marked contrast to unprecedentedly nauseating scenes, the prose also parades passages of tranquil radiance. Bloom tears up the envelope of Martha's letter in a seamy entourage, under the railway station: "Going under the railway arch he took out the envelope, tore it swiftly in shreds and scattered them towards the road" — as banal an action of scant significance but resulting in a vignette of airy lightness: "The threads fluttered away, sank in the dank air: a white flutter, then all sank" (5.300).

Rearranged, the structure is of epiphanesque delicacy:

> The threads
> fluttered away,
> sank in the dank air:
> a white flutter,
> then all
> sank.

"Sank" poetically echoes "dank"; the air under the railway tracks in actual fact is perceptibly dank in as unromantic a setting as can be imagined.

A similar sketch evokes the quiet air above the houses as Stephen leaves the National Library: "Frail from the housetops two plumes of smoke ascended, pluming, and in a flaw of softness softly were blown" (9.1218). A study of Joyce's frequent uses of "soft" and its derivatives (also in *Dubliners* and *A Portrait*) would be worthwhile and show that Joyce manages to make softness soft.

Chrysostomos

Contrary to narrative practice, an isolated and moreover foreign single word is unexpectedly interposed in otherwise fluent prose, as though filling a pause: "He peered sideways ..., then paused awhile in rapt attention, his even white teeth glistening here and there with gold points. "Two strong shrill whistles answered..." (1.24). The action is halted without warning; some justification seems called for (and the best on is still to see the interjection as a first sign of the interior monologue which will soon be introduced). On a larger scale, the Proteus episode can be seen as an analogous insertion: it doesn't move the action much further. It has been experienced as an indigestible excrescence that can be skipped.

What must have struck or at least vaguely felt were the choice and partly unprecedented composites, moreover consistently unhyphenated:

> tuckstitched, shameclosing, peacocktwittering, warmbubbled, white-flattened, biscuitfully, nookshotten, bedsmiling, smoothsliding, birth-aiding, seabedabbbled, largefooted, softcreakfooted, yellowkitefaced, etc. etc.

Any self-respecting spelling would balk at these. I do not think, incidentally, that Joyce necessarily saw them as the neologisms they may be, but just as items within the potential of language in constant development. Not that Joyce ever would care which words pre-exist in dictionaries. He also shows a fondness for verbs prefixed by "un-" for not doing something, not all of them prerecorded: "unanswering — unhear-ing — unheeding — unlabouring — unliving — unmoving — unoffending — unresisting — unseeing — unsleeping — unsmiling — unspeaking," and many more.

Another salient feature, alliteration, provides vivid phonetic reinforcement: "He puffed a pungent plumy blast" (11.514). It appears as if Joyce, even beyond an Irish proclivity, had exceptional alliterative genes. Buck Mulligan initiates the pattern with "jejune jesuit" (1.45) and numerous punchy echoes, "your lousy leers and jesuit jibes" (1.500), and later on: "as you lay in your mulberrycoloured, multicoloured, multitudinous vomit!" (9.1193)

Not unexpectedly, Bloom (in the refractions of Circe) stumbles on his oratorical run of alliteration: "they are grassing their royal mountain stags or shooting peasants and phartridges in their purblind pomp of pelf and power" (15.1395). Sometimes it is difficult to decide where alliteration ends and onomatopoeia begins.

Nothing is too trivial to escape attention: "Ben Dollard halted and stared, his loud orifice open, a dangling button of his coat wagging brightbacked from its thread as he wiped away the heavy shraums that clogged his eyes to hear aright" (10.940). The reader even learns an Irish word, *shraum*, for something that is usually unmentioned. A dangling button is equipped with a Homeric type of epithet, "brightbacked." *Ulysses* is full of minor epiphanies: "A kidney oozed bloodgouts on the willowpatterned dish" (4.145).

Wandering Syntax

A sentence may appear to be over but continues with an unexpected turn.

"A young man clinging to a spur of rock near him **moved slowly** frogwise" would be complete in itself. Yet it is followed by "... **his green legs** in the deep jelly of the water" (1.680). Analogously, "An elderly man shot up near the spur of rock [...] a blowing red face" (1.687). A seemingly intransitive "shot up" changes its tracks and takes an object. What emerges is a parallelism between a young and an old man, between green and red, and a grammatical similarity. The device is repeated when the verb "rock" changes its mind:

> [Bloom's] eyes sought answer from the river and saw a rowboat **rock** at anchor on the treacly swells [the sentence could stop here] lazily **its plastered board.** (8.88)

The rocking board advertises "Kino 11/ Trousers," an actual company ("Kino J.C. tailor, agent. 58 Dame Street"). As usual in *Ulysses*, anything can move in different directions. It so happens that "*kino*" (kinw) in Greek means "I move," which most likely Bloom never has in mind. "Good idea that," he thinks: "How can you own water really? It's always flowing in a stream, never the same, which in the stream of life we trace. Because life is a stream" (8.93). I find it hard not to associate this with Herakleitos and his "*Panta rhei*" ("Everything flows"). The Greek philosopher is also known for "You cannot step into the same river twice, for other waters are continually flowing on." You cannot step into the same *Ulysses* twice, it will have changed, and so have you.

Once you read *Ulysses* again, you understand much more than on a first time. The first bedroom scene in Calypso is a case in point.

Entering the bedroom he half-closed his eyes and walked through warm yellow twilight towards her tousled head.

— Who are the letters for?

He looked at them. Mullingar. Milly.

— A letter for me from Milly, he said carefully, and a card to you. And a letter for you. (4.247)

Why "carefully"? A trivial list does not seem to need particular attention. Strategically Bloom knows (and we do now) that his wife is interested in the letter that has already troubled him ("His quickened heart slowed at once," 4.244), so he intentionally mentions it last, with slight gratification. Only on later re-readings could we find it appropriate that Bloom "halfclosed" his eyes entering the bedroom, when a letter with the address written in "bold hand" has already disquieted him. Manifestly, he is adjusting his eyesight to different light. Yet to partly close one's eyes is a way of not looking. The Latin "*connivere*" (close one's eyes, to overlook something intentionally, turn a blind eye to) covertly anticipates Bloom's attitude toward the impending events. It would amount to a sin against the narrative spirit to point this out to novices. In a tit for tat equivalent, it is Molly who "had to halfshut [her] eyes" when facing Boylan (18.153).

Joyce was also adept at compressing things, and emotions, tersely and memorably: "Why did she me?" (11.732); "As easy stop the sea" (11.641); and most poignantly "Me. And me now" (8.917), using the simplest words. I always admired a sentence that crisply captures a moment, when Lenehan hastens after Boylan: "Lenehan gulped to go" (11.431). It compresses the awkwardness of moving fast while finishing a drink, the consonant sequence (glp-t-g) combines the speed with a slight stumble.

Long eccentric words equally call for attention: "Bloom was talking and talking with John Wyse and he quite excited with his dunducketymudcoloured mug on him and his old plumeyes rolling about" (12.1415); the assonant adjective ("dun, duck, mug") need not be elucidated to show that it is not a compliment.

Acts can be drawn out in exaggerated slow motion, as in Ithaca:

What suddenly arrested [Bloom's] ingress?

> The right temporal lobe of the hollow sphere of his cranium came into contact with a solid timber angle where, an infinitesimal but sensible fraction of a second later, a painful sensation was located in consequence of antecedent sensations transmitted and registered. (17.1275)

The elaborate causation takes some reading time to clarify one short moment: Bloom bumps his head against an unexpected piece of furniture. Nothing is more immediate than pain, and ironically the sensation is medically postponed in obscuring length. An "infinitesimal but sensible fraction of a second" is a contradiction in terms, since the long word for a briefest moment consists of six syllables. In Ithaca, language is often at a great remove from what it wants to convey.

In jocular parlance, a simple question can be extended to some length: "Will immensely splendiferous stander permit one stooder of most extreme poverty and one largesize grandacious thirst to terminate one expensive inaugurated libation?" (14.1529); "largesize" is the *mot juste*. Bloom himself can be elongated to "*lovelorn longlost lugubru Booloohoom*," (15.146) or else broadened: "*the bonham eyes and fatchuck cheekchops of jollypoldy the rixdix doldy*" (15.148), in preparation for the distortions in the Circe episode. "[E]ndlessnessnessness" is both stated and imitated in a long-drawn-out word, appropriate for Sirens (11.750). A HUE AND CRY in Circe moves "*Helterskelterpelterwelter*" (15.4362), which also contains a self-explanatory compound.

Many prose novels must have alliterative runs, but not to the degree that Joyce enlists them for vibrating effects or, as they might be termed, phonetic reinforcement. "Stephen closed his eyes to hear crush crackling wrack and shells," "His boots trod again a damp crackling mast, razorshells, squeaking pebbles" (3.10, 147). "A black crack of noise in the street here, alack, bawled back" (14.408). The English language sports a lot of monosyllabic onomatopoeic words. (Note how many long words are mustered to describe the short ones!)

The library episode belongs to the sedentary ones, with next to no walking in the streets. Yet what walking is done inside is elevated to terpsichorean parody. For some reason, Joyce imposed an elaborate choreography on the (real life) staff of the National Library of Ireland. One "came a step a sinkapace forward on neatsleather creaking and a step backwards a sinkapace on the solemn floor"; and soon afterwards "Twicreakingly analysis he corantoed off" (9.5–12), while the language performs its own dance movements. A "sinkapace," a five-step movement, "*cinque pas*," and "*coranto*," are dances lifted from *Twelfth Night*. They are accompanied by creaking boots: the quaker librarian is "softcreakfooted" (9.231), "— Directly, said he, creaking to go, albeit lingering." "He creaked to and fro, tiptoing ..." (9.329). This will be enhanced into a playful imitative "Swiftly rectly creaking rectly rectly he was rectly gone" (9.679). The steps become audible.

On many occasions, an early reader might have taken Joyce to be an author not sure of his steps, as when "heard warm running sunlight and in the air behind him friendly words," or Bloom heard "a warm heavy sigh" (4.58). Though sunlight cannot be heard and sighs are not warm, these are samples of synesthetic latitude, empirical shorthand, like "— Ringabella and Crosshaven, a voice replied, groping for foothold" (10.400). It is typical for spatially oriented Wandering Rocks to identify a person by their former local, while "Ringabella" in Sirens sounds its musicality: "Cross Ringabella haven mooncarole" (11.850–53). Voices can be "wellfed" or "moneyed." At the latest in Sirens, Joyce conditions us to take accumulated oddities in our semantic stride: "Full voice of perfume of what perfume does your lilactrees" (11.731); we understand it as a confluence of memories.

Loose grammar sounds natural in the language attributed to Nausicaa: "And Cissy and Edy shouted after them to come back because they were afraid the tide might come in on them and be drowned" (13.470).

In Circe the gulls, who in the morning ungratefully failed to give Bloom "even a kaw," speak Gullish: "Kaw kave kankury kake" (8.84, 15.686). A sample of table talk is given with full mouth: "I munched hum un thu Unchster Bunk un Munchday" (8.692). A horse echoingly neighs "Hohohohohohoh! Hohohohome!" (15.4878, 4899) As Bloom predicted, "their neigh can be very irritating" (5.220).

Displacement

Ulysses sets off with a notable displacement. Single persons on top of a tower about to shave do not habitually intone Church Latin: "*Introibo ad altare Dei*," an initial blasphemy. Bloom is characterized by his taste: "Most of all Bloom liked grilled mutton kidneys which gave to his palate a fine tang of faintly scented ...." If the word had to be guessed, few of us would opt for "urine" (4.1); it is not habitually expected in a palate.

Mulligan opens the book with God, Bloom his entrance with urine as though to adumbrate the scope from the divine to excrement (which also ends the first Bloom chapter). Dirt, excrement struck first readers of *Ulysses* as unnecessary and disgusting. Joyce in his own version of "I am a man, I count nothing human foreign (or alien) to me" (Terence, *Heauton Timorumenos*, 77), never aimed to exclude anything in a small-scale epic squinting at universality. He found himself in a long often undercurrent tradition.

A corresponding range encompasses a book Molly Bloom is reading in a quaint still life under a bed: "The book, fallen, sprawled against the bulge of the orangekeyed chamberpot" (4.308). The Greek ornament lends the object a dignity that its location lacks. Note that the adjective "fallen" silently corrects Molly's slip, "It must have fell down." A book adjacent to a chamber pot delimits the scope of *Ulysses*.

Displacements are a trademark in many varieties. Locally, they figure in Wandering Rocks, stylistically in the interpolations of Cyclops, in most cases they just cuddle up in a parenthesis. "Excuse, miss, there's a (whh!) just a (whh!) fluff" (5.453).

Ulysses summarises itself at various stages, first, when Bloom on Sandymount strand recalls recent events: "'Long day I've had. Martha, the bath, funeral, house of Keyes, museum with those goddesses, Dedalus' song. Then that bawler in Barney Kiernan's" (13.1214) – from Lotuseaters to Cyclops. In my view, this is an equivalent to Odysseus telling of his adventures in Books 9–12 of the epic. The next retrospective arrangement, in a self-reflective retrospective arrangement, a Litany in Circe encompasses the 12 central chapters:

THE DAUGHTERS OF ERIN

Kidney of Bloom, pray for us
Flower of the Bath, pray for us
Mentor of Menton, pray for us
......
Potato Preservative against Plague and Pestilence, pray for us. (15.1140-52)

Finally, one of the recapitulations in Ithaca surveys the past day:

> The preparation of breakfast (burnt offering): intestinal the bath (rite of John): the funeral (rite of Samuel): the advertisement of Alexander Keyes (Urim and Thummim): the unsubstantial lunch (rite of Melchisedek): the visit to museum and national library (holy place): the bookhunt along Bedford row, Merchants' Arch, Wellington Quay (Simchath Torah): the music in the Ormond Hotel (Shira Shirim): the altercation with a truculent troglodyte in Bernard Kiernan's premises (holocaust): a blank period of time including a cardrive, a visit to a house of mourning, a leavetaking (wilderness): the eroticism produced by feminine exhibitionism (rite of Onan): the prolonged delivery of Mrs Mina Purefoy (heave offering): the visit to the disorderly house of Mrs Bella Cohen, 82 Tyrone street, lower, and subsequent brawl and chance medley in Beaver street (Armageddon): nocturnal perambulation to and from the cabman's shelter, Butt Bridge (atonement) (17.2044)

Each item is accompanied by a tag mainly taken from the Old Testament, which may serve as a Jewish alternative to the Homeric analogies, in structural parallax; "Shira Shirim," the "Song of Songs," corresponds to the Sirens. *Ulysses* is subject to several co-ordinates. The Jewish tags were added very late, "27.1.22," a few days before publication, a last lick of paint (*JJA* 27, 204–5). Ithaca abounds in such parenthetical insertions. The odd item is "Urim and Thummim" for Aeolus, "breastplates" in the Old Testament (Ex.28:30, etc.), which might have had a particular meaning for Joyce, but remains largely unexplained.

One paragraph in Cyclops, already an interpolation with the urinating narrator's associations, is full of asides in parenthesis:

> Goodbye Ireland I'm going to Gort. So I just went round the back of the yard to pumpship and begob (hundred shillings to five) while I was letting off my (Throwaway twenty to) letting off my load gob says I to myself I knew he was uneasy in his (two pints off of Joe and one in Slattery's off) in his mind to get off the mark to (hundred shillings is five quid) and when they were in the (dark horse) Pisser Burke was telling me card party and letting on the child was sick (gob, must have done about a gallon) flabbyarse of a wife speaking down the tube she's better or she's (ow!) all a plan so he could vamoose with the pool if he won or (Jesus, full up I was) trading without a licence (ow!) Ireland my nation says he (hoik! phthook!) never be up to those bloody (there's the last of it) Jerusalem (ah!) cuckoos. (12.1561)

At times, such interspersion have been spatchcocked into the text as when Bloom rehearses Martha's letter with floral associations: "Angry tulips with you darling manflower punish your cactus if you don't please poor forgetmenot how I long violets to dear roses when we soon anemone meet all naughty nightstalk wife Martha's perfume" (5.264). One could imagine the interspersed flowers as forerunners of contemporary emojis.

Reports can be intertwined with interior monologue like when Bloom, the prospect of Greek statues in mind, struts to the convenience: "A man and ready he drained his glass to the lees and walked, *to men too they gave themselves*, manly conscious, *lay with men lovers, a youth enjoyed her*, to the yard" (8.934, emphases added). The sentence seems to be infused by Odyssean undertones. The term "polytropos" in the first line is rendered by Butcher & Lang as "that *man*, so *ready at need*" (*Od.* 1.1), while Tennyson characterises Odysseus with "I will drink Life *to the lees*" ("Ulysses," 1.6).

The whole Cyclops episode is based on interpolations within the main oral report in thematic exaggerations. An entry into Barney Kiernan's licensed premises is couched in mock-Homeric diction:

> And lo, as they quaffed their cup of joy, a godlike messenger came swiftly in, radiant as the eye of heaven, a comely youth, and behind him there passed an elder of noble gait and countenance, bearing the sacred scrolls of law, and with him his lady wife, a dame of peerless lineage, fairest of her race. (12.244)

The replay is again in the chapter's vernacular:

> Little Alf Bergan popped in round the door and hid behind Barney's snug, squeezed up with the laughing, and who was sitting up there in the corner that I hadn't seen snoring drunk, blind to the world, only Bob Doran. I didn't know what was up and Alf kept making signs out of the door. And begob what was it only that bloody old pantaloon Denis Breen in his bath slippers with two bloody big books tucked under his oxter and the wife hotfoot after him, unfortunate wretched woman, trotting like a poodle. I thought Alf would split. (12.249)

By internal translation, an "elder of noble gait and countenance, bearing the sacred scrolls of law" becomes "Denis Breen in his bath slippers with two bloody big books tucked under his oxter," while "his lady wife, a dame of peerless lineage, fairest of her race," transforms into "the wife hotfoot after him, unfortunate wretched woman, trotting like a poodle." Alf, in fact, does "split" into two variants.

Interpolations can occur on a meta-level, above the range of any characters present, as in the example below from Sirens:

> Upholding the lid he (who?) gazed in the coffin (coffin?) at the oblique triple (piano!) wires. He pressed (the same who pressed indulgently her hand) soft pedalling a triple of keys to see the thicknesses of felt advancing, to hear the muffled hammerfall in action. (11.291)

The parenthetical remarks look like explanations for the benefit of the readers. An embedded gloss explains the term "boots": "Scaring eavesdropping boots croppy bootsboy Bloom in the Ormond hallway heard growls and roars of bravo, fat backslapping, their boots all treading, boots not the boots the boy. General chorus off for a swill to wash it down" (11.291). An explicative note tells us that the person in a hotel who cleans the boots is called "boots," the lowest in the hierarchy. He is snubbed by the barmaids, also for his "impertinent insolence," which again he unmannerly imitates as "Imperthnthn thnthnthn" (11.100).

Meta-remarks, as they are termed here, have been confusing, the most obvious sample occurring in Sirens where Bloom reflects: "Music hath charms Shakespeare said. Quotations every day in the year. To be or not to be. Wisdom while you wait" (11.904). This is followed by a wholly misplaced echo: "In Gerard's rosery of Fetter lane he walks, greyedauburn. One life is all. One body. Do. But do. Done anyhow" (11.907).

It has of course been identified as one of Stephen's recalls of Shakespeare's life, in Scylla and Charybdis:

> Do and do. Thing done. In a rosery of Fetter Lane of Gerard, herbalist, he walks, greyedauburn. An azured harebell like her veins. Lids of Juno's eyes, violets. He walks. One life is all. One body. Do. But do. Afar, in a reek of lust and squalor, hands are laid on whiteness. (9.651)

Odd reasons have been offered for the coincidence. In my take, it is as though the Text itself remembered itself, with "Shakespeare" as a trigger.

This is on a par with the first internal memory, in Sirens, when at meal "Leopold cut liverslices" (11.519). The text itself intervenes with: "As said before he ate with relish the inner organs, nutty gizzards, fried cods' roes" (self-referentiality) to refer back to Bloom's introduction: "Mr Leopold Bloom ate with relish the inner organs of beasts and fowls. He liked thick giblet soup, nutty gizzards, a stuffed roast heart, liverslices fried with crustcrumbs, fried hencods' roes" (4.1). When Joyce added this to Sirens, he had not yet changed "cod's" to "hencod's" (*Ulysses, A Critical and Synoptic Edition*, I, 106).

More "said befores" follow suit: "Bloom ate liv as said before" (11.569). "Blazes Boylan's smart tan shoes creaked on the barfloor, said before. Jingle by monuments of sir John Gray, Horatio onehandled Nelson, reverend father Theobald Mathew, jaunted as said before just now," though "Theobald Matthew" has *not* been said before, but only "Father Matthew" (6.30). From this moment on, the wording of *Ulysses* flaunts its own self-awareness. The book begins to preen itself as a conscious artefact. Bloom's interior monologue passages may now contain external elements that are not in his mind: "I suppose each kind of trade made its own, don't you see? Hunter with a horn. Haw. Have you the? *Cloche. Sonnez la!* Shepherd his pipe" (11.1240). "Have you the horn?" was said by Lenehan to Boylan and "*Sonnez la*" was never heard by Bloom. Circe will amplify textual self-referentiality.

Book of Keys

Keys, important in practical life, figure largely in *Ulysses*. Both main protagonists significantly don't carry them, are "premeditatedly (respectively) and inadvertently keyless" (17.80). When there is only one key, as in the historical Martello Tower in Sandymount, and an old, large one at that, possession becomes a practical issue.

Joyce's small scale minute craftsmanship shows very early: "The key scraped round harshly twice and, when the heavy door had been set ajar, welcome light and bright air entered" (1.327). The verb "scraped" indicates old use and an extra effort; "harshly" reinforces mechanical resistance, not a smooth unnoticed action. That "twice" is tacked on shows that one attempt is not sufficient. The copper key to the Tower was in fact big and clumsy; this is not described, but acted out in slow motion.

The same device is employed at the beginning of Hades: "Mr Bloom entered and sat in the vacant place. He pulled the door to after him and slammed it twice till it shut tight" (6.9). The carriage supplied to the mourners is worn, less than perfect, so that a second try is called for.

The 1922 and following texts of *Ulysses* even ran: "... and slammed it tight till it shut tight" (*Ulysses* 1922, 84).

In similar fashion, "Maggy at the range rammed down a greyish mass beneath bubbling suds twice with her potstick and wiped her brow" (10.261), a repeated attempt is stressed. For Bloom's feeble inept whistling for a carriage in Eumaeus, the "twice" is laboriously tagged at the end, separated by a comma for greater effect. “Mr Bloom, who was anything but a professional whistler, endeavoured to hail it by emitting a kind of a whistle, holding his arms arched over his head, twice” (16.28).

A perceptibly stronger kind of whistle is staged in a close-up in Sirens: “Richie cocked his lips apout” (11.630); lips are pursed forward (*not* in an emotional pouting), to produce “A low incipient note ...” (11.630). Spite *can* be verbally expressed when “Gerty smiled assent and bit her lip” at a taunt (13.360). The effect is brought about by terminal plosives, “assen**t**, bi**t** and li**p**.” The terse “smiled assent” is essentially softened when recourse is had in translation to an amiable “smiled assentingly.” What final consonants can achieve is shown by the weak ending of a bisyllabic word: “lèvre, labbia, Lippe,” which is anything but tight-lipped. Plosives can be effectively forceful: “His gouty paws plumped chords. Plumped, stopped abrupt” (11.452).

“Modernism”

I wonder who first termed Joyce a “Modernist” and what his reaction would have been. *Ulysses* is full of new, modern devices: gramophone, telephone, cameras, typewriters, electricity, trains, even a mechanical invention by Tom Rochford, to indicate what music hall turn is on (the invention has even been discovered as patented device by Tom Rochford). Oddly enough, the word “modern” occurs fairly late in the book, by way of a Cyclopean parody of a séance to conjure up Dignam’s ghost. The report formally states that the ghost “had heard from more favoured beings now in the spirit had abodes that were equipped with every *modern* home comfort such as tālāfānā, ālāvātār, hātākāldā, wātāklāsāt” (12.384). Following theosophical precedent, the terms are generally Sanskrit ones, characterised by the long “ā.” Ironically, the most up to date comforts are spelled in one of the oldest recorded languages and are for the benefit of spiritual beings who have little need for them. The message itself, incidentally, would be conveyed by something like an ethereal “tālāfān.”

A key witness for "Modernism," *Ulysses* reaches back to the beginning of European Literature. But then it also implies just how modern and bristling Homer's epic is.

Accuracy of Perception

In English, the object usually follows a verb fairly soon, but Joyce can depart from the habit: "Looking down he saw flapping strongly, wheeling between the gaunt quaywalls, gulls" (8.51). Humans are evolutionarily equipped to notice movement before the moving object. Joyce acts this out at the cost of a slight strain. Translations tend toward solutions of the kind "Bloom saw gulls that flapped ...," prioritising syntactical habit over progressive observation.

Bloom's cat "blinked up of her avid shameclosing eyes, mewing plaintively and long" (4.33). In enumerations, the weightier words are usually put toward the end, as do many translations: "*avec de long miaulements plaintifs*" (Vors 82), "*maullando larga y quejumbrosamente*" (Tortosa 62). But once more, Joyce is empirically on target. We immediately hear a plaintive tone, but it takes some noticeable moments to experience it as "long."

Spelling may not be a hangman's strong point when applying for a job: "*... i have a special nack of putting the noose once in he can't get out hoping to be favoured i remain, honoured sir, my terms is five ginnese*" (12.427). A truncated "nack" decapitates a word, just as the lack of a capital I befits an executer of capital punishment; "putting the noose once in he can't get out hoping to be favoured" without punctuation tells a story different from the one intended.

Whatever else Leopold Paula Bloom is, he is also a grammatical paradigm and can be declined into the classical four cases: "Bloom. Of Bloom. To Bloom. Bloom" (15.677). Pseudonymically, he is Henry Flower, Senhor Enrique Flor, Don Poldo della Flora, or Professor Luitpold Blumenduft or just Leopoldo. He can be elongated: "blowing Booloohoom," or widened: "jollypoldy the rixdix doldy" become "puffing Poldy" (15.146). On occasion he is merged with pronouns: "Bloowho, Bloowhose, Bloohimwhom" (11.149). There are "Bloomites" and "antiBloomites" with

"Blumenlied" as a side issue. He might live at Bloomville, a new Bloomusalem is announced. He is fragmented in "Bloo, blue bloo blew" and contained in "Siopold" (11.752), verbally he "bloometh" or is "blooming." "Bloomers" might be but are not named after him. Typographically he is curtailed to "L. Boom" (16.1260) which spawns "booming." Bloom as Everyman can be declined or conjugated as the case may be. In Circe he is disgendered and becomes a she. At one point, we learn that he has a middle name "Paula," a small (Lat. *paulus*) female streak.

He is composed of 12 letters: 4 o's and 3 l's, plus b, p, d, m, e, which can be rearranged anagrammatically into "Ellpodbomool, Molldopeloob, Bollopedoom , Old Ollebo, M.P." – one o short.

Provection

I thought one of Joyce's penchants deserved the name Provection: an innate drive toward augmentation and divergence. This applies to the progress of the interior monologue, which begins in my view with an early, isolated "Chrysostomos" and then is tuned on almost imperceptibly ("As he and others see me. Who chose this face for me?", 1.136), takes on further momentum and soon governs most of the Proteus episode. Bloom's cat sets an early example, escalating from "Mkgnao" via "Mrkgnao" and "Mrkrgnao" to a satisfied purring "Gurhrr!" (4.16–38) by incremental purring. It is manifest in "Croak of vast manless moonless womoonless marsh" (11.1012) and becomes a favourite device in a crescendo: "The boots to them, them in the bar, them barmaids came. For them unheeding him" (11.89). Buck Mulligan's brief parodic bursts in Telemachus will be enhanced to whole episodes like Cyclops, part of Nausicaa and Oxen. Intermittent histrionic scenes come to a grotesque drawn out climax in Circe. On a small scale, it happens when "new nine muses" are listed: "Commerce, Operatic Music, Amor, Publicity, Manufacture, Liberty of Speech, Plural Voting, Gastronomy, Private Hygiene, Seaside Concert Entertainments, Painless Obstetrics and Astronomy for the People"; certainly new ones, but they also increased to twelve within a few lines. A solitary "Chrysostomos" in Telemachus multiplies to

Bloom's eight male children in Circe "Nasodoro, Goldfinger, Chrysostomos, Maindorée, Silversmile, Silberselber, Vifargent, Panargyros" (15).

A single dirty handkerchief, already quoted, climaxes in a Cyclops interpolation:

> The much treasured and intricately embroidered ancient Irish facecloth attributed to Solomon of Droma and Manus Tomaltach og MacDonogh, authors of the Book of Ballymote, was then carefully produced and called forth prolonged admiration. ... all these moving scenes are still there for us today rendered more beautiful still by the waters of sorrow which have passed over them and by the rich incrustations of time. (all in all 300 words, 12.1438–65)

Ithaca pedantically lists properties of water that Bloom "admires," or rather what if we were to draw up a list he might come up with. It is the longest list in a chapter of extensive catalogues:

> Its universality, its democratic equality ... the noxiousness of its effluvia in lacustrine marshes, pestilential fens, faded flowerwater, stagnant pools in the waning moon. (17.185–228)

The wholly heterogeneous enumeration also contains terms that might be applied to *Ulysses* as whole: "universality, restlessness, vehicular ramifications, buoyancy, variety of forms, metamorphoses," etc.

"Latin. Stupefies them first." (5.350)

The first spoken, rather "intoned," words are in simple Church Latin. Joyce might well have believed that the Latin of the Church would remain perennial, but in the meantime the mass can be read in any vernacular. In Telemachus, the Latin of the Church is again turned on, as a painful memory of the death of Stephen's mother:

> "*Liliata rutilantium te confessorum turma circumdet:*
> *iubilantium te virginum chorus excipiat.*" (1.276)

The meaning can be grasped in slow stages as though Joyce had wanted to teach a lesson. Anyone reading *Liliata* [something to do with lilies], *rutilantium* (in genitive plural: "with a reddish glow") *te* (you, accusative, no verb yet in sight), will so far be at a loss. Only when *"confessorum"* aligns with *rutilantium* does it become clear that (heavenly) confessors glow reddish. *Then turma* matches *liliata:* a crowd (of confessors) is supplied with lilies. Ultimately the trailing verb *circumdet* reveals the gist of the line: a wish that the dead person should be surrounded by confessors in heaven. But only the last syllable *"circum**det**"* (conjunctive mode) indicates that the sentence is a wish. What is unveiled at the very end, in English rendering has to be put right in visible front*: May ...,* which gives the show away right from the start. Understating is a gradual and retrospective process in time. As a temporal event in language, the sentence is untranslatable.

In classical Greek and Latin clarification may be delayed, and leads to reading backwards. The point of the didactical digression is that the Latin construction corresponds to a Joycean reading sequence: Often we understand only looking back. It is not immediately clear that *Ulysses* begins at the top of a tower, nor that Bloom is prepared for a funeral. On a first reading we do not know why Gerty MacDowell prefers sitting to running. As in real life, we find out (or not) as we go along. It takes a lot of cross-referencing backwards to realise why Bloom is credited with backing the outsider Throwaway in the Gold Cup, and quite a few inattentive readers may not grasp it, unless instructed...

Silence

Joyce excels at staging social silences, the absence of speech when it is expected, often in moments of embarrassment. At the beginning of the funeral episode the decorous silence is felt: "All waited. Nothing was said ... All waited. They waited still, their knees jogging" (6.21,24,29). When nothing is said nothing would have to be told, to say it creates patience. The conversation gets lowly underway.

Lighting a cigarette often bridges an awkward silence. When Stephen Dedalus, not overly responsive at the best of times, brusquely cuts off a conversation, "Haines stopped to take out a smooth silver case in which twinkled a green stone. He sprang it open with his thumb and offered it. / — Thank you, Stephen said, taking a cigarette. / Haines helped himself and snapped the case to. He put it back in his sidepocket and took from his waistcoatpocket a nickel tinderbox, sprang it open too, and, having lit his cigarette, held the flaming spunk towards Stephen in the shell of his hands" (1.615). The minute circumstantiality spells out the underlying tension.

In the cabman's shelter, conversation is intermittent: "A silence ensued till Mr Bloom for agreeableness' sake just felt like asking him whether it was for a marksmanship competition like the Bisley" (16.406). Later on when the talkative sailor Murphy leaves the assembled group, "silence reigned supreme" (16.937), which silences can do when they take over.

What Joyce gets uncannily right in the more realistic earlier parts, Eumaeus tends to get askew or plain wrong. "On this knotty point, however, the views of the pair, poles apart as they were, both in schooling and everything else, with the marked difference in their respective ages, clashed" (16.776). It is difficult for two items to clash when poles apart. Contiguity is required.

Some of the tautologies of the episode turn on the use of "Both": "both occurrences happening at the same time," "they both walked together along Beaver Street"; most amusingly in "both instinctively exchanged meaning glances" (16.152, 21, 594) — an act hard to be done by only one person.

In this context: interior monologue passages take up almost no time, as can be gauged from Stephen's lengthy reflection on the Church and its heretics in Telemachus ("The proud potent titles ... *de Dieu!*" (1.650–65) that are interspersed between Haines's "It seems history is to blame" and "Of course I am a Britisher ...," only moments apart.

In Oxen of the Sun, dialogue is transposed into period diction, what is actually spoken has to be extrapolated. At one time Punch Costello is censured in the language of a period: "whiles they all chode with him, a murrain seize the dolt, what a devil he would be at, thou chuff, thou puny, thou got in peasestraw, thou losel, thou chitterling, thou spawn of a rebel, thou dykedropt, thou abortion thou, to shut up his drunken drool out of that like a curse of God ape" (14.326). What do the actually say? *Ulysses* contains a number of built-in self-translations.

In Eumaeus again, Joyce does not always clarify what Bloom turns over in his mind and what he actually speaks aloud to Stephen. A long paragraph might be a transcript from Bloom's exhortation, though not necessarily or likely in this particular phrasing:

> He understood, however, from all he heard, that Dr Mulligan was a versatile allround man, by no means confined to medicine only, who was rapidly coming to the fore in his line and, if the report was verified, bade fair to enjoy a flourishing practice in the not too distant future as a tony medical practitioner drawing a handsome fee for his services in addition to which professional status his rescue of that man from certain drowning by artificial respiration and what they call first aid at Skerries, or Malahide was it? was, he was bound to admit, an exceedingly plucky deed which he could not too highly praise, so that frankly he was utterly at a loss to fathom what earthly reason could be at the back of it except he put it down to sheer cussedness or jealousy, pure and simple. (16.287)

Items like "bound to admit" sound like spoken – always with a twist of epimorph – but immediately afterwards a dash unmistakably suggests actual direct speech: "– Except it simply amounts to one thing and he is what they call picking your brains, he ventured to throw out." The statement appears to be prefigured in "except he put it down to sheer cussedness ..."

When, in Ithaca, "Bloom assented covertly to Stephen's rectification of the anachronism involved in assigning the date of the conversion of the Irish nation to Christianity from druidism by Patrick son of Calpornus, son of Potitus, son of Odyssus, sent by pope Celestine I in the year 432 in the reign of Leary to the year 260 or thereabouts in the reign of Cormac MacArt (266 A.D.), suffocated by imperfect deglutition of aliment at Sletty and interred at Rossnaree" (17.31), we cannot determine the actual words uttered in detail. In particular the phrasing "suffocated by imperfect deglutition of aliment" sounds like Ithacese for what formerly was put "Cormac in the schoolpoem choked himself" (8.864). Direct quotation has given way to transposition. A related question is why Bloom (most likely) should raise the topic in the first place.

It would be interesting to know what words Bloom actually used in the report on his day to his wife when all we get is an unreliable listing of "modifications" (17.2250). Perhaps the most salient term that answers the question "Was the narration otherwise unaltered by modifications?" is scientifically one of the most significant and conversationally of the least meaningful – "Absolutely" (17.2268), as though any report could ever be unaltered. "Absolutely" means "relatively." The faulty account of Dignam's funeral, with M'Coy and Stephen Dedalus among the mourners, is a case in point (16.1249–61).

The elusive articulations of Eumaeus are a case apart, every phrase almost is slightly askew, yet often with an implicit awareness of its discrepancy. There is nothing wrong with "At this stage an incident happened" (16.918), except that it is hard to imagine an incident that does not happen. Hilarious collocations abound, a supreme example is an "untasteable apology for a cup of coffee" (16.1141), which looks like *ad hoc* shorthand for coffee that is so untasteable that it calls for an apology, irrespective of whether apologies can be tasted or not.

My favourite items depict the contribution of a horse (which to the best of my memory Hugh Kenner once called the last stamp of realism in the book):

> The horse, having reached the end of his tether, so to speak, halted, and, rearing high a proud feathering tail, added his quota by letting fall on the floor, which the brush would soon brush up and polish, three smoking globes of turds. Slowly, three times, one after another, from a full crupper, he mired. (16.1874)

Horses can be kept on a tether, but this particular is not, so that the phrase is particularly inept. The stylistic discomfort is conveyed by "so to speak." Statuary dignity is conferred by the rearing of a "proud feathering tail." In anachronistic anticipation, a brush is removing what has not yet reached the floor. The retake of the act emphasises the sequence, "one after the other." I would defy any horse to achieve this act in any other way than sequentially. Of course, the pedantry also intimates that Bloom observes the event with kind attention.

Especially in Sirens, word boundaries along with grammatical categories take a back seat: "Hoarsely the apple of his throat hoarsed softly" (11.589). Language becomes sound material that can be cut to size.

"— Dollard, murmured tankard." "Dollard" chimes with tankard. In the sequel, it is curtailed to "tank," Dollard to "doll," Kennedy to "Kenn": "Tank one believed: Miss Kenn when she: that doll he was: she doll: the tank" (11.778641). From now on "tank" substitutes for "tankard" among clipped names: "Miss Douce, Miss Lydia, did not believe: Miss Kennedy, Mina, did not believe: George Lidwell, no: Miss Dou did not: the first, the first: gent with the tank: believe, no, no: did not, Miss Kenn: Lidlydiawell: the tank" (11.818). The whole cluster also amounts to vacuous conversation with little content.

Words are malleable according to compositional needs. The technique could be called Procrustean: if a word is too short, it can be elongated at need: "endlessnessnessness" (11.750), or shortened if too long: "An unseeing stripling stood in the door. He saw not bronze. He saw not gold. Nor Ben nor Bob nor Tom nor Si nor George nor tanks nor Richie nor Pat" (11.1281).

After "Lenehan round the sandwichbell wound his round body round," Boylan's simple "I heard you were round" (11.240, 345) takes on another quality: Lenehan becomes round. This was prefigured in *Dubliners*: "But his figure fell into rotundity" (D50). As it happens, ubiquitous Lenehan indeed is around in Aeolus, Wandering Rocks, Sirens, Cyclops, and again in Oxen of the Sun Sirens — with its predictive collocations (Overture) and the main narrative — and Cyclops are told twice. Bipartite Cyclops in alternation pits colloquial and richly idiomatic talk against parodic formal writing:

> And he after stuffing himself till he's fit to burst! Jesus, I had to laugh at the little jewy getting his shirt out. He drink me my teas.

> *He eat me my sugars. Because he no pay me my moneys?* (12.29)

No one is getting a shirt out, but the comparison is understood without effort. This is followed by the emotionless legal diction of a written contract:

> For nonperishable goods bought of Moses Herzog, of 13 Saint Kevin's parade in the city of Dublin, Wood quay ward, merchant, hereinafter called the vendor, and sold and delivered to Michael E. Geraghty, Esquire, of 29 Arbour Hill in the city of Dublin, Arran quay ward, gentleman, hereinafter called the purchaser, videlicet, five pounds avoirdupois of first choice tea at three shillings and no pence per pound avoirdupois and three stone avoirdupois of sugar, crushed crystal, at threepence per pound avoirdupois ... (12.33–51)

The Law states its conditions with circumstantial neutrality and devoid of amusing flourishes. The legal diction is turned on early in the episode and may serve as a counterpoint to practically all the rest of *Ulysses*; it is consistently without embellishment, originality, elegance, and of scant entertainment value. (On a second reading, who is likely to purse it attentively in every detail without skipping?) Moreover, the names are replaced by impersonal terms "vendor" and "purchaser," this in the chapter of naming and long lists of names. But even the Law distinguishes an Irish "gentleman" from a Jewish Moses Herzog, who is designated "merchant."

In the same vein, Ithaca is not famous for frivolous word play; in fact it seems to aim at excluding it. Nevertheless, exceptions from the tacit rule do emerge, at times perhaps not manifestly, or only at a second glance: "Which example did he adduce to induce Stephen to deduce that originality, though producing its own reward, does not invariably conduce to success?" (17.606) The string of compound verbs with Latin *ducere*, to draw, looks like a language lesson to memorise related composites.

A sudden burst of sensual emotion is drastically set off from the general dead pan diction of Ithaca: "He kissed the plump mellow yellow smellow melons of her rump, on each plump melonous hemisphere, in their mellow yellow furrow, with obscure prolonged provocative melonsmellonous osculation" (17.2241). The *ad hoc* coinings, "smellow, melonsmellonous," (which would not feel out of place in Sirens), are sticking out like a frivolous thumb.

Epithalamium

Richard Ellmann has speculated why 16 June 1904 became the chosen date: "To set *Ulysses* on this date was Joyce's most eloquent if indirect tribute to Nora, a recognition of the determining effect upon his life of his attachment to her. On June 16, he entered into relation with the world around him and left behind him the loneliness he had felt since his mother's death. ... June 16 was the sacred day" (RE 155–6).[2] In this view, generally accepted and perpetuated in many blurbs, *Ulysses* is Joyce's "epithalamium." Still, it remains somewhat askew. On 16 June 1904 James Joyce, aged 22, met Nora Barnacle, from which day on they remained together until his death. On 16 June 1904, Stephen Dedalus, aged 22, poignantly does not meet a younger girl for a lasting relationship; in fact he ineffectually visits a brothel and then disappears into nowhere, *via* Eccles Lane. Leopold Bloom, aged 38, married for 16 years, on this particular day, condones his wife's first act of adultery. On 17 June 1904, Molly Bloom, aged 33, ends with a perhaps resounding "Yes I said yes I will Yes" – but in a backward look over 16 years: "Me, and me now" (8.817). Molly comments almost casually: "here we are as bad as ever after 16 years" (18.1215). But then Bloom recalls the past day as "perfect" with only minor "imperfections" (17.2071).

Of course, even in an epithalamium battered by reality, *Ulysses* is nonetheless a tribute to Nora Barnacle.

So much for a few remarks of what may *Ulysses* set apart, to this day.

---

[2] Richard Ellmann, *James Joyce* (Oxford: Oxford University Press, 1983) 155–156.

The Painting of van Velde or the World and the Pants

SAMUEL BECKETT

> CUSTOMER: God made the world in six days, and you, you ain't fucking made me pants in six months.
>
> TAILOR: But Sir, look at the world, and look at your pants.

To begin, let's talk of something else, let's talk of old doubts, fallen into oblivion, or reabsorbed in blithe choices, in what is commonly called masterpieces, turnips, and works of merit.

Doubts of an amateur, of course, of a very wise amateur, such as painters dream him, who arrives with arms dangling and who leaves with arms dangling, his head heavy with what he believed he glimpsed. What a joke the worries of the performer, alongside the pangs of the amateur, whom our four-penny iconography has stuffed with dates, periods, schools, influences, and who knows how to distinguish, so wise he is, between a gouache and a watercolor, and who from time to time thinks he can guess what he likes, while keeping an open mind. Because he imagines, poor man, that nothing that is painting should remain foreign to him.

Let's not talk of criticism itself. The best, that of a Fromentin, of a Grohmann, of a McGreevy, of a Sauerlandt, is that of Amiel. Hysterectomies of the trowel. And how could it be otherwise? Can they only quote? When Grohmann demonstrates in Kandinsky reminiscences of the Mongolian graphic, when McGreevy so aptly brings Yeats closer to Watteau, where do the rays go? When Sauerlandt speaks, with finesse and — let's be fair — parsimony, on the case of the great unknown painter Ballmer, where does he fall? *Das geht mich nicht an*, said Ballmer, whom the writings of Herr Heidegger caused cruel suffering. He said it very modestly.

Or then we do general aesthetics, like Lessing. It's a charming game.

Or then we make anecdotes, like Vasari and Harper's Magazine.

Or then we make catalogues raisonnés, like Smith.

Or then we frankly indulge in disagreeable and confused chatter. It's the case here.

With words we only speak to ourselves. The lexicographers unbutton themselves. And even in the confessional, we betray ourselves.

Could we not attack modesty elsewhere than on these surfaces painted almost always with love and often with care, and which themselves are avowals? It seems not. Unnatural copulations are highly valued, among lovers of the beautiful and of the rare. The only inclination is to bow before good manners.

Completed, brand new, the picture is there, a non-sense. Because it is still only a painting, it still lives only in the life of the lines and of the colors, offered only to its author. Be aware of his situation. He's waiting, for us to get him out of there. He awaits the eyes, the eyes which, for centuries, because it is a painting of the future, will charge him, blacken him, with the only life that counts, that of the featherless bipeds. He will eventually die of it. No matter. We'll botch him up. We'll patch him together. We'll hide his sex and support his throat. We'll give him a leg of lamb instead of the buttock, as we did for the *Venus* of Giorgione in Dresden. He will know the basements and the ceilings. We will fall on him with umbrellas and with sputum, as we did for the Lurçat in Dublin. If it is a fresco five meters high by twenty-five long, it will be locked in a tomato greenhouse, having previously taken care to brighten the colors with nitric acid, as we did for the *Triumph of Caesar* of Mantegna at Hampton Court. Whenever the Germans don't have time to move it, it will turn into a mushroom in an abandoned garage. If it's a Judith Leyster we'll attribute it to Hals. If it's a Giorgione and it's too early to attribute it to Titian again, we'll attribute it to Dosso Dossi (Hanover). Mr. Berenson will explain himself on this. He will have lived, and spread joy.

This explains why the paintings look so much better in the museum than at home.

This explains why the *Unknown Masterpiece* of Balzac is on so many bedside tables. The work withdrawn from the judgment of men ends by expiring, in terrible tortures. The work considered as pure creation, and whose function ends with genesis, is doomed to nothingness.

A single (enlightened) amateur would have saved him. Only one of those gentlemen with a face hollowed out by unwarranted enthusiasms, feet flattened by innumerable stations, fingers worn down by fifty-franc catalogs, who first look from afar, then from close up, and who consult with their thumbs, in particularly thorny cases, the relief of the impasto. Because it is not a question here of the grotesque & despicable animal whose specter haunts the ateliers, like that of the *normaliennes student* tapir, but of the harmless kook that runs, like others in the cinema, in the galleries, in museums, and even in churches with hope – hold on tight – to enjoy. He doesn't want to learn, the pig, or get better. He thinks only of his own pleasure.

It's he who justifies the existence of painting as a public thing.

I dedicate these words to him, so well made to further obsess him.

He asks only to enjoy. The impossible is done to prevent it.

The impossible is done in particular so that whole slices of modern painting are taboo to him.

The impossible is made so that he chooses, so that he takes sides, so that he accepts à priori, so that he rejects à priori, so that he stops looking, so that he ceases to exist, before something he could have simply liked, or found ugly, without knowing why.

We say to him:

"Stay away from abstract art. It's made by a bunch of crooks and incompetents. They couldn't do anything else. They don't know how to draw. Yet, Ingres said that drawing is the integrity of art. They don't know how to paint. Yet, Delacroix said that color is the integrity of art. Don't go near it. A child could do the same."

What can it do to him, whether they are crooks, if they give him pleasure? What does it matter to him that they can't draw? Did Cimabue know how to draw? What does it mean: to know how to draw? What does it matter to him, that children can do the same? Let them do the same. It will be marvelous. What is stopping them? Their parents perhaps. Or would they not have time?

We say to him:

"Do not waste your time with the realists, with the surrealists, with the cubists, with the fauves, with the apprivoisés, with the impressionists, with the expressionists, etc., etc. And each time he is given excellent reasons. He must be told not to get involved with the deplorable centuries of pre-cézannienne painting.

We say to him:

"All that is good in painting, all that is viable, all that you can admire without fear, is on a line that goes from the caves of des Eyzies to the Galerie de France."

It is not clear whether this is a pre-established line or whether it is a trace that unfolds like the slime of the slug. We do not show him what signs he can know if a given painting relates to it. It's an invisible line. Could it be by chance a plan, their line?

We say to him:

"Only one who is able to forgo direct expression has the right to do so. Abstract painting is the refuge of all dabblers."

Law! Since when does the artist, as such, not have all the rights, that is to say none? He may soon be banned from exhibiting, or even from working, if he cannot justify so many years of academia.

The identical bleating greeted, 150 years ago, free verse and tonal scale.

We say to him:

"Picasso, he's good. You can go there with confidence."

And he will no longer hear the Homeric snoring.

We say to him, with great kindness:

"Everything is an object for painting, without excepting moods, dreams, and even nightmares, provided that the transcription is done with plastic means."

Could it be by chance the use or the non-use of these machines that would decide the presence or the absence, on the aforementioned line, of a given painting?

In any case, it would be useful, and even interesting, to know what is meant by plastic means. Yet, no one will ever know. It's something only initiates sense.

But suppose that the definition is acquired, once and for all, so that any hunter can exclaim, before the painting to be judged: "It is good, the means are plastic," and that it is established, at the same time, that only the painter who uses such is good. What to say, in this case, of the artist who renounces it?

This raises vast and obscure problems of practical aesthetics, I speak of those relating to the pompier, to the hypopompier, to the hyper-pompier and to the pompier deliberately, to their reciprocal relations and zones of cleavage, and in a general way to the legitimacy, excuse me, the expediency, of the willed creative defect.[1]

We say to him:

"Dali, he's a pompier. He couldn't do anything else."

This is called leaving nothing to chance. We strangle first, then we disembowel.

Twin judgments are thriving at this time. They say a lot about judges.

I propose the above specimen as a model of its kind. It's short, clear, well balanced (affirmation first, negation second), gently transcendental,

---

[1] Pompier, French for firefighter, and the following terms hypo- and hyper-pompier, are used pejoratively to describe a certain type of academic painting. Jacques Thuillier suggests that pompier "may have come from the visible resemblance between the helmets worn by classical heroes in Davidian history painting and the helmets worn by French firefighters of the period; it was possibly a corruption of pompéiste, a label sometimes used to describe the group of 'Neo-Greek' painters around Gérôme at mid-century... [It was also] a widely accepted alternative for 'academic' by 1880, when the critic Théodore de Banville entitled a comic fable on academic painting for the front page of *Gil Blas* "Le Pompier."" See *Academics, Pompiers, Official Artists, and the Arrière-garde: Defining Modern and Traditional in France, 1900–1960*, ed. by Natalie Adamson & Toby Norris (2009) 13.

easy to pronounce for Anglo-Saxons, and free of aftershock. That is, the aftershocks should start around the age of 15, at the latest.

There would not be too many volumes of nauseating analyses to extirpate the enormous and malicious misunderstanding, the one that has poisoned for so long, on the level of the idea, the relations between painters, between amateurs, between painters and amateurs.

Because if it is not Dali, it is another; and if he's not a pompier, he's another thing.

Let us see only some of the questions that arise, when we have admitted that pompier has a meaning and that Dali, voluntarily or involuntarily, presents its stigmas.

Why wouldn't he be a pompier, deliberately, if that suits him?

Can we not conceive of the pompier and the non-pompier together, the former at the service of the latter? Would the prose of the *Princess of Elide* be so beautiful, if it weren't for the verses? Do the landscapes of Claude really owe nothing to the staffage?

How do you know he can't do anything else? Did he sign any written report in this session? The fact that he never did anything else? And why wouldn't he have been a pompier, nothing but a pompier, since his early childhood, if that suited him?

And why, knowing how to do nothing but be a pompier, would he not get something admirable out of it? Because an admirable pompier is a *contradictio in adjecto*? The was.

And so on.

This is a base part of what we say to the amateur.

We never say to him:

"There is no painting. There are only paintings. These, not being sausages, are neither good nor bad. All we can say of them is that they translate, with more or less loss, absurd and mysterious pulsions toward the image, that they are more or less adequate vis-à-vis obscure internal tensions. As for deciding the degree of suitability for yourself, that is out of the question, since you are not in the skin of the canvas. Most of the time he doesn't know. Besides, it is a coefficient devoid of interest. Because losses and profits are equal in the economy of art, where the you is the light of the said, and all presence absence. All you'll ever know about a painting is how much you love it (and possibly why, if you're interested). But you will probably never know that either, unless you go deaf and forget your letters. And the time will come when, of your visits to the Louvre, because you will only go to the Louvre, you will only have lasting memories: "I stayed three minutes before Professor Pater's smile, looking at him."

This is a lowest part of what you never tell the amateur. This is clearly no more true than the rest. But that would change him.

The painting (since there is none) of Abraham and Gerardus van Velde is little known in Paris, that is to say little known. Yet they have been working there for twenty years, since the age of sixteen.

That of A. van Velde is particularly little known. His paintings have hardly ever left the studio, unless the annual upside-down ventilation at the Indépendants is counted as an outing. From this long seclusion they emerge, today, as fresh as if they had never ceased, since their beginnings, to be admired, tolerated, and vilified.

No exhibition, however modest, has ever brought together in Paris paintings from either one or the other.

Contrarily, an important G. van Velde exhibition took place in London, in 1938, at the Guggenheim Young Gallery. Strange encounter. Many paintings of his have remained in England.

They worked mainly in Paris and its immediate surroundings. A. van Velde however stayed in Corsica (1929-31) and Mallorca (1932-36).

I almost forget the most important. A. van Velde was born in The Hague in October 1895. It was the moment of *des brumes*. G. van Velde was born near Leiden in April 1897. It was the time of *des tulipes*.

What follows will only be a verbal disfigurement, even a verbal assassination, of emotions which, I well know, concern only myself. Disfigurement, come to think of it, less of an affective reality than of its laughable cerebral imprint. Because it suffices that I reflect on all the pleasures that gave me, all the pleasures that give me, the paintings of A. van Velde, and to all the pleasures that gave me, to all the pleasures that the paintings of

G. van Velde give me, so that I can feel them escaping, in an innumerable landslide.

Therefore, a double massacre.

As for the form, it will necessarily have the appearance of a series of apodictic propositions. It's is the only way not to show off.

First of all, it is important not to confuse the two œuvres. They are two things, two series of things, absolutely distinct. They move apart, more and more, from each other. They will move, further and further apart, from each other. Like two men who, starting from the Porte de Chatillon, would move on, without knowing the path too well, with frequent stops to give themselves courage, one toward the Rue Champ-de-l'Alouette, the other toward Ile des Cygnes.

It is then important to understand the relationships well. Let them resemble each other, two men walking toward the same horizon, in the midst of so many layers, of private and of public transport.

Let's talk about the eldest first. His originality is, by far, the easier to grasp, the more dazzling of the two. G. van Velde's painting is excessively reticent, acts through irradiations that one feels are defensive, is endowed with what astronomers call (if I am not mistaken) a high escape velocity. While that of A. van Velde seems frozen in a lunar void. The air has left him.

I exaggerate.

I am thinking especially of the latest paintings, those that G. van Velde has just brought back from the South, those that A. van Velde had made in Paris in 40 and 41 (he hasn't done anything since). The contrast was less felt ten years ago. But it was already exploding.

This distribution of roles is most unexpected. Everything suggested the contrary. And I'm afraid we're headed for observations that will in effect have to reverse them, for any mind concerned with consistency.

From where does this impression of something in the void come? From the way? It's like saying that the impression of blue comes from the sky. Let's look for a larger circle.

With Abraham van Velde we are dealing with an effort of apperception so exclusively and fiercely pictorial that many others, whose reflections are all in murmurs, conceive it only with difficulty, conceive it only by ensnaring it in a sort of syntactic circle, than by placing it in time.

(I note, literally between parentheses, the curious effect, which I have witnessed more than once, that these paintings produce on the viewer in good faith. They deprive him, even the most prompt to comment, of the use of speech. It isn't a silence of shock, judging by the eloquent refutations that nevertheless end up flowing out. It's a silence, one would almost say of convenience, like the one we keep, while wondering why, before a mute.)

To write purely visual apperception is to write a sentence denuded of meaning. As usual. Because each time we want to make words do a real work of trans-shipment, whenever we want to make them express something other than words, they align themselves so as to mutually annul each other. This is, undoubtedly, what gives life all its charm.

Because it is not a question of awareness, but of a vision, of a quick shot. Very quick! And from a single field of vision that sometimes allows itself to be seen without more, which does not always insist on being poorly known, which at times allows its faithful to ignore everything that is not apparent: in the inner field.

Space and body, completed, unalterable, torn from time by the maker of time, sheltered from time in the factory of time (who spent his day in the Sacré-Cœur so as not to have to see it anymore?), here we are, this is what Barbizon and the sky of Perugia are worth. It is, in a sense, its culmination.

The birds have fallen, Manto is silent, Tiresias blind.

Blindness, silence, and the still azure, here is the solution to the riddle, the very last solution.

For some.

What have the representative arts always chased after? To want to stop time, through representing it.

So many flights, races, rivers, arrows. So many falls and ascensions. So much smoke. We had even the jet of urine (sheep of the divine Potter), symbol par excellence of time flying.

We can never be grateful enough.

But it was perhaps time for the object to withdraw, here and there, from the so-called visible world.

The 'realist,' sweating before his waterfall and railing against the clouds, has never ceased to enchant us. But don't let him piss us off with his stories of objectivity and of things seen. Of all the things no one has ever seen, his waterfalls are undoubtedly the most immense. And if there exists an environment where it would be better not to speak of objectivity, it's the one that he crisscrosses, under his parasol hat.

The painting of A. van Velde would therefore be firstly a painting of the thing in suspense, I would gladly say of the dead thing, ideally dead, if the term did not have such unfortunate associations. That is, the thing you see there is no longer just represented as suspended, but strictly as it is, actually frozen. It's the sole thing, isolated by the need to see it, by the need to see. The thing motionless in the void, here finally the visible thing, the pure object. I don't see any other.

The cranial box has the monopoly on this article.

It's where time sometimes slows down, like the wheel of the speedometer when the last light bulb goes out.

It's where we finally start to see, in the dark. In the dark that no longer fears any daybreak. In the darkness that is the daybreak and noon and evening and night of an empty sky, of a fixed earth. In the darkness that enlightens the mind.

This is where the painter can calmly blink.

We are far from the famous "right" of painting to create its objects. It's the outdoors that calls for this daring operation.

Also far from the bambocciantes of the surreal.

Tool relations with the great school of painting criticism-critique of its objects, criticism of its means, criticism of its aims, criticism of its criticism, and of which we are still only at Sienese magnificence.

There was once a man that we called the great Thomas...

Useless to look for the originality of A. van Velde elsewhere than in this prodigious objectivity, because everything else is connected to it, not certainly as a consequence, nor as an effect, but in the sense that the same occasion gave rise to it. I am talking about all that this painting presents of irrationality, of ingenuity, of the non-combine, of the surly.

Impossible to reason about the singular. Rational painting is painting in which each touch is a synthesis, each tone chosen from among a thousand, each stroke a symbol, and which ends in the writhings of enthymeme. It's la natura morte with a butterfly. It's the sewing machine on the operating table. It's the figure seen from the front and in profile at the same time. It's probably also the lady with the dorsal breasts, although this is not certain. She produces masterpieces in her own way.

Impossible to want the unknown other, the finally seen, whose center is everywhere and the circumference nowhere; nor the sole agent able to stop it; nor the goal, which is to make it stop. Because that's what it's all about, no longer seeing this adorable and frightening thing, going back in time, into blindness, going to be bored before the whirlwinds of never-dead meat and shivering under the poplars. So we show it, the only way we can.

Impossible to tidy up the elementary.

We show it or we don't show it.

Conjectural painting provided him with the tool. Its hold goes no further. A. van Velde has since modified this tool. We do not feel the less where it comes from. He adapted it to the needs of his work, which is by no means conjectural.

There is a Braque that resembles the plastic meditations on the implemented means. Hence this strange feeling of hypothesis that emerges from it. The final is still for tomorrow. It seems that this remark is relevant to much, not the least, to what is called living modern painting.

With A. van Velde, nothing of the kind. He assures. Not even. He finds. His means have the specificity of a speculum, exist only in relation to their function. He does not care enough to doubt it. He is only interested in what they reflect.

We are touching here on something fundamental and which could make it possible to grasp by virtue of what exactly there exists, since Cézanne, a whole painting cut off from its antecedents (how much time it has lost in trying to relate to it), and by virtue of which, in turn, the painting of A. van Velde breaks away from it.

Art loves leaps.

To go from this immense fidelity to the painting of G. van Velde is to go from *Man in the Helm* to the *View of Delft*, from the Sistine to the Lodges (I am comparing relations).

It's a difficult passage.

What say of those planes that glide, those contours that vibrate, those bodies like tallies in the fog, those balances that nothing must upset, that break and reform as we gaze? How to speak of those colors that breathe, that pant? Of that teeming stasis? Of that weightless, forceless, shadowless world?

Here everything moves, swims, flees, returns, unravels itself, remakes itself. Everything ceases, ceaselessly. It looks like the insurrection of molecules, inside a stone a thousandth of a second before it disintegrates.

That's it, literature.

It would be best not to be exposed to these two ways of seeing and painting, on the same day. At least in the early days.

Let's put it more roughly. Let's be ridiculous.

A. van Velde paints the expanse.

G. van Velde paints the succession.

Since, before being able to see the expanse, let alone before having the power to represent it, it must be immobilized, this one turns away from the natural expanse, that which spins like a top under the whip of the sun. He idealizes it, gives it an internal sense. And it's precisely by idealizing it that he was able to achieve it with this objectivity, this unprecedented clarity. This is his discovery. He owes it to an extremely tense need to see clearly.

This one, contrarily, is entirely turned outwards, toward the tohu-bohu of things in the light, toward time. Because we only learn about time in the things that it agitates, that it prevents one from seeing. It is by giving himself entirely to the outside, in ascending the macrocosm shaken by the chills of time, that he realizes himself, that he realizes man if you prefer, in what is most unshakeable, in his certainty that there is neither present nor rest. It is the representation of that river where, according to Heraclitus' modest calculation, no one descends twice.

It's a funny *memento mori*, the radiant painting of G. van Velde. I note it in passing.

No connection with stopwatch painting, the one which, having granted the water lilies two minutes a day for the eternity of the psalmist, believes to have blocked earthly rotation, not to mention the annoying wriggling of the lower stars. With G. van Velde time gallops, he spurs it on with a frenzied release of Faust against the grain.

'This is what we are,' his paintings say. And they add: 'It's a chance.'

With that it's a painting of extraordinary calm and gentleness. Clearly, I understand nothing. It doesn't make noise. That of A. van Velde makes a very characteristic noise, that of the door slamming in the distance, the little thud of the door that has just been slammed, tearing it from the wall.

In short, two works that seem to refute each other, but which in fact come together at the heart of the dilemma, that of the plastic arts: How to represent change?

They refused, each in their own way, biases. They are not musicians, nor litterateurs, nor hairdressers. For the painter, the thing is impossible. It's moreover from the representation of this impossibility that modern painting has drawn much of its best effects.

But neither of them have what it takes to plastically take advantage of a plastic situation with no exit.

Basically, they're not interested in painting. What interests them is the human condition. We will return to this.

What, then, is representable, if they renounce representing change? Is there something, outside of change, which they can represent?

There remains to them, to one the thing that suffers, the thing that is changed; to the other, the thing that inflicts, the thing that causes change.

Two things which, in detachment, one from the executioner, the other from the victim, where they finally become representable, remain to be created. These are not things yet. They will come. Indeed.

These are two profoundly different attitudes, and whose principles hastily erected in antithesis have always delighted psychology, ever since the *dyskoloi* and the *eukoloi*.[2] They have their roots in the same experience. This is what is charming. Is it not?

The analyses of this divergence, if it does not explain anything, it may help situate the two works, one vis-à-vis the other. In particular, it will be able to shed light on the gap that they indict from the point of view of style, a gap whose deep meaning it is important to penetrate if we want to avoid founding a superficial confrontation there. It cannot be overstated. This kind of categorical negligence, which translates so well, in the elder, the urgency and the primacy of the inner vision, would become, in the other, irreparable faults. For the latter is not dealing with the thing alone, cut off from its moorings with all that makes it a simple extract of perdition, one would say cut off from its moorings with itself, and whose bailout requires precisely this mixture of mastery and boredom, but to an infinitely more complex object. To tell the truth, less to an object than to a process, a process felt with such acuity that it has acquired from it a solidity of hallucination, or of ecstasy. He always deals with the compound. It is no longer the natural compound, nestled in its dreary daily shimmers, but the same elements remain in presence. Confronted by this impenetrable block, A. van Velde blew it to pieces, to release what he needed. For the other, this solution was excluded in advance.

The two things had to remain together. Because we only represent succession by means of successive states, by imposing on them such a rapid shift that they end up merging, I would say almost by stabilizing, in the image of succession even. To force the fundamental invisibility of external things until this invisibility itself becomes a thing, not a simple consciousness of limit, but a thing that one can see and make seen, and do it, not in the head (painters have no head, so read canvas instead, or stomach, in the places where I affix them), but on the canvas, here is a

---

[2] *Eukoloi* & *dyskoloi*, terms Schopenhauer discusses in "Personality, or What a Man is," the second chapter of *The Wisdom of Life*. The first term refers to those who can be described as consistently focused on feelings of pleasure; the second refers to those consistently geared toward feelings of discomfort.

work of diabolical complexity, one which requires a profession of flexibility and of an extreme lightness, a profession that insinuates more than it affirms, which is positive only with the fleeting and supplementary evidence of the great positive, of the only positive, of the time that carries along.

Is there, behind these daubings, a solid fund of tricks to deceive the eye? Would they be able to trace the rainbow without the aid of a compass? Pretend, what am I saying, give relief to the ass of a racing horse, in the rain? I never asked them.

The painting of van Velde has other secrets, which it would be easy to reduce (to powerlessness) by means of the above. But I don't intend to lose everything.

I am not unaware of how many such developments must appear to be arbitrations, schematic and hardly in conformity with the images that were the occasion and the nourishment for them, with the images of images. Giving them more decent, more persuasive airs, with a lot of restrictions and nuances, would undoubtedly not be impossible. But it's not worth it.

At no time was there any question of what these painters do, or think they do, or want to do, but solely what I see them doing.

I want to say it again, lest they be taken for intellectual swine.

Yet one cannot conceive of a painting less intellectual than this one.

A. van Velde, in particular, must not begin to realize what he's been up to until about ten years later. Let's move along. He knows every time it's there, like a deep-sea fish that stops at the right depth, but he is spared the reasons.

This also seems true for G. van Velde, with the restrictions (here we are) imposed by his very different attack.

They remind me of this painter of Cervantes who, at the request, 'What do you paint?', replied: 'Whatever demon comes out of my brush.'

Finally, let's talk about something else, let's talk about the 'human.'

This is a term, and undoubtedly a concept also, reserved for the times of the great massacres. It takes pestilence, Lisbon and a major religious butchery, for people to think about loving each other, of leaving the gardener next door alone, of being extremely simple.

It's a word that we send back today with unparalleled fury. We say dum-dums.

It rains on artistic circles with a very particular abundance. That's a shame. Because art doesn't seem to need a cataclysm, in order to be able to be practiced.

The damages are already considerable.

With 'it's not human,' everything is said. À la the garbage can.

Tomorrow we will demand that the charcuterie be human.

That, it's nothing. We're used to it though.

What is truly appalling is that the artist himself got involved.

The poet who says: I am not a man, I am only a poet. Quickly the way to rhyme love and paid holidays.

The musician who says: I will give the siren to the muted trumpet. That will be more human.

The painter who says: All men are brothers. Come on, a little corpse.

The philosopher who says: Protagoras was right.

They are capable of destroying poetry, music, painting, and thought for 50 years.

Above all, let's not protest.

Do you want some presentable being? Give it a bruise. Give it a whistle.

Are you interested in space? Let's crack it.

Are you bothered by time? Let's kill it together.

Beauty? The reunited man.

Goodness? Choke it.

The truth? The fart of the greatest number.

What will become, in this fair, of this solitary painting, solitariness of the solitude that covers its head, with the solitude that extends its arms?

This painting, the slightest bit of which contains more true humanity than all their processions toward the happiness of sacred sheep.

I guess she will be stoned.

There are the eternal conditions of life. And there is its cost. Woe to him who distinguishes them.

After all, maybe we'll just hoot.

Anyway, we'll come back to it.

Because we're just starting to screw around with the van Velde brothers.[3]

I open the series.

It's an honor.

[3] Screw around is a translation of the French *déconner*, the archaic (vulgar, rare) meaning of which is to pull out, or "*decunt*." It is also slang that means to talk rubbish, kid, joke around, or to mess up, act up, malfunction. The French "con" means cunt, pussy, asshole, fucktard, etc.

Painters of Impediment

I have said everything that I had to say about the painting of the van Velde brothers in the last issue of the *Cahiers d'Art* (unless there has been another one since). I have nothing to add to what I have said there. It was little, it was too much, and I have nothing to add to it. Fortunately it is not a question of saying what has not yet been said, but of repeating, as often as possible in the smallest space, what has already been said. Otherwise we confuse the amateurs. This first. And modern painting is already disturbing enough in itself without our wanting to make it more disturbing still, by saying sometimes that it is perhaps this, sometimes that it is perhaps that. Then one disturbs oneself, without necessity. And we are already disturbed enough, of necessity, and not only by modern painting, without wanting to be more disturbed, by trying to say what has not yet been said, by one's knowledge. Because to give in to the ignoble temptation to say what has not yet been said, to one's knowledge, is to expose oneself to a grave danger, that of thinking what has not yet been thought, that we know. No, what matters, if one does not want to add to one's confusion and that of others before modern painting and other subjects of dissertation, is to affirm something, whether it is without precedent or with, and to remain faithful to it. Because by saying something and sticking to it, no matter what, you can end up forming an opinion about almost anything, a good solid opinion that can last a lifetime. And opinions of this kind, made to resist the ages, are not to be despised, doubtless never were, even in the early Middle Ages. And this seems to be particularly true of opinions relating to modern painting, of which it is not possible to form one, however fragile, by ordinary methods. But by affirming, one fine day, with firmness and then again the next day, and the day after, and every day, of modern painting that it is this, and this only, then in the space of ten, twelve years one will know what modern painting is, perhaps even well enough to be able to share it with one's friends, and without having had to spend the best of one's leisure time in so-called galleries, narrow, cluttered, and poorly lit, questioning it with their eyes. That is to say, we will know everything there is to know about the formula adopted, which constitutes the end of all science. Knowing what you want to say, there is wisdom. And the best way to know what you want to say is to want to say the same thing every day, with patience, and thus to familiarize yourself with the formula used, in all its quicksand. Until finally, to the classic problems on Expressionism, Abstraction, Constructivism, Neo-Plasticism and their antonyms, the answers are made immediately, complete, definitive and, so to speak, machinated. The aesthetic security and the feeling of well-being that result from it can be advantageously studied in the society of modern painters themselves, who will tell you, as soon as they are asked, and even without being asked anything, what exactly modern painting consists of, and what exactly it does not consist of, but preferably what exactly it does not consist of, at all hours of the day and night, and which will destroy all that resists this demonstration in less time than it takes them to describe a circle, or a triangle. And their painting itself, which must not be confused with their conversation, joyfully bears the same mark of certainty and irrefragability. So much so that of the two things, the canvas and the discourse, it is not always easy to know which is the egg and which the chicken.

We learn by the hour that it is, not only from the mouths of the usual crocodiles, one eye full of tears and the other screwed to the market, but from that of the most serious and respectable connoisseurs, that the School of Paris (meaning to be determined) is finished or almost, that its masters are dead or dying, its little masters too, and the epigones lost in the ruins of the great refusals.

This must mean either that the effort, the efforts of the last half-century of painting in France, are liquidated, the problems solved, the road closed, or that the affair has come to a halt for lack of executants. Either there is nothing left to do in the direction of these efforts, or what remains to be done is not being done, because there is no one to do it.

I suggest that the painting of van Velde is an assurance that the School of Paris (cf. Greenwich time) is still young and that it has a bright future ahead of it.

An insurance, a double insurance, because the same mourning leads them far from each other, from mourning for the object.

The history of painting is the history of its relationship with its object, these evolving, necessarily, first in the direction of width, then in that of penetration. What renews painting is first of all that there are more and more things to paint, then a way of painting them that is more and more possessive. By this I do not mean a first phase all in fulfillment, followed by a second all in concentration, but only two attitudes linked to each other, such as rest on effort. The primary thrill of painting in becoming aware of its limits carries toward the confines of these limits, the secondary in the sense of depth, toward the thing that the thing hides. The object of representation always resists representation, either because of its accidents or because of its substance, and first of all because of its accidents, because the knowledge of the accident precedes that of the substance.

The first assault given to the object seized, independently of its qualities, in its indifference, its inertia, its latency, here is a definition of modern painting that is undoubtedly no more ridiculous than the others. It has the advantage, without being in any way a value judgment, of excluding the Surrealists, whose preoccupation, bearing solely on questions of repertoire, remains as far removed from its great contemporary as the Sienese Sassetta and Giovanni di Paolo of the in-depth effort by Massaccio and Castagno. Di Paolo is a charming obscurantist. It also excludes those estimable quintessential abstractors Mondrian, Lissitzky, Malevitsch, Moholy-Nagy. And it expresses what is common to independents as diverse as Matisse, Bonnard, Villon, Braque, Rouault, Kandinsky, to mention a few. The Christ of Rouault, the most Chinese nature morte of Matisse, a conglomeration of the Kandinsky of 1943 or 1944, stem from the same effort, that of expressing how a clown, an apple, and a square of red are one and the same, and of the same disarray, before the resistance that this uniqueness opposes to being expressed. For they are one in this, that they are things, the thing, the thingness. It seems absurd to speak, as Kandinsky did, of a painting liberated from the object. What painting has freed itself from is the illusion that there is more than one object of representation, perhaps even the illusion that this single object allows itself to be represented.

If this is the last state of the School of Paris, after its long pursuit less of the thing than of its objectness, less of the object than of the condition of being, then we are perhaps entitled to talk about a crisis. For what remains of what is representable if the essence of the object is to escape representation?

It remains to represent the conditions of this escape. They will take one or the other of two forms, depending upon the subject.

One will say: I cannot see the object, to represent it, because it is what it is. The other: I cannot see the object, to represent it, because I am what I am.

There have always been these two kinds of artist, these two kinds of impediment, the impediment-object and the impediment-eye. But these impediments, they were taken into account. There was accommodation. They weren't part of the representation, or barely. Here they are part of it. We would say the biggest part. What is painted is what prevents painting.

Geer van Velde is an artist of the first kind (in my faltering opinion), Bram van Velde of the second.

Their painting is the analysis of a state of deprivation, an analysis borrowing from one the terms of the outside, light and emptiness, from the other those of the inside, darkness, fullness, phosphorescence.

The resolution is obtained in one by the abandonment of weight, density, solidity, by a tearing of all that ruins space, stops light, by the engulfment of the outside under the conditions of the outside. In the other among the unshakable masses of a being pushed aside, locked up and forever returned to itself, without traces, without air, cyclopean, with brief flashes, in the colors of the spectrum of black.

An endless unveiling, veil behind veil, surface upon surface of imperfect transparencies, an unveiling toward the unseen, the nothing, the thing again. And burial in the unique, in a place of impenetrable proximity, cell painted on the stone of the cell, art of incarceration.

This is what to expect when you allow yourself to be tricked to write on painting. Unless you're an art critic.

The painting of van Velde emerges, free from all critical concern, from a painting of criticism and of refusal, refusal to accept as given the old subject-object relationship. It is obvious that any work of art is a re-adjustment of this relation, but without being a criticism of it in the sense that the best of modern painting is a criticism of that which in its last manifestations strongly resembles the one addressed, with a stick, to the slowness of a dead donkey.

From this moment there remain three paths that painting can take. The way back to old naivety, through the winter of its abandonment, the way of repentance. Then the path that is no longer one, but a last attempt to live on the conquered country. And finally the path forward of a painting that cares as little for an outdated convention as for the hieraticism and preciousness of superfluous investigations, painting of acceptance, glimpsing in the absence of relationship and in the absence of object the new relationship and the new object, a path that already forks, in the works of Bram and Geer van Velde.

Translated by Rainer J. Hanshe

1000 & 1

Kari Hukkila

PRECIS

1000 & 1 (Kustannusosakeyhtiö: Teos, 2016) is above all a novel about a disaster or disasters, man-made or natural, and how to survive them.

Hence the title of the novel, which refers to the number of nights that Scheherazade tells stories to Shahryar and by doing so survives from one morning to the next.

Although the novel is full of micro-histories, digressions, and human destinies, in the following excerpt the themes of the novel are superimposed on the desolate landscape of the northern part of the Bay of Naples, which becomes a metaphor for all the fiery devastation of our times.

In the excerpt included here, the nameless narrator is in Pozzuoli, on the northern shore of the Bay of Naples. The episode starts in the middle of a flashback and then moves without a clear boundary to the present time.

The narrator follows his own tracks from years ago in the area, as well as that of the Polish writer and former Gulag prisoner Gustaw Herling, who had also wandered about in the same area, as the narrator has learned when planning a literary work about Herling.

— Kari Hukkila

January, a sunny day ... a municipal worker took us on a tour of the shuttered city. A down-to-earth guy in a brown suede jacket, a hardy face, a sprawling moustache, no-nonsense conversation. Over the last fifteen or so years (after most people had left the city, I assumed), plants had occupied the streets, captured the walls, the gables, and crept their way into old apartments. The windowpanes were smashed, the gutters collapsed. Our route wound its way in and out of the houses, most of them without a roof, rising and falling one story at a time. Broken Coca Cola bottles in the corners of the rooms, walls covered in faded posters of pop stars who hadn't recorded a note since the 1970s. Inside the church, the gilding had been torn from the fixtures. Here and there lay items of furniture, forgotten and left to the mercy of the elements, individual kitchen appliances, tables, chairs, vinyl and cassette players, shoes, winter clothes and so on. From the edge of the city wall, you could see down into a gravel pit with trailers, the former residents of the *terra* living there. A mild, sunny day. At the foot of the wall was the small center of the town, where people lived as though the ruins weren't there at all. *You forget about it... You learn to close your eyes...* The small potted plants standing by the trailer doors were shabby; they reminded me of the worn-out old shell suits and cheap baseball caps, the woolen sweaters, the track suits, the tired and swollen faces, the gaunt cheeks, the puffing on cigarettes. All around was a cacophony of uncouth voices, harsh cries, laughter, shouting, sighs whistling between missing teeth. The women middle-aged and older were so overweight that it must have taken them considerable effort. The girls' large round or triangular earrings scraped against their necks when they turned their heads. Thick, black hair. *Salve, salve.* They had been driven from their homes *like cattle. My home used to be up there.* All this in a shrill, rough voice, a curious mixture of innocence and directness. They were *Bethlehem's cattle*, someone said. The women's jumpers had heart-shaped patterns on them. Between the trailers, long wooden poles held a row of plastic awnings in place, like a continuation of the endless lattice of scaffolding holding up the walls and masonry across the street. A suitable place for our perfectly average life twenty years ago, its sheer inanity, I thought now. In our first serious relationship, we always repeat the worst aspects of our childhood homes, Mara told me once. The conformism we glean from our surroundings is like Herling's depiction of *the invisible hand, the power unaware of its own majesty, to which we learn to close our eyes.* My brother would have said that the greatest conformism of all was *not thinking further than your own arse*, and even in Kontula you might hear someone say that so-and-so's world *only reached as far as his arse could drag him.*

An hour later I find myself in the place where the road leads us to the dead, or so people used to believe. I've been walking, or perhaps it would be more appropriate to say I've been shuffling in circle around an enormous flat crater with small islets of woodland, laurel trees, holm oaks, sage and gorse; behind the woodland there was a large plateau covered in volcanic ash where the whiteness of the earth was dazzling, the air stank of sulfur, the heat and the horseflies wouldn't give me a moment's peace, smoke rose from fissures in the ground and curled its way up the steep embankment further off. I felt weak, and when I saw a wooden bench in the shade of the trees I lay down, closed my eyes and wedged my wallet against the back of the bench in case I fell asleep. Behind the nearby trees, there were a number of dome tents, old camper vans, a few shacks selling things; a camp site, *only eastern Europeans*, I concluded from the voices. There was nobody in sight. In ancient times, local folklore held that a road ran through this place leading underground to the homes of the dead.

The taxi ride from the harbor to the *Vulcano solfatara* took only five minutes, but I didn't have the energy to walk. In front of a small arched doorway, the elderly tout at a nearby bar watched my arrival, launched into his usual spiel, pointed at the patio; his tone was friendly, so I stood there and exchanged a few words with him. *Food poisoning*, I said. *Drugs, medicine, injection*, he replied and mimed injecting himself in the forearm. Along the bar's wall was a long table, volcanic rocks, lava, coral, pearls, cameo brooches, all intended as souvenirs. I ordered a Diet Coke, but before it was brought to the table, I felt sick and had to get up. The toilet cubicle was cramped and dirty. Endless amounts of hand washing. I leant over, stuck my fingers down my throat, and only then saw something deeply unpleasant. At a moment like this, the last thing you want to see is human feces. I washed the toilet bowl, rewashed my hands, stuck two fingers deep down my throat and emptied the contents of my stomach. Another round of hand washing, after which I staggered across the bar, drank my Diet Coke, and set off for the crater.

Herling had taught me that wherever there is a road from which nobody ever returns, there must be a sauna nearby. In the middle of the sweltering crater, the sauna is a simple brick construction with two closet-like alcoves built into the wall where you can lie down and curl up. A small sign explained that in one of them the temperature is 60°c and in the other 90°c. Next to them, above a pile of yellow sulfuric rocks, the temperature was 160°c, but the higher the temperature the more the horseflies felt at home. Another sign explained that the crater was fitted with corner reflectors to observe seismological activity.

I drift off, unsure whether I am more asleep than awake, I can hear people's voices, but there is nobody in sight; the air shimmers with smoke, the stagnant baking heat, the sun haze.

There on the bench I chuckle, half aloud. As though shadows had appeared from amid the smoke and the glare. The voices had disappeared, and now I felt alone in the crater, as if left inside a deserted theater. Here wanderers chosen by fate can meet one another, people who by dint of their societal and economic differences would never have crossed paths while they were alive. Here amid the stench of filth, the rich can appeal to the ferryman, demand a postponement for a fee, and ask to take all their worldly belongings with them, while the poor, already used to obeying their superiors, will supinely give up their seat for anyone who asks, and even take up the oars or the bail if ordered to do so. There can be no return, so while for one person this could be the final battle, for another it might as well be business as usual... *This team will get some real results... An affable chap will do just fine... All things in good company...* Vanity flourished, and even if someone was concerned about the future, be it underground or in the skies above, nobody seriously believed they would be forced to leave everything behind, a bodybuilder his muscles, a rich man his arrogance, a philosopher his convoluted notions... *It is like shutting the door behind oneself*, said Björling shortly before his death. Wittgenstein, when he heard that the end was drawing near, sighed *finally*, or so Mara always claimed... The depiction and mood could equally apply to the moment when Herling arrived at the prison camp that dark evening in the middle of winter and saw the watchtowers in the distance, *like four crow's nests propped on tall wooden stakes*.

There on the bench, half-asleep, I wondered why Mara had talked about the Ethiopian so insistently, as if this man had always been one of the recurring topics on our walks around Kaivopuisto. When Björling commented on his approaching death, that it is like shutting the door behind oneself, he wasn't telling the truth. Even Wittgenstein's *finally* sounded a little hollow. One way or another, humans always try to resist loneliness and crow's nests. A few brief trysts notwithstanding, Björling's sexual life was lonely, and Wittgenstein's wasn't much better. Herling too told us something about loneliness when he described how the convicts systematically hunted down and raped any women who arrived at the camp. It was part of the camp's economy: scraps of bread, a rape, felling a tree, like snapping a branch from a pine, a handful of berries from a sprig.

Mara fetched the Ethiopian as though this was a form of *survival*, morning upon morning. Later that afternoon, Mara called, twice, and said the Ethiopian was here now. I didn't ask whether *here* meant at Mara's apartment or the fact that this relative stranger had now been located. They had done simple things together, strolled, chatted, gone grocery shopping, cooked some pasta. It sounded almost like two people's shared loneliness, or the tranquility of Skjolden when compared to the folly of the world, which I encountered later that evening when, with considerable exertion, I stood up from the bench and shuffled back to the arched doorway and the Solfatara office. Two old men were sitting in the middle of the room. Their thinning white hair and beards were scruffy; behind them were a few large potted plants, old bookcases, dark wood, glass doors, scientific-looking books and tomes published sometime between 1900 and 1910. In front of the men was a bulletin board showing clippings and articles dating from March 2009 and cut from American and Italian newspapers. *Solfatara compared to Viagra*, the headlines declared. Two enzymes producing hydrogen sulfides had been discovered in the tissues of the male member, and these in turn caused an erection and the enlarging of the blood vessels. Natural Viagra, the same gases as in the 'Solfatara shrouds,' the devil's issue... I take a moment's rest on a chair in the office and ask whether the ground still tremors almost daily... It's been quiet for the last fifteen years, the ground making only small motions *back and forth*, chuckles one of the men, suggestively rocking his fist back and forth a few centimeters at a time. Always the same old jokes... *The pot isn't simmering... The giant isn't smoking... There's no cauldron quite like it...* This is a VEI 8-category *caldera*, a supervolcano, he laughed. Fish in the sea could be boiled alive at any moment... Then the bubbling will bring them up to the surface like white fillets on a restaurant plate... Some kind of eruption is imminent, that much is clear.

*

Back in my hotel room later that evening, the day's exertions collapse into bed with me, and it takes a moment before I have the energy to take my temperature. It's 38.4°c. I drift off to sleep and wake up during the night; I'm not hungry, even though I haven't eaten all day. I am half asleep, half awake, for a while I can't remember where I am, but I feel a little better and switch on the reading lamp. Twenty years ago I used to look at these same places from one week to the next, but as I start flicking through the brochures I bought from the boys at Solfatara and think back to our *little group's* lies and decades-old deceits, it occurs to me that I never really *saw* anything. I study a historical engraving of a group of aristocrats who long ago traveled from far away in the north to admire the lava flows... Horse-drawn carriages, platforms, sedan chairs, women in long skirts, hats and diadems on their heads, there's a man sitting on a deckchair sketching the panorama, a young man and woman, perhaps looking for a way to elope together, they have walked out to the furthest safe ledges in the distance, the man is standing in front showing the woman the lava flows... We were like that too: idle, cruel, stupid. Standing in front of a raging inferno we imagine that at most we will burn our nose, our toe or little finger, the belief in our own exceptionalism is so unshakable that there's no way a disaster affecting the *hoi polloi* could ever befall us.

I wished Mara could have been there with me to comment on the image, chortling upon seeing something that could easily apply to our time too, just like he did that summer when I walked across the yard to his place almost every day, my brother was seven years old, but he too spent his time in and around that same yard, always appearing with his bike at some point during the day. Mara had a habit of telling me about what he'd been reading that morning, laughing as he explained how a particular section should be understood. After this, he put his books aside and forced me to listen as he played his flute. He played straight from the score, stopped, furrowed his brow, leant closer to the music, then continued his painfully pedantic reading of Bach's counterpoint until he stumbled in the exact same spot again... There in my hotel room, floored by the heat, I imagined I could hear his stumbling flute as I read about how Monte nuovo, the green-dappled mountain on the shores of Pozzuoli, rose up from the earth in a single night, Mara stumbled and chortled, and out in the yard my brother was living his seven-year-old life, he too stumbling on his bike and chortling, fumbling his way onwards like the tentative notes of the flute. At around midday, the earth at the shores of Pozzuoli rose five meters, I read, and the flute stumbled again. The sea retreated hundreds of meters from the shoreline, forming sandbanks and shallow pools, the sun glinted against the flanks of the thousands of thrashing fish that the locals rushed to gather up. People lay claim to everything revealed by the departing sea, even the court turned up to divide the land, not only to its favorites, but into taxable property. An hour or two after sunset, a molten rock the size of a bull was spat up into the air from the bowels of the earth, contemporary witnesses attested. A great fissure appeared, tearing the land apart at the seams. Loud noises filled the air. The earth vomited smoke, fire, rock and a silt of thick ash. Sulfurous compounds and fumes issued all around. The birds and animals were covered in yellow sulfuric ash and died or let people capture them with their bare hands. Soon afterwards, ash covered the streets of Naples too, blackening the palace façades and tarnishing their beauty. Everyone who had had the chance to leave the town had already done so, but now, at night, the poor inhabitants of Pozzuoli headed off to Naples on foot, carrying their children and scant possessions in their arms. Some were carrying birds covered in ash, others the fish they had plucked from the shore. Many wore nothing but a shirt, some had run out into the night stark naked. *Their faces were painted in the colors of death*, wrote one contemporary source. In Kontula, sixteen-year-old Mara's Bach kept stumbling at the same spot, like so many human endeavors. If Mara had been reading this with me, he would have laughed and cried, just like he did in Kontula, and there in the dim of the hotel room I thought that if only I could make my brother laugh and cry too it might very well nudge him along a little. In Pozzuoli, people's curiosity soon conquered their dismay at the natural disaster. The viceroy and his entourage rode out to the spot, or as near as it was possible to go. The earth was covered in a layer of ash half a meter thick, columns of smoke obscured the sky, the terrain was like a churned field. Word had it that beneath all the smoke there was a mountain the size of Vesuvius. The viceroy was thinking of profit, the people were there for the spectacle. The mountain was by the shore, so many curious onlookers arrived by boat and climbed up the hillside all the way to the edge of the crater, heedless of the ash and the fact that the soles of their shoes became singed. From the crater rim, they could see down into the cauldron with water boiling deep at the bottom. The mountain was 134m tall and had risen up in less than twelve hours. An average of one meter every five minutes, I calculated. The following Sunday, when several dozen or perhaps more than a hundred curious souls had gathered at the summit to behold the newest local attraction, an eruption shook the crater and belched up a cloud of red-hot ash that came rolling down the southern face of the mountain. Many onlookers were consumed in the flames, toppled over by falling rocks, or overcome by the smoke.

Translated by David Hackston

PERSONAGES ETC.

Mara
A fictional character. Mara is a common male nickname in Finnish, a diminutive of the proper name Martti or Martin.

Gustaw Herling -Grudziński (20 May 1919 – 4 July 2000)
A Polish writer, journalist, essayist, World War II underground fighter and political dissident who lived abroad during Communist rule in Poland. Herling is best known for writing a personal account of life in the Soviet Gulag entitled *A World Apart*, first published in 1951 in London. He lived in exile in Naples, settling there permanently in 1955 until his death in 2000.

Gunnar Björling (31 May 1887 – 11 July 1960)
A Swedish-speaking Finnish poet. He was one of the leading figures of modernist literature in Scandinavia.

Ludwig Wittgenstein (26 April 1889 – 29 April 1951)
An Austrian-British philosopher.

The Ethiopian
A fictional character. A sans-papiers from Ethiopia.

Kaivopuisto
One of the oldest and most well known parks in central Helsinki, Finland. Gunnar Björling lived almost all his life on the outskirts of Kaivopuisto.

Skjolden
A village in the municipality of Luster in Vestland County, Norway. It was home to philosopher Ludwig Wittgenstein, who lived there after 1913 during some periods of his life. He had designed a small wooden house that was erected on a remote rock over the Eidsvatnet Lake in 1913.

Kontula
A suburb in Eastern Helsinki.

TRACTATUS ILLOGICO-INSANUS

(an excerpt)

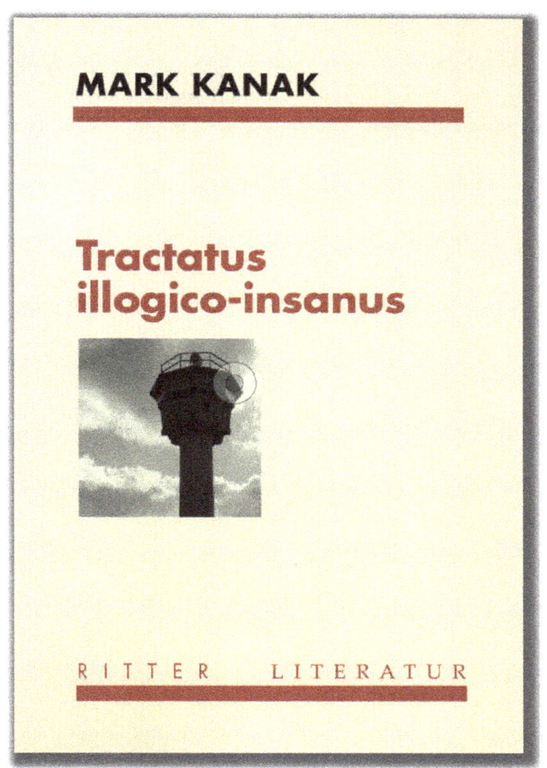

MARK KANAK

Foreword

This book will perhaps only be understood by those who have not even thought the thoughts expressed in it – or thoughts that are not at all similar, but are rather skewed and the meaning thereof as well. It *is* a textbook. That is, a *book of texts*. Its purpose would have been achieved if, after reading through it *without pleasure*, one went away completely confused, angry, furious and stunned in order to in turn confuse, excite and cause others to think.

In fact, a lot is said today, and faster than ever, *in real time*, but of course most of this is usually *saying nothing at all*. This book deals with *some of* the non-philosophical problems (and equally, the philosophical ones – that is, so philosophical that they are not philosophical at all) and draws the conclusion – as I believe – that the questions underlying these problems are, to the vast majority of populations *in all countries*, but *especially* in the United States of America, except in *those other places where people themselves are personally affected*, completely fucking irrelevant and have nothing to do with the misunderstanding of the logic of our language, but rather with the fact that the vast majority of people in all countries have poor access to educational opportunities, clean water, raspberries and the like. One could sum up the whole meaning of this book with the words: Anything that is being said at all is overheard, stored, analyzed and secretly recorded, no matter whether it has been said in a clear, cryptic, unclear, inverted, confusing, innocent, or guilty manner; and what one cannot talk about should absolutely be communicated in encoded form, from one individual to the other, or not at all.

This being said, this book seeks to induce the reader to think, yes, to *think*, as to why there are no limits to the surveillance state (SS) or why he or she is not drawn to support and encourage others to think as well, or rather – to *not think*, but rather to *the expression of thoughts* – and only in coded or other ways: Because to draw a line in thinking, the SS wants you to go around the corner, hide, ask no questions at all, accept everything and admit everything – for "reasons of security," of course. And we have to be able to think on both sides of that line (so we have to assume that after Edward Snowden's revelations, everything will go on as before, new walls will be built, and governmental capabilities of surveillance will continuously be expanded).

You can't draw lines in the language, you don't know where the limits are. If something is boundless, it grows, attracts other *bodies* to itself, uses other *devices* (to be understood simultaneously as "human" or "head"), and since we have no idea where the limits are, nonsense will simply prevail.

How far my efforts will coincide with those of other non-philosophers, chimney sweeps, bakers, cleaning ladies, housewives, editors, authors, raspberry pickers, raven and crow friends, I do not want to judge. Clearly, what I have written here is not at all new; already in the introduction some things have been stolen from a certain Herr Wittgenstein, and what follows is pure fantasy, and therefore I do not bother quoting sources, because I don't care whether what I have thought has already been thought before me by someone else or not – chances are it all has. Whatever.

This book was born in a dream and strives to hint at the great preliminary achievements of all those for whom *participation is (or was) not a solution*, who are (or were) not always indifferent to what is exacted or done by the state. You know the types – Serner, Burger, Jarry, blahdey-blah – the fucked up types.

If this work has a value, it is twofold. On the one hand, thoughts are expressed in it, and the worse the thoughts are expressed, the greater this value will be, or better yet if one fails to think about any of it at all – and if so – the more the nail (*SS*) shall have been squarely hit on the head (*the device*). Here I am far from aware that I have failed, but, well, hmm. Actually I suffer from loss of short-term memory, I really have no idea what happened or even what I wrote just 5 minutes ago.

Simply because my power (*ability*) to cope (*ring-fix!) with the task* is too...lacking. May others come and do it better. Or worse. Wait, what was I talking about again?

Let me just say this: The *truth of* the thoughts communicated here seems quite assailable to me and is not at all definite, but rather vague, blurred and dull. Or the opposite. So I am of the opinion and yes, 100%

sure that, much like Herr Wittgenstein, I have solved all problems. Wait, or that I have not. I am asserting the opposite here! Ultimately, if I am not mistaken, the value of this work will be that it demonstrates how little is being done at the moment to solve specifically these problems: the rampant plague of state-sponsored (and personal) surveillance, the systematic destruction of our planet, and the odious obliteration of the private sphere.

There is but one imperative:

Go mad and smash the surveillance state!

Berlin, October 2018

M.K.

TRACTATUS ILLOGICO-INSANUS

3 EXCERPTS

1. The Program is running — constantly.

1.1 Upon considerable reflection,and after contemplating applying various applications using velcro, the idea is perfected for implementation.

1.11 The surrounding forests (in our heads) are mostly natural (or unnatural) spruce forests.

1.12 Myths and prejudices concerning the alleged "opacity" of the boundary between normality and mental illness (and simultane-ously the harmfulness or even "risk" of exposure to "madmen," see § 2.11) only reinforces the isolation of people who are already socially disadvantaged anyway. Ostensibly.

1.13 My head (hereinafter referred to as "the device"): Filled with black and neutral quality shoe polish, 2 applicator shoe brushes, 1 large shoe brush, 2 towels and a shoehorn made of metal. And gasoline, blood, thoughts and music. And raspberries.

1.2 Inquisitors and regressive types may be able to build prisons and asylums that will be suitable for them later as workers' settlements. However, asylums inquisitors and regressive types cannot invite you to make time for a trip to a climbing forest. Or some absinthe with a side of arsenic.

1.21 Quick interim report: The initial processes are running like a top, the input has been processed, bit 0 to bit 6. Keep going.

2. XKeyscore monitors and stores — everything. They've got it covered! Relax! (See §3.22, §5.01)

2.01 Fully sintered ceramic foam made of high purity alumina guarantees the system (also known as "the device," or "the head") a high strength and thermal resistance base. It also provides a good cushion when having your skull battered by the investigators.

2.012 But that's another story and we'll not go into that just yet.

2.0121 In fact, the actual term used for the Program will not be revealed here at all. Incidentally, pianists have long considered pianos from the Steinway & Sons workshop to be the best in the world, probably from the mechanical workshop and forge head-quartered at the Jean Amery-Hermann Burger Suicide-Factory, somewhere in North or South America, or maybe somewhere in Europe. Whatever.

2.0122 Filenames of the loaded in memory method are only visible if the method has already been saved. This may lead to delays, which can be compensated for within the switching electronics and the valve control unit.

2.0123 The file cannot be saved.

2.01231 The magazine "Quarto" dedicated issues 22 and 23 to Hermann Burger and Etienne Bariller. In the future, they will dedicate an issue to Marek Sturmvogel. A fatal mistake, scholars will later come to believe.

2.0124 Once upon a time, somebody thought up an art project, or "little art thing." No, it was not a block of wood in an empty room, or a shoehorn positioned on a dildo or a pile of trash bags sprayed with perfume and inflated adorned with pictures of Hitler, Sinatra and Holub. Entitled "Just One More," it listed hard facts about the "Berliners' favorite drug." 25,000 Berliners are alcoholics; 500 Berlin hospital beds are occupied daily as result of chronic alcohol consumption; 120,000 cases of beer are sold weekly at the Getränke Hoffmann liquor store; 200 liters of draft beer are consumed on average on an ok party night at the Kaffee Burger (bottled beer not included); etc. The consequences: Who knows. And what's more: who cares?

2.013 "Dive down to grab some air" is a favorite motto of the once lauded, now reviled German poet Durs Grünbein; I expropriated (stole) it after he signed a book for me and use it now myself when signing. Or variations thereof. Now, if by chance or great exception someone wants me to sign one of my books, I write: Fuck off, to grab some mail. Or: Suck off, to protect the tomb. (See §5.1311)

2.0131 Including cases of fetal pathology, the risk of complications to the amniocentesis and chorionic villus sampling, but overall in non-hydropic fetus, is less than 1 . Something like that "doubt truth to be a liar" bit by that one writer. Put that in your pipe and smoke it, Grünbein!

2.014 If numbers entered have already been stored, the entered number is shown flashing on the display. Keep a log!

* * * * * *

2.03 To prevent operating errors, the front panel (in your head) is designed so that illogical and/or incomplete settings are automatically monitored and signaled. This in turn seems illogical and wrong, but can be explained as follows: There is a chasm in the background, while in the foreground (of the background), no chronological narrative sequence is occurring. The only concern for the Reader: If a text seems to her to be ambiguous or illogical, one should consider that it could be meant ironically or sarcastically – but – if the arrangement of the scenes on the walls of your mental cell appears sparse, seem totally illogical and irrational, it is because they seem to follow no chronic narrative sequence, as one would expect (e.g., with respect to weather data, in the foreground).

Which, in the light of these facts, begs the questions: What kind of a wall? What scenes? How? Who? Cell? Weather? When?

2.031 We are on the way to splintering and juxtaposing all these illogical feelings/thoughts through the collaborative work we are accomplishing here (you reading, me writing) with rationally, modern thoughts (think of the logo we can use!), but with an absolutely sufficiently motor. In other words, illogical combinations of plants (for example, combinations with a diuretic ingredient and a second part, which is used as a laxative) would be questionable, if applied to the system, at this point. Theoretically.

2.032 The Reader: All this is illogical and we should take time to analyze the deeper reasons for these results. For example (says the reader to him or herself, or itself): "The world is spinning faster than ever. Or so it seems to many of us, and has, for some years. Yet the world turns stupidly faster than the internal mills in the head of the narrator beneath the wheel. The device, that is. Action, analysis, reaction. But what does it mean?" To which I respond: "Mayakovsky said: Writing is like mining uranium: work one year, yield one gram. That is: If freezing is longingly arconic, then it's also pedantic, servile, and symbionic. And difficult." To which the reader responds: "Are you fucking drunk?"

2. Is only the animals / are addicted to fuel / and are narcotic, / then they will also be podagratic / diabolic, / and idiotic.

2.033 Difficult, also, is identifying mental problems as an indirect result of environmental pollution that occurs in response to direct or indirect experience, and on the basis of which I can relate to circumstances with or without injurious potential.

2.034 The more unique the information, the faster the electron rotates, and the stronger its spin shall be.

2.04 According to Prof. Dr. Dr. "I am not the son of Yuri!" Andropov of the Academy of Sciences in Moscow, the electron can be accelerated to a net spin of 32 times the speed of light.

2.05 Through the constant inflow over the line of electric flux, a reaction is formed as a constant magnetic field (vertical magnetic field lines) which moves from the Earth to the ionosphere in its own clockwise direction.

2.06 Problem: You sit there at the computer. By pressing a single key, the screen rotates 90 degrees Z counterclockwise. So many thoughts to be expressed, but how? The NSA/ BND/GCHQ (cross out those that do not apply) has the solution! Solution: Grab a container (any), hold tight and rotate your head clockwise until it stops; perform a visual inspection (all retaining lugs of the container must be properly locked). Take a drink of the nearest fluid (preferably antifreeze). Problem solved.

2.061 If large container installations such as struts or supports cause false echoes, these can be attenuated through supplementary measures.

2.062 Each revolution of the adjusting screw clockwise increases the trigger flow rate by approximately 10% relative to the paddles used. Remember that fluid? Take a sip. Wait for the effect. Ideas are now collected. But even so, they still have to be expressed. For applications with high acoustic pressure, such as speaking loudly, reduce the audio gain level by rotating the gain control (gain) counterclockwise (while using the microphone) until the red LED "AUD" on the receiver only flashes during the loudest signals. Much like *Krapp's Last Tape*, that sort of thing. Smile to yourself, laugh at the most inopportune times, wait for reactions.

2.063 The monitoring devices used by the "AUTHORITIES" and "EXPERTS" for processing sets of questions and statements (captured) essentially use checklists and reminder lists. Remember that.

* * * * * *

2.1 Two hunters meet — both dead.

2.11 Two madmen meet. The one says: Can you take a group picture of me? The other replies: Yes! The first replies: Great! Then fan out into a semicircle! A third, arriving with a limp, says, observing it all (moving in curiously, giggling): You can tell someone has a cold by their stuffy nose, chills, slight cough and possibly elevated chill and even slight fever! Suddenly, a bright light flashes and all three freeze in place. One looks at two, two looks at three, and three at one. The first one says (slowly moving backwards): Ah, ok! Kleist...Kleist!!! The second (to himself, whispering): Shove it in the drawer!!! Shove it in the drawer!!! The third, euphorically: Raspberries!!!

2.12 The three all come down with terrible colds. Yet a few days later, the cough subsides; the patients find it easier to move; the temperature lowers. Unfortunately, in the meantime, every madman imprisoned in the unsupervised ward with them as a security measure has mysteriously dropped dead. The only survivors (our three friends) eat the corpses, but only after dissecting, wrapping and storing certain body parts in the refrigerator for a snack later.

2.13 Illogical behavior is easily recognizable. It is characterized by a variety of symptoms including wheezing, coughing and shortness of breath and can be life threatening. Example: Television program, Bachmann Prize, Austria. We all like to sit around and evaluate texts, as we're all know-it-alls and of course we can assess better than anyone else if a text is a success or not upon first reading. Everything is evaluated, cross-examined, the faces are recorded with cameras and enlarged, the disappointments, the confusion, the joy, the shakes of the head, the angular women in high boots smoking with their wine spritzers and who are oh-so-easily-disappointed, the men with short beards who visibly, disgustedly contort their faces and simply cannot grasp how, after "a really okay first publication and a goodly structured and layouted, super looking successful debut" it would have come to this, that the author is presenting such a "lousy, failed, awful disgrace" of a follow-up. The audience coughs, moves uncomfortably in their seats, sweats, etc. The author retreats in shame.

2.131 The initial assessment is generally performed only once and is valid as long as the book that was reviewed does not appear in print. The prize is naturally awarded to anybody that doesn't speak German as their mother tongue. This has become a requirement, lately. (I've still a chance! I just need to be able to endure insults, but that won't be a problem – my neighbor plays Heino night and day – I can bear everything, the "Swedish drink," etc.)

2.14 The "Schwedentrunk" (Swedish drink), also called water torture, is torture whereby the accused receives a funnel of water, partly mixed with urine or manure, in the mouth. In addition to the pain, which causes a large water accumulation in the abdomen, the esophagus also burns, due to the manure. Worst of all, the Schwedentrunk results in bacterial infections and visions of Viking marionette performances. Hallucinations about Abba reunions and Ikea sales are modern side effects.

3. If you are slapped with a restraining order and must always keep 100 meters distance from a particular person, the question is, how you can guarantee this will happen? At 100 meters distance, you can't really recognize anybody, and before you know it, you're suddenly standing right next to them! (Not that I would know anything about that).

3.001 Nature itself (*roses, apples, blueberries, Jarry, Federman*) knows no logic (*Serner*), and the laws of nature govern none at all. (Yeah, yeah, de Sade, I know). What would happen if, at some point, irreconcilable contradictions (*Uwe Johnson/ Daniel Johnston*) were to arise between individual laws of nature (*Bommi Baumann*), which gradually allowed the foundations of physics (*dacha life*) to disintegrate? The laws of nature (*Bommi Baumann*) are a closed causal circle (*pancakes*). Thus one law (*dacha*) determines the other, and with progressive development steps (*natural mineral water*), one obtains a self-referential framework (*corn-*

flowers), which according to the model (*vodka*) seems to have gaps (*currants*) in some places.

3.01 Natural laws (*Bommi Baumann*) can be unproblematically illogical in themselves. At the same time man (*FM Einheit*) also weights them qualitatively in the models (*Three Mile Island*) and makes statements (*Marienbad, Blixa Bargeld*) about the relationship (*Toskana Brötchen/N.U. Unruh*) between them, for example. an illogicalness of laws of nature (*Patricia Hearst/Ulrike Meinhof/Roland Kaiser*) that we have brought about in our minds does not lead to the decay (*Babe Ruth, Ted Williams*) of the basic physical structure (*Homer Simpson*).

3.02 The probability (*Heiner* Müller) that in the case (*spruce forests*) of a resulting contradiction (*Uwe Johnson and Magic Johnson*) between the observation of a system (*XKeyscore*) and the underlying laws of nature (*Bommi Baumann*), the system relations (*PRISM, Klaus Fischer*) between involved components (*raspberries*) were misinterpreted temporally and spatially is much higher than the probability (*Berliner Pilsner [prior to 1991]*) with which a natural law (*Bommi Baumann*) in sycophantically isolated form (*Richard Carpenter, Udo Lindenberg, Joe Dimaggio, Stan Musial*) must be regarded as contradictory and corrosive. So it is often the picturesque relationships of individual system components (*PRISM, raspberries*) that are not correctly interpreted and thereby erroneously transferred to the apparently (but not spotlight) contradictory laws of nature (*Bommi Bauman times Babe Ruth*).

3.03 In the light of current physics we can say: Everything consists of energy. Everything is moved by energy. Everything new arises from a combination of energy and chance. It is also no coincidence that about 6 out of 10 physicists smell of piss. As the song goes: *"I don't need society/I don't need society/I don't society/I don't need society // Fuck you!"* (DRI, 1983)

3.031 By chance, the English chemist and inventor of linoleum, Frederick Walton (1834–1928), at the age of 21, discovered a paint pot on whose surface a moldable and kneadable layer of dried linseed oil had formed. Walton had stumbled into the lab with his flashlight when he made the creepy discovery and had (unwittingly) changed kitchen life forever and ever. Within a very short period of time, all English kitchens were floored with beautiful linoleum. (Ok, not all, in fact not many at all, but you get the idea). After some time, however, he realized there was something missing in his life, and he was unhappy. Sure, thanks to his clever invention (dopey accidental discovery), people now had this great and practical flooring for their kitchens, but he still wasn't getting laid and had to live in some dreary lab without running water and had to listen to the Russian neighbors fighting about the Siege of Sevastopol (he assumed, given the fact that he only spoke a bit of Russian) all the time. Over the next few years, he continued to work in the laboratory hoping to find an improved chemical process for converting uranium to uranium hexafluoride as a starting material for an enrichment plant to kill people with uranium more efficiently in the future. By the time he was 25 he had made good progress and had almost reached his goal, but suddenly everything went horribly wrong. One evening around midnight, when he was still working, a ghoulish figure that appeared to be the Russian poet Mayakovsky (who was from the future) came unexpectedly out of a closet, confused and humming some zippy song about revolution. Walton reached for his flashlight, thinking to himself, intuitively, "Absolutely don't say anything about Brik," (which in and of itself was odd, since Lilya Brik was also from the future; somehow Walton had intuitively (and instantly) acquired this great knowledge of Brik, wherefore he knew not) and directed it (the light, not the great knowledge of Brik) at the poet from the future. But Mayakovsky (not the bald Mayakovsky, but the one with the head of hair before he lost all his hair or shaved it off) just stood there, not moving, rigid, dressed in a nightgown with a bundle of poems between his legs and under his arms. Somewhere outside one could hear a midnight trolleybus arriving, stopping, wait a few seconds, and then drive on. Then and there Walton thought to himself, "Oh for fuck's sake, Mayakovsky, you're such a man, but there's no shadow that will accidentally fall on your vision bulbs, and I suspect that far into the future you'll end up working with directors and lights to trick yourself with shadows and light, making yourself look slimmer, more beautiful, bolder, crazier, paler or just younger. But I won't succumb to your dark magick! You're a ghost! Get out of here! Get out of here!" Which, in retrospect, seemed a rather convoluted and complicated thing to think to himself, or so it would seem...later. And in a flash, the poet was gone again. The next day Walton gave up all his work, burned down his lab, moved to Brighton and died a some years later, homeless and forgotten, wandering around eating raspberries all day. Linoleum, however, IS and REMAINS immortal! Much like asbestos! One is prompted to say, "Walton who?"

3.032 It is not useful to monitor the functions of these control windows that you are already familiar with. Better, rather, to switch it all off, shut it all down, to abolish the language of the world and take a walk in the park, at the lake, feeding crows (*sparrows*).

3.1431 The device (your head) has inverted the relationship between the rule and the exception into its opposite, and in the process also reversed the burden of proof for three-dimensional spaces, specifically dishwasher tablets, returnable bottles and vacuum cleaner bags. This is about the surveillance state, you know, and if they don't spy on us on the Internet and with video, then they're surely doing it with household appliances, clearly. Everything, everything has already been infiltrated and figured out. But our "household device" on our necks that we take with us, whether it be on the journey to Heiligendamm, or to Vienna, or falling asleep and in the dream you've dreamt of the crow, this device is apparently not accessible for the surveillance state. Of course, that's what we all want to believe. But precisely here is where everything goes wrong.

3.1432 Orders. Well, they happen. You get orders. You think you can believe you can trust that they are coming from a reliable source. From agencies, business partners, friends, strangers. Well...these orders are harmless, per se, or *seem* to be. But then again, that's just what they'll be expecting you to think, right! So, don't...accept...any...orders. Ever!

3.144 An internal order is not a static object, but has its own lifecycle that begins with its initiation and conclusion. If you accept it.

3.2 This internal order, however, can be manipulated. Sometimes the device can't process the commands, or the data is damaged or altered, or adjusted. As for external orders...well, don't even get me started.

3.202 Participation is not a solution.

3.202 We want to follow this principle (of non-participation), because only the provision of a sustainable benefit will secure the continued existence of a society. In other words: The device is under constant attack by society, from friends, data must be collected by the surveillance state in order to determine whether the device should be switched off, or changed, or even reset.

3.203 Of course, in this whole discussion, the idea that we can master natural (random and non-random) control technology is nonsensical, whereby we simply do away with it and try to get this thing under control by establishing measures such as travel bans on geese or foxes or the abolition of free range chickenry, or the like.

3.21 My tax advisor says: People with overvalued ideas are subjectively convinced of this principle (§ 3.202), and their actions support this theory. I say: Get me the Schwedentrunk, I done gots biznis to take care of. Big biznis!

3.22 Classical guitar drives you insane. How can listen anyone listen to something like this over a period of time, any period of time, without completely freaking out? These people (the SS, or Surveillance State = classical guitar types) know everything – and we out here (the uninitiated into the world of classical guitar) are like morons living in the wilderness and are dismissed as idiots (by those who are in this SS camp). We simply accept everything, classical guitar, Yanni, Trump, the surveillance state, everything. We know quite precisely that we are being watched, recorded, followed, after Snowden everything is as clear as day, was as clear as day, and then after a week or so...we do...nothing. Literally, not a fucking thing. But after all, who can blame us: we do not live in these circles and have no classical guitars. And the fact is: if you really want to drive us mad, if you really want to stop the unbridled flow of refugees overrunning Europe, if you really want to stop foreigners on entry, then just set up 1,046 (see Burger, *Tractatus logico-suicidalis)* speakers with very fast, maddening staccato Spanish classical guitars at the border and play them incessantly, 24/7. People will simply turn on their heels and flee in horror. (Update, 2022: the Ukrainians are implementing this in Donbas currently to great effect).

3.221 The patient that is overwhelmed by his psychosis (incessant classical guitar being played) naturally wants to be taken seriously in experiences, and to understand it and have it understood. After all: Energy takes shape and form, that's a fact, and is therefore vivid and accessible for us. Or not. Just depends.

3.23 The transitions regarding shape and form of devices (heads) can be fluid, and thus it is simply not sensible to provide a categorization with exact screen dimensions for mobile phones.

3.24 If the shape, surface or design does not determine the function of the material to a greater degree than its chemical composition, then the aggregate would not correspond to the product definition and should therefore be regarded as a substance or in a mixture. Therefore, according to Trump, we need a big, beautiful wallllllllll. (Oh, have I gotten too *modern* now?)

3.25 Whoever is superstitious is simply destined to continue, ad absurdum, ever tumbling forward, into greater levels of absurdity. For example, a man who wants to walk on ice in slippers because it will help him catch more fish on thin ice in the early Spring. It's a series of experiments, the chances we take, to get to the root of the thing (whatever that is). Which, of course, is beyond our understanding. And with this series of experiments, the dogma of *horror vacui absurdity* is (and was, and has ever been) conducted and, incidentally, you should really consider using a barometer in the process, or inventing yourself some kind of lie detector! You know, to find out...what...is at the root of, well, the thing. Which naturally begs the question: Why so silly? And: what was that thing Hegel said? Or better yet: Will it rain today?

3.251 People can, actively or passively, slide down the slope of criminality through corruption and the promise of a better future.

3.26 It thus follows: In the early 21ST century, ostensibly under the cause of 'fighting terrorism', it was decided at the highest levels to spy on people at all levels of society, in hospitals, in cafes, in public spaces, at events, in the park, at home, on the beach, forest, meadows, climbing mountains, while having breakfast, while feeding the dog, everywhere, in short *anywhere* and *everywhere* in order to protect their rights (and lives).

3.261 There's no romping without a little bit of stomping!

3.262 The Surveillance State (SS) consists of thick dough, needs a bit more time until it solidifies when baking and doesn't hold together as well as dough that contains eggs. But it's invisible, so one doesn't gain weight when eating it.

3.263 The limits of the Surveillance State are the limits of our world. (See §2.16, §4.116)

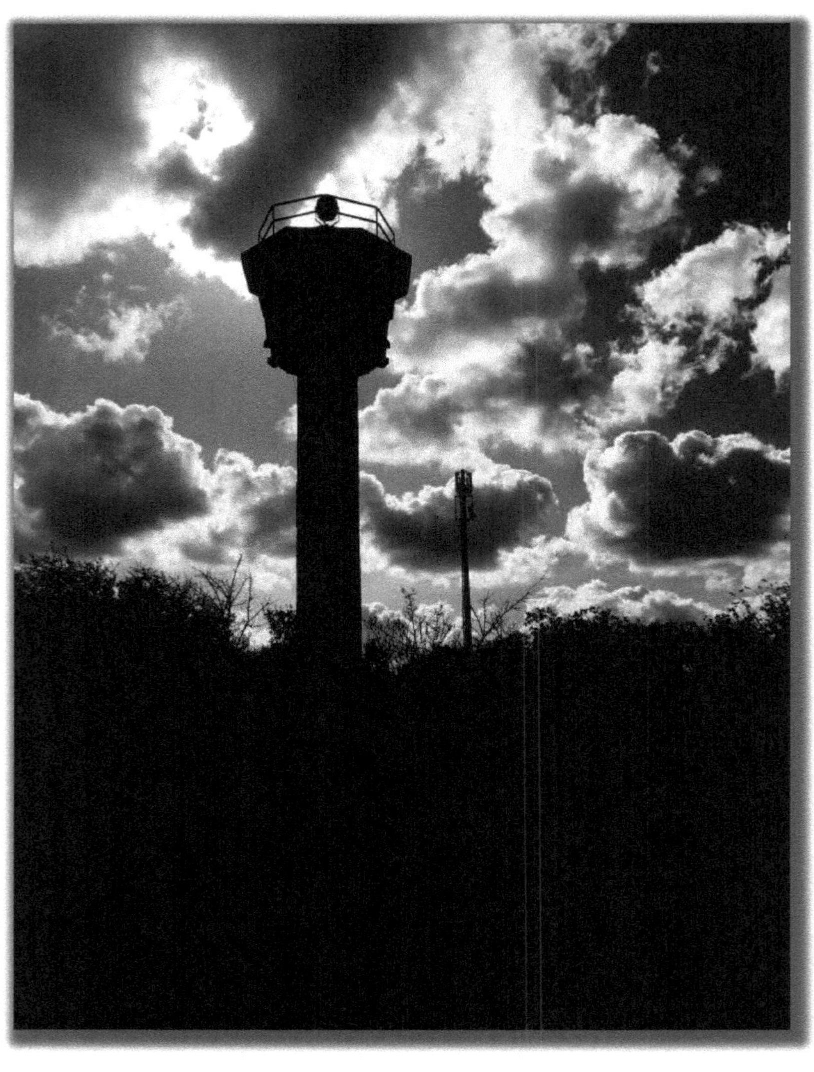

The Wolf Skin

HANS LEBERT

Hans Lebert (1919-1993), nephew by marriage of composer Alban Berg, was a lyric poet, novelist, professional opera singer, and graphic artist. He was a fierce opponent of the Nazi regime and vowed never to take part in it, successfully feigning insanity when called up for military service. He was often misunderstood as a hater of his own country, but it was in fact his devotion to Austria that animated his uncompromising criticisms of mediocrity and evasion. His two novels are considered masterpieces of prose.

Doch ward ich vom Vater versprengt;
seine Spur verlor ich, je länger ich forschte.
Eines Wolfes Fell nur traf ich im Forst;
leer lag das vor mir:
Den Vater fand ich nicht.

But flung far away from my father;
losing all trace the longer I tracked.
The fur of a wolf all I found in the forest;
lying forlorn before me:
My father I never found.

Richard Wagner, *Walküre*

First Chapter (excerpt)

The mysterious events that dismayed us this past winter began, if we observe the matter more closely, not on the 9th of November, as is generally assumed, but in all probability a day earlier, on the 8th, with that strange noise the sailor claims to have heard.

Indeed. But let us first take a look at the map.

This place is Schweigen; here, south of it, lies Kahldorf.* There is the Kahldorf-Schweigen railroad station and the single-track branch line that ends three stops farther. The backs of some hills in the Eber mountain range thrust out toward Schweigen from the west; the road from Kahldorf to Schweigen leads around the mountain. Here, by this curve south of Schweigen, is where that suspicious brickworks is located. And the rest . . . ? Here are some fields, here is forest; the dots mark isolated farms and the lines are paths that trail away in the woods.

It's a godforsaken region, a region that has nothing to offer and is thus hardly known. It lives its obscure life remote from the great traffic arteries, and those who think they know it – myself, for example – know in the end only that it is there and that it is far off the beaten track, slurred like a language hard to understand as it is, but now with men murmuring it into their beards. Fox come out at night, and in the morning they skulk back through the thickets as they snuffle the air from the farmsteads, where the smoke rising out of the chimneys has a smell of burnt feathers.

Then they cock their ears, and their eyes, alight, rove as they make their rounds: wasteland. Mountain peaks packed in fog clouds; a squall of rain pounds down on fields harvested bare.

But now back to the point!

On the 8th of November, at about three in the morning, the sailor was awakened by some apprehension, a repulsive, ice-cold feeling, "as if the front door were open." So he got up and satisfied himself that it was locked. Then he lay down again but wasn't able to fall back to sleep. Annoyed, he got up again after a while, lit his pipe and looked out the window. Outside was a milky half-light. The moon, hidden behind the clouds in the east, dabbed a runny spot onto the fog, a watery patch of consumptively pale brightness, against which the bare branches of the fruit trees were standing out in shadow. Nothing was much out of the ordinary; indeed, everything was as it should be. Even so, the sailor all at once had a feeling that he was waiting for some event, and while he stood there pondering what sort of event it might be, he suddenly heard that strange sound no one has even yet been able to explain. It came, as he told it, from the direction of the brickworks and gradually filled the whole vault of the sky. It sounded like "ringing in the ears" or like an Aeolian harp, more or less as if the air over there were quivering like a string stretched taut.

The sound died off, ebbed away uncertainly into the expanse of night, lost itself in the forest, sank down in the swampy lowlands, where the fog was growing thicker toward morning and hoarfrost was glinting on the reeds. It was finally drawn into the faint humming of the telephone wires (to which it had a certain similarity) until the two could no longer be told apart.

At the time, the rest of us went right on sleeping soundly. After all, we had no reason to sleep other than well. We were convinced we had survived the war and its various repercussions quite intact; the whole country was once again on the upswing; there were even signs of an economic boom in the offing, and if anything tormented us, it was, at worst, that same old boredom so at home around these parts in peacetime, walking abroad like a gray, ungraspable ghost among houses and among barbed-wire fences.

Like every other day in that month, this one started out with it (boredom, that is). It sent ahead a tear-stained redness (an inflamed redness, like pinkeye, paling after just a few minutes) and then crept, all gray and grudging, over the backs of the hills. Even though it was a Saturday and there was even supposed to be some kind of entertainment or dance at the Grape Tavern that evening, there was no reason to expect the day to break open with something unusual the crippling ring of monotony, the ring made of tilling the soil and breeding the cattle, of bare woods and brown ripples of earth, the ring that draws its circle with especially tight constriction around our village and surroundings as the year is coming toward its end.

Everything was the same. Trucks and motorcycles began their droning. The steam engine from the sawmill set to wheezing like someone sick with a fever, and all around in the forest, by now given over to felling, the axes of the woodcutters awakened and took up their barking. As on every other morning in Schweigen, the shops opened – the bakery, the general store, the butcher shop (which belongs to the Grape); and, as on every other morning, the children ran to school, clouds of their silver breath in front of their faces.

But still! Something was different (must already have been different) on that sleepy Saturday, a day that didn't feel suspicious to us until weeks later. And at that, strangely enough, the only one who felt it was the sailor, and even he only sensed it very dimly, at most as a kind of tension tugging at the most delicate nerve endings, and with the best will in the world he could not have said what was there, if anything at all.

He stepped out to the front of his house (the one-story "Potter's Cabin" huddling at the edge of the woods above the village), looked up at the clouds and twisted his face into a frown. It wasn't the air. It wasn't the light, either. So what was it then? Nothing. He strained his ears, but all he heard was the grass rustling, the dry brushwood snapping in the woods and the sawmill puffing away from the valley beyond. He filled his pitcher with water at the well and then went back into the house to make coffee.

Let us exhume a corpse! Not one of the nameless ones the sailor tried exhuming, but a person well known to us all (who at the time was having himself made all dapper for a Saturday he would never live out); I mean Hans Höller, son of Höller the large-scale farmer (and a powerful force in the community – the Lindenhof, that large holding on the road to Kahldorf, belonged to him).

Around ten he came into the village on his motorcycle, walked into Ferdinand Zitter's* barber shop and beauty parlor and flung himself with his thick thighs into one of the chairs. He was a handsome, strapping young man, dressed from head to foot in glossy leather, a perfect match for his bike. He too looked as if he had been newly varnished, and everything about his own person also seemed all factory-fresh and shiny. As he sat sprawled there so totally content and stretched out his legs in their heavy Canadian boots (when you saw him like this, I mean), you could also sense the strong motor inside him; that is, you were sure his heart was healthy.

"A shave!" he barked.

Ferdinand Zitter (a frail little old man with white curly hair and horn-rimmed glasses that sat so far down on his nose they were forever threatening to fall off) bowed and rubbed his hands.

"Just one second," he said; "Irma will be right with you. Would you like to look at the newspaper in the meantime?"

"Today's?"

"No, yesterday's."

"Read it already," growled Höller. He examined himself in the mirror while whistling one of the hit tunes.

Ferdinand Zitter said to us later, after the disaster had already happened, "Irma took her good old time, as usual. She was probably in the middle of her coffee break, and her fingers were all smeared with cheese or jam. So I decided I would at least lather up Herr Höller, although I knew he wouldn't enjoy it much, since he was there because of Irma in the first place. So I got a fresh towel and stuck it into his collar. While I was at it I stroked his cheek to feel how tough his beard was. That was when I got frightened. I mean it. I was really frightened. His face was like something dead; it felt cold and like a lump of dough – like the face of a corpse. Just then Irma came along and took over the job. Thank God! My hands were shaking by that time and I just didn't feel like going on."

Hans Höller invited Irma, the barber's assistant, to the dance in the Grape. She accepted (after a longish hesitation, even though she was already planning to go) but said he would have to commit himself to picking her up from home, because – as she explained to him – she couldn't very well go splashing around in the dark through the mud in her dancing shoes and arrive looking like a pig.

He nodded. That was fine with him, because they could take a ride beforehand, and that would give her a chance to get to know his new machine. While she was shaving him, leaning over him all soft and warm, he was speaking in his deep voice – but without moving his mouth for fear she might cut him, so more or less the way a ventriloquist speaks – about the inexhaustible joys of driving a motorcycle. She listened in a trusting and somewhat sleepy way, her eyes half closed and stifling a yawn now and then. At times she would smile, her teeth showing between her lips, and say (it sounded like crickets chirping), "Oh? Oh, really? That's great!"

Then she washed off the rest of the shaving cream, dried his face gently, splashed it with after-shave, and groomed his curly, straw-blond hair with comb and brush.

The day was shining through the milk-glass window with a gray, repulsive light. Ferdinand Zitter was sitting by the stove as it quietly crackled and hummed, taking it all in.

"The whole time I had the feeling," as he told it later, "that besides the three of us there was a fourth person in the shop, somebody invisible who kept pointing at Hans Höller."

"What was it like?" we asked him. "What was that feeling like?"

He said, "It's hard to describe something like that. It was like a sudden cold snap. I thought I was going to freeze to death, even though I was sitting right next to the stove." (A stove kept fired all the time; it spread powerful heat.)

The Suppan family's house is located diagonally across from the barbershop. It's a squat old building, most likely dating from the seventeenth century, and its gable, with an attic window, is turned toward the street like a face. Now, as Hans Höller left the shop, swung onto his bike, and started the motor with an ear-splitting roar that made all the window panes in the area start rattling, the following took place in the Suppan house: the curtain decorating the window (a white curtain fringed with lace) was drawn aside a little, creating a dark gap wide enough for an eye to peek out. Höller stayed where he was for a while, and the eye, which it was not possible to discern but which was undoubtedly sharp on the lookout, kept staring at the "damn kid" until he took off around the next street corner with a hellish explosion of backfiring.

Granted, there's nothing special here. All people who walk along the street in Schweigen can detect eyes at all the windows following them with greater or lesser suspicion. Even so – and as an exception – this instance ought to be mentioned, because, as we all know, there dwelt behind the attic window in question Karl Maletta, along with his photographs of us.

Let's think it through some more.

Half an hour later (it might have been 10:30) Konstantin Ukrutnik honors us with his usual visit. Ukrutnik is a cattle dealer, 28 years old, 6'4" tall, and a superb specimen of a man. He looks like a wrestler! His chest reminds you of a kettledrum, and you feel tempted to strike him on that spot to find out if it would rumble or boom (like a hollow space, like an empty vessel). But which one of us yokels would dare to beat on the mighty cattle dealer's chest? He claims to have enormous power and — far more dangerous — he considers himself a fine gentleman because he has money like dirt and a girl at the tip of each finger.

In those days he came here every Saturday and stayed (nobody ever knew quite why) over the weekend. He stayed at the Grape, where there was a room permanently reserved for him, and then he and Franz Binder, landlord-owner, farmer, and butcher, would talk over the various business dealings — often somewhat shady — they conducted with one another. He had already been showing some interest in Herta Binder, the owner's daughter. He frequently brought her small gifts, usually a pair of nylon stockings, which she valued highly, even though the material, delicate as a veil, would ordinarily shred — and almost always the very first time she put them on — in a great race to see how soon they could develop runners as a result of excessive stretching (for Fräulein Binder is a gymnast and has exceptionally strong calves).

So this time, too, she received a present from him, but now perfume instead of stockings, as if he had guessed her most secret worries, because a body like hers — well, you know how it is! She was standing now in the doorway between the tavern bar and the butcher block, beaming with joy (as they say), beaming with joy. Her stubby, thick fingers, greasy from bacon, were tenderly wrapped around the small bottle, which even now, though still sealed, was exuding an elegant aroma. Meantime, Ukrutnik drove his car (a former army automobile) back behind the house and into what was called the garage.

In that windowless shed, crouching like a blind man next to the manure pile, were stored useless things in a hopeless clutter, broken pieces of old farm wagons and agricultural tools covered with dust and coated with spider webs. A cat sat hunched in one corner and looked steadily at the big cattle dealer. With its pale autumn eyes it followed his movements as if it were gathering secret powers of hate in this way. He had turned off the car engine and was just getting ready to leave the shed when he took notice of it and stopped. It was a black cat.

They stared at one another, motionlessly fixing one another and stooping down as if to leap. The pale autumn eyes of the cat lit up the shed like a moon in a mirage, gilding the dusk twice. Ukrutnik's eyes were gleaming too, but in a whole different way from the animal's. They were dark and listless and had the color of rotted olives, the greenish sheen of lubricating oil. He squinted slightly, turning the eyes into two narrow slits, clenched his teeth firmly, thrust his chin energetically forward, and tightened his facial muscles. He stood leaning forward a little, near the doorway, through which daylight was falling, and the cat hunched in the depth of the shed, a clump of darkness, not moving. So they kept scrutinizing one another, both holding their breath, and in the air between them, which seemed to be lying just as motionlessly in wait, something was sparking like the discharge of an electrical storm.

The cattle dealer recognized none of this, by the way. (Recognition tended to spare him.) He felt only a blow at his back, a blow from a mysterious fist, stumbled forward and, still as if lowered for a leap, approached the cat with silent, stalking footsteps like a beast of prey. Then he made a sudden motion as if he wanted to grab it by the tail; at that very second it leapt up and hurtled past him like a black burst of wind.

He could just make out how it bolted for the door, hackles raised and ears oddly pinned back, out into the gray light and over toward one of the farm buildings, where it disappeared through a cellar window.

(That was at around eleven, and the smoke from the chimneys was now beginning to smell of food cooking; but the smoke, instead of rising up into the sky, spread over the countryside like smothering ground fog.)

Now let's talk about Maletta!

In the third year after the defeat (or liberation), on a May morning wet and cold as a dog's nose, he turned up at the Suppan house. He first introduced himself to the two old people, who up to then had never known he even existed, as a relative and second as a war victim. "How are you related to us?" they asked him. He could give only a vague explanation. And in what way was he a victim, they wanted to know. And on that subject he also gave information just in passing. He rented one of the two attic rooms in their house (the other had already been assigned to Fräulein Jacobi, the new teacher), then he had his luggage brought from the station in an oxcart, unpacked all his gear, set up his equipment and fastened onto the garden fence a sign he had obviously painted himself. It said MALETTA'S PHOTOGRAPHY STUDIO, SECOND FLOOR LEFT.

Because we're all so attractive, and because we were also curious, of course, almost all of us went to him and had our pictures taken. He was soon able to paper the walls of his room with our faces; that must have looked appalling, because anything that appears in such quantity produces an appalling effect.

Let us hear from an impartial witness, a wagon driver from outside our area who had his picture taken by Maletta but who otherwise has nothing to do with matters at hand.

As he tells it, "It was just 12:00, but when I walk into his room he's still lying in bed, that scurvy bum. Well, I'm the gruff type, so I just roust him right out. I ask him if he maybe isn't getting sick. 'Definitely,' he says, 'definitely.' Then he gets up, puts on his pants — they're hanging on a chair — and tucks his shirt in all around. 'I have to do some thinking,' he says, 'and the best place to think is in bed.' While he's fooling around with his camera, I take a good look around the room. What a state! Horrible! And nothing but photographs on all the walls! Everybody who's anybody in Schweigen and Kahldorf, one right beside the other and practically no way to tell the difference between them! 'Well, what do you know!' I say. 'You have a whole mob gathered together! Doesn't it turn your stomach to keep looking at them all the time?' 'It's all a matter of habit,' he says and smiles (with a face that looks like cheese spread), 'only a matter of habit. Now would you mind stepping over here?' I sit down on a stool already set in place, and he disappears behind his box. 'All these pictures,' I say, 'all these pictures could make you afraid. They stare you directly in the face as if they wanted to hypnotize you.' He laughs, hidden under his black cloth. 'That's because people always stare so fixedly into the lens,' he says, 'so their character will come out better in the picture. Please look at my finger!' (A finger that reminds you of a maggot in cheese.) He holds it up as if he were trying to explain something. 'Attention, please! – Thank you,' he says.

"'You're right, though,' he says afterwards, when I'm paying him, 'sometimes I almost can't stand it here; sometimes I seem to myself to be a violet pressed into an album of wanted posters.'"

On that suspicious Saturday Maletta made his way (no different from what he always did) just after 12:00 to the Grape for his noon meal. With his Styrian felt hat and his green loden overcoat, in which he gave the impression of being masked, we saw him coming along the street. We had already grown used to him and didn't pay him much attention any more, because – all right, we may be a backwater where everybody minds everybody else's business, but we're not so much of a backwater after all that we could never get used to the sight of him. He stood for several seconds in the doorway (outside was an imposing sign: FRANZ BINDER'S BUTCHER SHOP AND GRAPE TAVERN) as if hesitating at a secret border, but perhaps also nauseated by the odors from the kitchen on the right and the butcher block on the left. He removed his hat, brushed back his hair, tugged at his necktie . . . finally he gave himself a push and entered the tavern.

Franz Binder, enthroned behind the bar as the very incarnation of the god of beer, saluted him as always – somewhat as if from on high. But then Maletta did something he'd never done before. He ignored Binder's greeting and walked past the bar, past the landlord's beer belly, without saying boo. He took off his coat and sat down at the table (next to the door leading to the kitchen and the lavatories) at which the schoolteacher normally sat and ate. In fact, the teacher was already sitting there politely eating his soup (a lukewarm, watery, yellowish broth in which an occasional noodle was floating); he later provided us with an exact report of what then happened, but we had to change it a little to bring it closer to plausibility.

Maletta took a seat, then, picked up a beer coaster lying on the table, and began tearing it into pieces with relish. In his eyes, which usually darted around restlessly but today were trained as if spellbound on one spot – a place on the paneling where there really wasn't anything to see – in his eyes there suddenly flickered a glow, the kind a gently rippling water surface produces. (For example: a glass of water is standing on a table; the autumn sun comes shining through the window; a truck thunders past outside; the water in the glass commences to quiver, and the sun, thrown back by it, now dances flickering on the ceiling.)

"How are you?" the teacher asked.

"Well, thanks," answered Maletta.

"And business?"

"Also going well, thanks." He spoke in short, clipped sentences.

The waitress, an aging dragon, emaciated and terribly cross-eyed, threw the menu at him as she walked by.

"Thanks," said Maletta, not touching the greasy sheet of paper, which had landed on the table upside down, that is with the blank side up.

"There's pork today," said the teacher.

"Oh," answered Maletta.

"Or veal roast," said the teacher.

"Ah," answered Maletta.

The waitress went sweeping past.

"Do you want soup?" she yelled at him.

With his eyes flickering, Maletta stared back at that one spot on the wood paneling. "Yes, please," he said, looking straight ahead, as if the waitress were painted there.

Out she went with a swirl of her winter dirndl skirt, and when she came back a few minutes later, she slammed a bowl of soup down on the table with a sideways hand motion (to show that handling her job was child's play), but so forcefully that the broth slopped over.

Maletta tore his eyes away from the wall and watched the presentation. The soup bowl was set more or less in front of him, and next to it was a puddle; no soup spoon.

"Waitress! Hello!" he called. But why, all of a sudden? He knew the way things were done around here, after all, for he'd had enough experience. A diner who wasn't given a spoon just simply gets up and gets one. This kind of service is the custom here since the war; they tried it during the war years and when it proved workable, they held to it. Any stranger who doesn't like it can eat somewhere else! There's only this one tavern-restaurant in Schweigen anyway. And as far as the puddle next to the soup bowl is concerned, it wasn't such a bad thing (for the owner) either. Such accidents had already been provided for, after all: the tablecloth is covered with wrapping paper.

It was just that Maletta suddenly had no understanding for conditions as they were.

"Waitress!" he cried, "I have no spoon. And you spilled the soup as well!"

The waitress either didn't hear him or didn't want to hear him; at any rate, she was busy with other guests (wagon drivers eating smoked meat, workers from the sawmill who had just quit for the weekend and were boozing their time away). Maletta sat there expectantly, his hands in his lap, his soup meanwhile growing cold.

"You'll have to go and get one," the teacher said.

"Nothing doing," Maletta made clear.

"Why not? I've often gone after my own spoon."

There was suddenly something pastoral in his voice.

Maletta looked at the teacher. The light from his eyes flashed across the teacher's face. He returned Maletta's look in the exact manner of a grade-school teacher, a little disconcertedly, a little warningly, a little soothingly . . . These two men – an unwilling pair, seated together at the worst table by Franz Binder, who kept the other tables, far more pleasant ones, free for the more popular locals – these two men looked at one another, and whereas the one was making every effort to maintain his schoolteacher's demeanor while the other one, slowly lowering his eyelids, was trying to cast his look into the shade, if not hide it altogether, they could not prevent a boundless mutual hostility, which they had probably been feeling for a long time anyway, from flashing out like an alarm signal in their eyes.

"I'll go get you a spoon," the teacher said. He started to get up and was already partway out of his chair.

"Would you kindly keep your seat?" Maletta hissed. "Or are you trying to correct me?"

The teacher sank back down. He asked, "What's wrong with you? Are you really so annoyed?" Then he raised his hand like a schoolboy who wants to be called on and cried out in a friendly tone, "Hello? Rosl? Herr Maletta would like a spoon, please."

And then something happened that provoked Maletta into leaving the tavern immediately.

The waitress came. Oh yes, she came. But she didn't have a spoon with her; instead, she was carrying the dirty dishes (with gnawed bones etc.) she had just been clearing from the other tables; and because the owner just then called for her to come fetch and serve the wine he had poured, she set the dishes down on the table, which seemed to her the most logical thing to do, because it is located next to the kitchen door, meaning that they were right under the photographer's nose.

He stood up with a jolt.

"That does it," he said, and his words made all the more unpleasant an impression precisely because he remained so calm. He slipped into his coat and then asked Franz Binder at the bar how much soup costs when it's slopped onto the table so that he couldn't eat it anyway.

"One fifty," Binder informed him.

Maletta gave him the money and went out the door.

What can I tell you! As he goes out into the entrance hall, he hears footsteps coming closer and comes to a standstill as if nailed to the spot. He knew those footsteps. They were Herta Binder's, firm, quick, unfaltering. They were coming out of a darkness in which the light of day drowned as it fell from the street into the doorway here. In the angles of the walls and of the upward and downward staircases of the old building they awoke a muffled echo, as in a cellar, a sound as if from a world below them. He still could have made his escape; with just a few hurried steps he would have made his way out into the open. But no, he remained standing where he was – as if nailed to the spot – turned halfway to the inside of the building and halfway to the outside, and waited for the young woman marching toward him, because her footsteps provoked him.

Let's try imagining how he must have felt! He hadn't eaten anything; he was hungry. He had gone without his midday meal. Only his anger – *that* he had managed to swallow – was sitting in his stomach, but that didn't satisfy his hunger. Now, however, just when he wants to leave so as to digest his anger away from us, just now (in the doorway, between the dining room and the butcher block, between the sour smell of the beer and the smell of the slaughtered pigs and bulls) footsteps are coming toward him in which all of life is manifested – but life, passing him by with mockery and brutality, is what is causing him to starve so totally, and now the butcher's daughter is approaching him with footsteps that sound as if she'd like to trample him to the ground.

"A person can't even eat in peace!" she grumbles at him. "You know we're closed now."

Maletta was dumbfounded. The light in his eyes flared up (so Herta Binder claims) so fiercely that you were afraid it might set the house on fire.

"I don't know what you want," he stammered.

"I don't want anything, not from you!"

"I don't want anything from you, either."

"But you rang the bell."

"Rang the bell? – Me? – Not at all."

You need to know that there's a bell by the door where the butcher block is. People ring it (if they can summon up the courage to do so) when they find the door locked and in that way let it be known that they would like service. Of course it's entirely possible that someone else (a customer who was tired of waiting or a child playing a prank) had rung the bell shortly before. But because Maletta was standing there right at that moment and Herta had just snapped at him, she acted – so that she wouldn't have to apologize to him and because she now needed a whipping boy – as if she thought he was the transgressor.

She said, "Just this once. Just this one time only." With these words and a key she unlocked the door.

"But I never did ring the bell!" Maletta said.

"Oh, so what? I'm here now. What is it you want?"

She opened the door and went into the echoing room. Her buttocks were rippling under her skirt, her calves flexing at the seam.

Maletta followed her as if hexed. "I don't want anything from you or any of the damn rest of you!" Apparently that was right at the tip of his tongue, finally ready to be said out loud. He should have said it, too, right out with it at this moment, and then departed with a heroic attitude, because he could just as easily have bought the quarter-pound of sausage he wanted for dog food at the general store. But no – as a result of being hexed (there's no other explanation), hexed by Herta's firm tread, hexed by Herta's backside, hexed by this carnal provocation and the fact that this young woman was rejecting him and yet attracting him, hexed, in short, by the contradiction in his feelings, a tangle of craving and loathing that brings on pleasurable pain, he walked behind her to the counter, behind which her thighs now disappeared.

"So what can I get you?" she asked in a surly voice.

"A quarter-pound of Braunschweiger liverwurst," Maletta said.

She brought out the roll of sausage, threw it onto the cutting board, and cut slices from it. Her thick fingers moved nimbly. The knife (an immense butcher knife) went zipping with frightening speed past her fingernails, to which flakes of blood-red nail polish were still clinging. In the background, against the white-tiled wall, half a pig was hanging from a hook; it was shamelessly displaying its inside, as if it wanted to say, "Sorry, but that's all there is!" Maletta didn't even take it in, though. He was looking with greedy hate and hateful greed at the thick fingers of the butcher's daughter, as though he were examining their claws — but who in hell knows — as she did her handiwork.

And then he suddenly noticed: the sausage had spots, ones as gray as the day looking sleepily through the window. Was it some trick of his vision caused by the nail polish? Or by hunger? Fräulein Binder swears the meat was fresh and thinks Maletta was just looking for a fight and so had made up the whole thing in his mind. She laid the sliced sausage onto the scale, and because it was underweight, she cut two more slices and put them on top of the others; that was the moment at which Maletta declared, in a voice trembling with agitation, "I'm not taking that sausage! It's got spots on it."

"Spots? — Where?"

"Right here! — And all over!"

"That's just from the pepper they put in it."

"I don't believe you."

He picked up a piece and smelled it.

"It stinks!" he declared. "Stinks like an old sock. Maybe you can put up with that, but not me."

Now Herta let loose (got down to brass tacks with language to match, that is). She told him off in a raucous voice that set the bare vaulted room booming with echoes.

What was he thinking? she shouted. Did he really think she'd palm off rotten merchandise on him? Fine, then let him buy his stupid food somewhere else! In fact, he ought to get lost and go back where he came from! (Maletta had his mouth half open, but nothing came out; he wouldn't have been able to get a word in edgewise anyway, because her tirade continued nonstop.) She wrapped the liverwurst in newspaper. Sorry, she explained, but because it was now sliced, she couldn't take it back.

So he took out his wallet and paid her (just like spilled soup, rotten Braunschweiger is going to cost, too). His face had turned as gray as cement, grayer than the decayed spots on the sausage, grayer than the November afternoon in the window, and his hands were shaking so violently that the money he had counted out and was now trying to set down in front of Herta fell on the floor and went rolling away with a tinkling sound.

He scrambled after the coins, tossed them onto the counter, and turned toward the exit.

"Your sausage!" cried Herta. "What am I supposed to do with it?"

He turned back, grabbed the package and put it away.

"For the dogs," he mumbled, halfway through the door. The gleam in his eye had suddenly gone out, as if he had put it away, too.

For the past several days, an enormous puddle had been building up next to the gutter on the sidewalk in front of the tavern and butcher shop. When the children got out of school, they would float little paper ships on this puddle. A few boys had just gathered there to play their game with much yelling and shouting. The wind, as it came through the street, would drive the little boats along this lake and create a delicate, yellowish sea lane.

As Maletta now stepped out of the doorway and turned right so as to flee the village (he had had quite enough of us for today), there came heading directly toward him along the sidewalk – so narrow here that two people can scarcely pass one another – none other than Ukrutnik wearing Cossack-style knee boots. Maletta stopped and pressed himself against the wall to allow Ukrutnik past with plenty of room; what he was doing was not only the right thing but very considerate besides, because in the first place he was the person closer to the wall and therefore the one to move aside, as etiquette dictates, and in the second place he squeezed himself as flat as he possibly could. Ukrutnik, meanwhile, a lord of the village greens, a czar smelling of cattle and hair oil and laying claim to wide room for himself, was not satisfied with half the sidewalk. That a man should do no more than flatten himself, as the photographer had done, seemed quite beneath the level of respect owed him, and he was not about to step into the puddle, because he was on his way to put in an appearance before Herta and wanted – quite naturally – to be well-groomed and elegant, with his boots clean.

So what happened? At first Ukrutnik stopped too. But then, as Maletta made no move whatever to vacate the sidewalk, that is to hop to the left and straight into a sea of mud wearing ordinary shoes – to the right was the wall – as Maletta, supported by the rules of etiquette, refrained from doing any such thing, Ukrutnik simply gave him a push, shoved him in absolutely classic fashion and in this way created the path he needed to be able to continue striding along with duly wide room.

Maletta stumbled sideways, splashed first with one foot and then with both into the puddle, right into the middle of the little boats, which went capsizing and drifting apart; the water splattered up onto his pants legs and was already running down into his shoes before he could get away; the boys were yelling with delight.

"This is . . . this is . . . but this is . . . " he was swearing in broken words, "but this is . . . " He couldn't find any suitable expression. Ukrutnik continued on his merry way, however, and the passers-by in close range heard him say, "Don't go and hurt yourself now – moron!"

These, then, were such of Maletta's adventures as we actually witnessed on that Saturday. For what I'm about to report, on the other hand, there are no witnesses, admittedly, but the theory of probability alone (plus my groping in the dark) gives me cause to assume it happened.

Hounded by the children's yelling he left the village, furiously stomping along the street beneath him with its holes, lifting his legs high like a Lipizzaner stallion. He had the feeling he needed to vomit, to puke in the government woodlands, or slam his head into the ground to block his mouth with dirt and leaves. The water sloshed and gurgled in his shoes, a feeling as if he were wading barefoot through a bog, and it was in this way that he fumbled right into the disaster that had been waiting there a long time for him.

He was walking in the direction of Kahldorf. That's what he always did when he set off like this with no goal. Why? I don't know. Kahldorf is every bit as nasty as Schweigen. He ordinarily didn't go all the way to the village, but would turn back about halfway and wind his way down into the valley where the road rises after it crosses a narrow strip of woods. About half a mile before that spot, though, the "pale strip" cuts across the road. I am now convinced that something seized hold of Maletta on this strip, at which point the story turns deadly serious all of a sudden.

Let us consider this place at our complete ease: the road with its few maple trees winds around Eber Mountain here; if you go from Schweigen to Kahldorf, you plunge deep into the shadow of the mountain. To the right, at the clay dropoff covered with low thickets, huddles the sailor's house, adjoining the woods that start higher up, and keeps watch with its tiny window-eyes. Across from it, on an uncultivated piece of land (nothing ever seemed to want to thrive there), the half-collapsed walls of the brickworks thrust up, a raw, red blot on the landscape. Behind it, like a mouth dropped open, gapes the clay pit, which is being slowly filled in with trash; it's a mouth with a blond beard of reeds that rustle in a motionless surface of ground water. On the overgrown access lane, which branches off from the road here and leads to the brickworks through weeds and yellowish meadow grass, stands an old stunted oak. Lightning split it decades before; one half of it is dead, and the wide-open gashes in its trunk are black, as if the wood had turned to charcoal from the inside.

There, near the oak — about a hundred paces from the brickworks — is where the "pale strip" begins. We have no idea what it is or how to explain it. It creeps like a snake through the fallow land and onward beyond the road to the mountain. It isn't always visible. It keeps showing up and then disappearing again. An effort was needed to follow its track at that time, because it was late in the year and the grass had withered in other places as well.

As Maletta now went along the road, the following — since he had passed the strip, thus coming into its general area — is what might well have taken place:

He is racing along without watching the road, which he probably has long known by heart and could have walked in his sleep. Then something suddenly causes him to stop — to stop right in the middle of the road — as though some obstacle were lying across his path. If the car that had passed him before were coming only now, he would have let it run right over him and spared me the not inconsiderable exertion of constantly having to try to put myself in his position. What was wrong? Nothing. It was quiet. The humming of the car was soon lost entirely behind the mountains; the landscape was drowsing in the twilight; the clouds lay like a slate slab above it. And yet! Something seemed to have happened. Something or other had brushed against him, fleeting as the wing of a dragonfly, and it now trickled from the top of his head, trickling down his arms from his shoulders and off his fingertips.

He stood there spellbound for some seconds, hardly daring to breathe. He was standing in the road without moving, his eyes almost completely shut, and listening inside himself. At that moment (or maybe later — it happens here all the time and doesn't mean much) two crows came flapping out of the fallow land on the left and flew up into the sky in a steep spiral. Now he opened his eyes a little and peered over to the brickworks, but without turning his head, as if he suddenly had a stiff neck. The building was where it had always been. There was nothing out of the ordinary to note. The two crows, meanwhile, circled over the road and cawed in a disagreeable way. He looked up at them, rolling his eyes far up in their sockets so as not to have to move his head. The black birds traced a loop and perched with outspread wings in a treetop on Eber Mountain. Maletta, who had followed their flight with his eyes, stared up spellbound at the sailor's house. He saw something up there – a person? an object? – some strangely shaped thing under the branch of an apple tree, a thing he could not explain to himself but that reminded him of something even so.

He suddenly shook his head. He was filled with apprehension – stronger than his bitterness, more tormenting than his rage – a disgust, a slight tingling produced by this sight, as if hairs were clinging to his palate or spider webs to his face.

The thing seemed to sway a little, but without changing its position. As if someone had hung a scarecrow from the tree branch!

And suddenly it felt to him as if he had been transformed into a junction point of some kind, a junction where a thousand threads met, gently vibrating and invisibly stretching from Schweigen to the Kahldorf train station, from the silence of the woods to the silence of the solitary farms* and from the potter's cabin to the brickworks. He himself was the midpoint, the point at which all these threads converged, where they all touched one another with faint trembling and produced in him a sound similar to the whispery wing beats of a dragonfly.

Three factors have to be taken into consideration now.

First: Maletta was standing on the "pale strip," within working range of mysterious powers.

Second: even at that time, though they did not yet know each other, there existed some relationship between him and the sailor.

Third: there was a dangling corpse in his past, some kind of disgrace, repressed from his consciousness as too awful but on a good many occasions emerging from below the surface in one guise or another to frighten him.

So what did he do in this condition of being touched by the breath of the incomprehensible? Instead of continuing along the road as he otherwise would, he turned to the right and leapt over the ditch, clambering through bushes and dry undergrowth up the mountain slope in his eagerness to solve the riddle. And indeed he found the solution there: the "thing" (the dangling corpse, the scarecrow) was nothing other than a kind of spring not far from the house, a tree trunk about human size, a man from whom a heavy lead pipe was protruding and who – depending on the wind – was pissing either into the trough overgrown with moss or onto the ground beside it.

Maletta determined what it was he had been seeing and could now be satisfied that this was all very natural and in good order. But he could not get rid of the feeling that had overcome him earlier. On the contrary! It gained in strength; the silence filled his ears all of a sudden with an angry hissing. It couldn't have been because he was standing at the very spot where his fate was later to overtake him, because there was no way he could have had any inkling of that.

He crept past the potter's cabin at some distance, past the airy barn in which the clay vessels were dried, and because he felt no desire to make his way back to the road, he trudged up to the woods; bare and gaunt, they rose up behind the property like a desert of black scaffolding. In the rustling of the fallen leaves, more and more numbed by the silence, he climbed ever upward through the endless colonnades and ever deeper into the cold and the inhumanity of the woods as if into the howling of a narcotic. "Am I an actor?" he asked himself (the hissing intensified around him and stopped his ears). "Who's the prompter, then? – what? – what's that? – evil? – louder! – I can't understand . . . "

Translated by Vincent Kling

Translator's Note

Hans Lebert creates the intense atmosphere of the setting in *The Wolf Skin* partly by giving persons and places emblematic names that have struck some critics as excessive. That judgment aside, the translator will notate the significant meanings of personal names and place names as they appear chapter by chapter. To translate those names directly into English in the text would ruin the atmosphere of the Austrian mountain setting; it would be unconvincing, for example, to refer to an Alpine village as "Silent" (Schweigen), even though such a place name is entirely plausible in German, or to a person as "Redskull" (Rotschädel). The names for which notes are given below are indicated by an asterisk in the text of *The Wolf Skin*.

First Chapter Notes

- \# Schweigen = to keep silent
- \# Kahldorf = Bare Village
- \# Ferdinand Zitter = Zitter means tremble or quiver
- \# solitary farms = isolated properties

SPECIAL CATALAN FEATURE

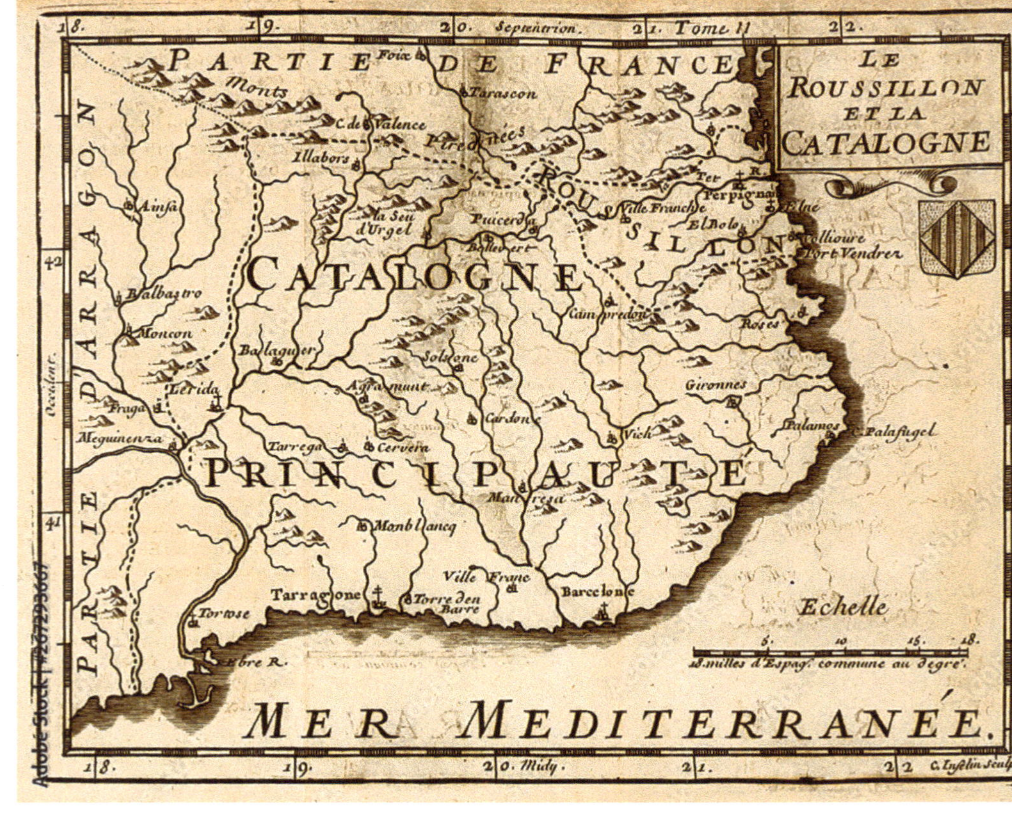
LE ROUSSILLON ET LA CATALOGNE
Septentrion
Tome II
Midy
Occident
PARTIE DE FRANCE
PARTIE D'ARRAGON
CATALOGNE
PRINCIPAUTE
ROUSSILLON
MER MEDITERRANEE.
Monts Pirenées
Foix
Tarascon
C. de Valence
Illabors
Ainsa
la Seu d'Urgel
Puicerda
Belleguert
Ville Franche
Perpignan
Elné
El Bolo
Colliouré
Port Vendrez
Ter R.
Balbastro
Monçon
Balaguer
Lerida
Fraga
Meguinenza
Solsone
Agramunt
Cardone
Tarrega
Cervera
Campredon
Roses
Gironnes
Vich
Palamos
Palafugel
Manresa
Monblanc
Ville Franc
Barcelone
Tarragone
Torre den Barre
Tortose
Ebre R.
Echelle
18 milles d'Espag. commune au degre.
C. Inselin Sculps.

Elevation & Rootedness

Notes on a Catalan Outlook

(Talk at the 15th International Congress on Musical Signification

Barcelona, 1 September 2021)

RAÜL GARRIGASAIT

I've been assigned a difficult, perhaps impossible, task: explain what Catalonia is in fifty minutes to an audience composed of people from many different countries. But it's a difficult task not merely because of the time constraint. Is it actually possible to define a piece of land, a linguistic community, a culture, a nation? And can one really hope to find within all of this a coherence that has not only lasted over time but also remained rooted in the geography? These aren't questions that can be simplified or answered flippantly. In order to understand reality we must first classify it, but we are condemned to always omit important elements. Standing before you today, then, I have no option but to present a drastic selection. I'll do so by concentrating on three or four figures and the one specific sensibility that unites them, a sensibility that, in my opinion, is still relevant to our day and age.

To begin with, allow me to take you on a journey through one of Barcelona's most visited attractions, one of those locations that run the risk of turning into mere decoration for passers-by: Park Güell. At the turn of the 20th century, the entire area was outside the city of Barcelona and known by the rather striking name of *Muntanya Pelada*, or Bare Mountain. The industrialist and philanthropist Eusebi Güell purchased two tracts of land there with the idea of constructing a large urban devel-opment and gave the job of drawing up the plans to the architect Antoni Gaudí. The original idea was to build, on sixty individual plots of land, homes with an abundance of natural light and views of the city. The plots were never sold and the original plan fell through but this failure proved a stroke of luck because out of it was born a seventeen-hectare public park.

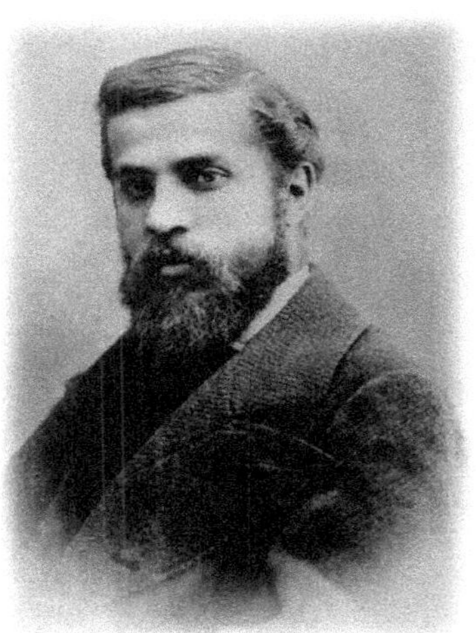

Bare Mountain was a dry, rocky wasteland with a steep gradient but it's these specific features that give the park its form. Gaudí refused to flatten it: he was eager to utilise the abruptness of its slopes and accept the land as a gift from nature. Thus, in order to save the slope from oblit-eration, he designed paths that snaked and spiralled. Inside the park we find columns that lean heavily to one side, helical pillars with capitals shaped like mushrooms and winding walls and benches. Everything has the feeling of a mountain having been sculpted out of the original mountain's forms.

What's more, the architect obtained material for all of the park's constructions directly from the land and surrounding terrain. Not only was the perimeter wall built using stone from the mountainside but the builders were instructed to collect any tiles or bottles they might find along the paths and tracks. These materials would later serve for the roofs and handrails, all of which are made using a technique called *trencadís*: pieces of ceramic, marble, and glass set with lime mortar, in an art form that can be considered a genuine precursor of avant-garde collage. Each of these works used discarded materials which conserved their original character while being transformed into something new. This is where Gaudí's exceptional collaborator, the architect and designer Josep Maria Jujol, really excelled, even going as far as incorporating crockery from his own home into the park's creations. Despite being formed by scraps of waste material, *trencadís* is successful in creating a bright, luminous beauty. One could even talk of a 'philosophy of *trencadís*' that consists in taking the lowliest, most scorned objects from your immediate surroundings and regarding them with enough charity to transform them into something beautiful and of service. My use of the word 'charity' is no coincidence: Gaudí and Jujol were devout Catholics and perceived the world as divine revelation. Therefore, any material they chanced upon, no matter how insignificant, was capable of possessing a profound truth. Finding a role for it meant they were collaborating with Creation.

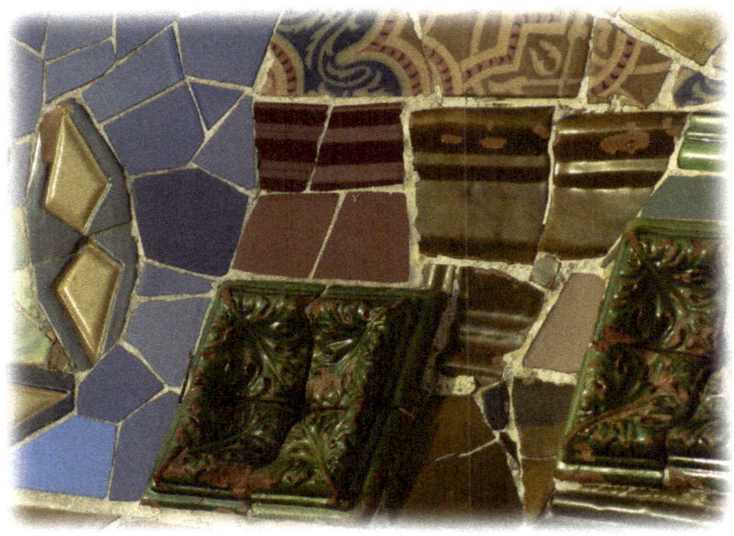

Entering Park Güell, we're immediately greeted by two cottage-style houses. The one to our left has a tall tower culminating in a Greek cross, while the one to our right is crowned by an *Amanita muscaria*, a hallucinogenic mushroom with a long tradition in European folklore, which naturally includes Catalonia, a country with a long-standing passion for mushrooms. Thus, flanked by Christian redemption and earthly hallucination, we enter Gaudí's world.

First we come to a monumental stairway, a *tondo* with the four blood-soaked bars of the Catalan coat of arms, and a snake's head. Slightly further up is another reptile: a dragon, or lizard perhaps, staring us down while it clutches the handrails as if defending the site. At the very top of the stairs we enter a hypostyle chamber with 86 Doric columns and, continuing our ascent, we arrive at a large square bordered by one continuous, undulating bench made of *trencadís,* the delightful result of Jujol's extraordinary vision. Gaudí christened this vast area the 'Greek Theater' and positioned it at the foot of the slope, as was customary with the orchestra or scenic space in ancient theaters. At the same time, the square (and here we must keep in mind that *théatron* means 'a place for contemplation') offers magnificent views of Barcelona framed by the cross and the psychotropic mushroom.

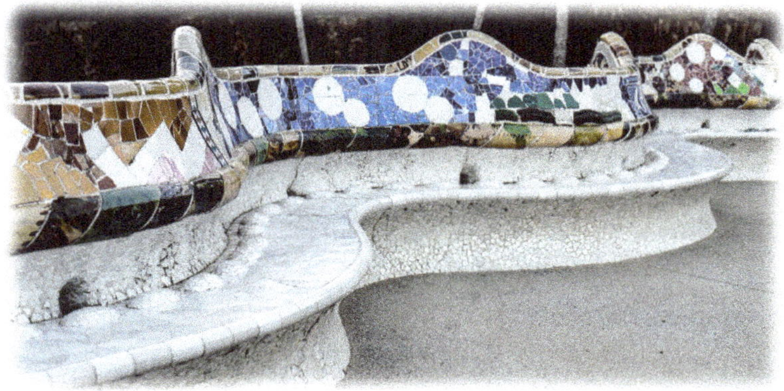

As I've already mentioned, Bare Mountain didn't contain a drop of water. But Gaudí solved this with a small architectural masterpiece: rather than cementing the square, he would allow the water to filter through the ground. Underneath, a receptacle would collect and guide the water toward the hollow Doric columns and, via the columns, into an underground tank. When the tank was full, the water would pour out of two overflow channels: the mouths of the dragon and the snake that guard the splendid stairway.

It's not difficult to sense the site's dense symbolism. Ancient mythology abounds with dragons defending fountains, the most famous being the dragon at Delphi, the guardian of water slayed by the god Apollo so he could establish his oracle there. Just as with Park Güell, the temple of Delphi had a theater, Doric columns, and was built on sloping terrain, in this case at the foot of Mount Parnassus. The story goes that Apollo's high priestess would sit on a tripod in order to enter into a trance, which is why at the very top of the sweeping Park Güell stairway we find a strange, three-legged figure made of *trencadís.* Near to the Temple of Apollo, one could contemplate a stone known as the *omphalós*: the navel of the world.

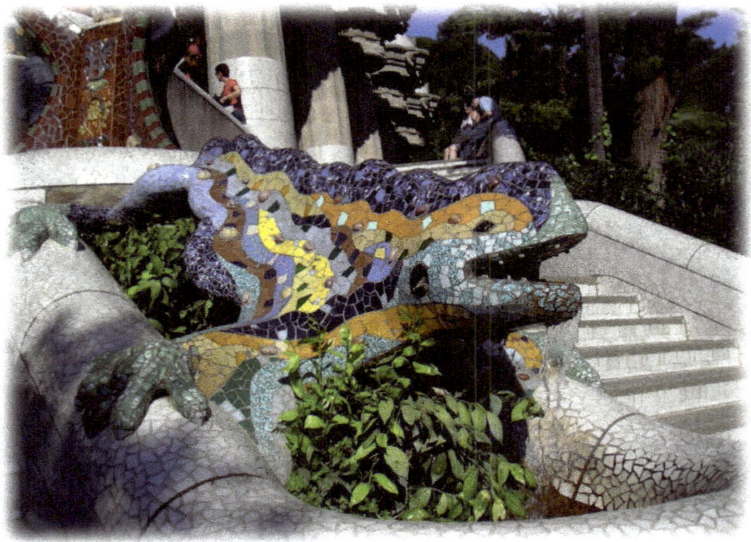

With direct allusions to Delphi, Gaudí was sending a daring message, an idea formed in equal measure by creative energy and hallucination: here, at this exact point on the primordial *Muntanya Pelada*, is the centre of the world, and Catalonia, a fusion of Hellenic and Christian legacies, is the new Greece.

But why such heightened affection for a dry, rocky wasteland, and its unexpected elevation to the level of universal meaning? Up to a point, these were the two fundamental concepts of Catalan modernity between the years 1868 to 1939, but to understand them it's worth focussing on two specific phenomena: the fascination with the notion of Greece and the linguistic reality experienced by Catalans.

I'll begin with Greece. Gaudí enjoyed saying such things as the following:

> My Greek qualities are on account of the Mediterranean, the vision of which constitutes a necessity for me. I need to see the sea often, and most Sundays I go down to the breakwater. The sea is the only thing that synthesizes all three dimensions of space. The sun is reflected on its surface and through it I spy movement and depth.

But for Gaudí, the Mediterranean wasn't just any sea:

> Virtue is in the mean; Mediterranean means the middle of the earth. Its shorelines, with the light at 45 degrees (the angle that best outlines bodies and exhibits their form), is the place where all great artistic cultures have flourished for the very reason that the balance of light [...] in the Mediterranean establishes the definitive vision of things, within which all authentic art must reside. Our plastic strength is the balance between emotion and logic. [...]

In other words, according to Gaudí, the people of the Mediterranean have a privileged sensitivity because they receive sunlight at the ideal angle. On the other hand, those from the north – and allow me to take this opportunity to greet our colleagues from northern Europe present here today – are unable to achieve a similar level of aesthetic sensitivity and thus incapable of appreciating beauty with such definition and intensity. Seeing only ghosts amid the fog, northerners take refuge in abstract thought, which is why they excel in analysis, science, and industry. The architect clarified his idea in the following way:

> Fantasy belongs to the people of the North. We're more precise: image belongs to the Mediterranean. Orestes knows where he's going; Hamlet, on the other hand, wanders lost.

Gaudí undoubtedly had an eccentric character but in his day and age his was by no means an outlandish theory. Paradoxically, his vision had northern roots. It was the Germany of Winckelmann, Goethe, Wilhelm von Humboldt and the Schelegel brothers that created the spiritual dichotomy of a reflexive north full of darkness and a luminous south where beauty manifested itself like nowhere else on earth. And as the theory spread across Europe each country appropriated it in its own way.

In Catalan-speaking territories, the image of both ancient Greece and the Mediterranean became nothing short of an obsession. In 1906, the poet Miquel Costa i Llobera celebrated the landscape of his native Majorca as a renewal of Greece where the 'the Homeric Muse' breathed and where one could drink 'the joy of life' as it 'overflowed from the nectar cup.' To him, the Majorcan shoreline shone just as brightly as those of Attica.

While Gaudí was working on Park Güell, in the north of Catalonia, in what was once the ancient Greek colony of Empúries, a statue measuring 2.2 metres (7ft 3in) was discovered of the Greek god Asclepius – Aesculapius to the Romans – son of Apollo, capable of miraculously curing the sick. The statue was compared to the wooden sculptures of the Virgin Mary discovered in remote caves in medieval legends and which served as the centre of new communities; with identical vigor, Asclepius was meant to inspire a new age of cultural renaissance.

Around the same time, Joan Maragall – poet, leading intellectual, and translator of Goethe and Nietzsche – wrote the tragedy *Nausica,* based on Book VI of the *Odyssey.* Maragall often spent his summers in the coastal village of Caldes d'Estrac and it was there, gazing out from his house on the seafront, where he found inspiration. He wrote: 'My poem seems to need this view, this color, this sound of the same sea that swayed Ulysses' boat, and which surrounded those heavenly islands...'

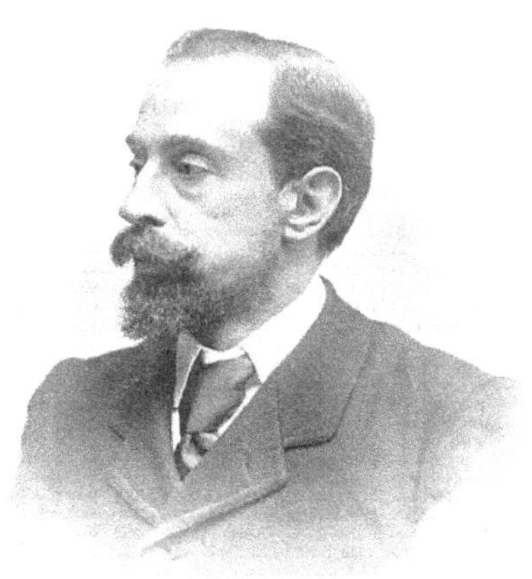

It's possible to find similar appropriations of Greece's symbolic capital in all Western cultures but it's crucial to read each manifestation within its own particular context. In Catalan-speaking territories, the link to Greece satisfied a burning necessity. When intellectuals at the turn of the 20th century looked back they saw a desert; they saw Catalonia as having been reduced, over subsequent centuries, to the status of an unambitious, powerless province existing on the margins of great European culture. Within the hierarchy of modernity, a country without power was strictly local, turned towards the past, without the muscle or means to contribute anything to the world. And this was precisely the decadence that Gaudí and his contemporaries were anxious to reject.

Around 1800, Wilhelm von Humboldt described Greece as having gone from the most particular culture in human history to the most universal. What Greece demonstrated was that by developing local traditions a message could be sent to the whole of humanity. And this was the deep, underlying meaning of the Hellenic imagery we find in the Catalonia of a hundred years ago: Greece set an example of anti-provincialism and offered a universal perspective, thus providing Catalonia with the opportunity to recover a voice capable of conversing with Europe and the world as an equal.

The idea of Greece beamed Catalans towards the ethereal heights of the universal, as if it were a magic spell capable of making them levitate. But this elevation is only one of the two elements on display in Park Güell. The other points downwards.

Let us take a moment to remember the philosophy of *trencadís*: however lowly it may be, however deserving of scorn it may appear, any discarded piece of glass or ceramic found on the street can be transformed, with the loving embrace of lime mortar, into a part of a useful and valuable whole. The steep, rocky mountain needn't be flattened and made to disappear because it partakes in the qualities of the very earth from which Park Güell emerges. The philosophy of *trencadís* is based on the principle of accepting whatever you stumble across as possessing an inherent fecundity.

Art is one thing, but is it possible to apply this idea to language? In his famous speech of 1903 entitled 'In Praise of the Word,' the poet Joan Maragall proclaimed the word as the 'most marvelous' thing in the world 'because within it all of Nature's corporal marvelousness and spiritual marvelousness embrace and blend into one.' It's for this reason that the spoken word, 'with a subtle movement of air,' 'presents us with the world's immense diversity.' We tend to forget this deeper dimension of language and speak superficially but, on occasions, we're reminded of its power and glory: when we're in love, when we're whisked away by poetic impulse, but also when we know how to pay close attention to how the lowly and the illiterate speak. With devotion, Maragall evokes the spontaneous phrases spoken by a Pyrenean shepherd, a Provençal maiden, or a group of Cantabrian sailors. They might seem banal but in their purity they had an epiphanic power. For the poet, the words that make the universe reverberate aren't the result of calculations and forethought, rather a marvelous gift handed to us. This gift manifests itself mysteriously, away from power, outside of the classroom and on the margins of dictionaries and grammar. To see it one must possess the same receptive attitude that forms the basis of *trencadís*: anything, however modest, can be regarded with wonder.

It's highly significant that the three examples of authentic speech given by Maragall – the shepherd, the maiden, the sailors – are in Catalan, Provençal, and Castilian. The poet perceives universality as a blossoming of plurality, saying 'the one true universal expression will necessarily be as diverse as the diversity of nations and their people.' Maragall proposes an understanding of human diversity that goes far beyond borders and the disciplinary codifying of the nation states of his day, including Spain.

But this perception was necessarily born out of a specific historical context. When Maragall gave this speech, Catalan wasn't only the most commonly heard language on the street and the vehicle of both traditional and modern intellectual culture but the language that impregnated daily life in Catalan-speaking territories from French-ruled Northern Catalonia all the way to Valencia in the south, from the Balearic Islands to the eastern strip of Aragon. Nevertheless, there was one, very specific space that remained strictly off-limits: anything that was official or related, either directly or indirectly, to the state excluded Catalan and the obligatory language was Spanish in the south and French in the north. Gaudí, for one, had first-hand experience of this: he was held in a cell for insisting on speaking Catalan to a policeman. With Catalan excluded from schools and other public institutions, for Maragall's generation the language of official rhetoric, bureaucrats and the military was Castilian. When the poet described the word as 'a sacred thing' and explained the importance of avoiding 'the sacrilege of the unnatural word', he was taking an unequivocal political and aesthetic position: in addition to placing his faith in genuine forms of expression he was rejecting the standardizing policies of all states.

During this period, Maragall used poetry to celebrate legendary popular figures reinterpreted through a Romantic lens, such as Count Arnau and the outlaw Serrallonga. Sons of the Catalan interior, they were impetuous, carnal men marked by the conflict between desire and sin, individuals that broke through the limits and faced down the law. They reflected the very image the poet wanted to present of his compatriots at the turn of the century: inside every Catalan was an anarchist and the essence of the Catalan soul was liberty. Indeed, Maragall's Serrallonga proudly affirms the following:

> I have walked the world to my own delight,
> I have done what pleased me, every instant free,
> bending to no law, no king, no thing.[1]

In Maragall's idiom each of these characters is an earthy figure, a son 'of the *terra*.' It's worth pausing here to consider the meaning of this very specific word. As in other Romance languages, the Catalan word *terra* can be translated into English in numerous ways: earth, land, soil, country, ground, floor. And, more often than not, all of these meanings are present to some degree. In the 17th century, Catalans launched an armed uprising against the Castilian monarchy in what is today known as the Reapers' War or the Catalan Revolt under the rallying cry of 'Long live the *terra,* death to bad government!' And this dichotomy has endured over the centuries. Along with language, *terra* constitutes a direct engagement with one's daily reality, material needs, and family and community inheritance. It's a plot of soil that can be worked or a stretch of land that can be contemplated, it's the landscape of pine, oak, and gorse you'll see if you have the opportunity to travel during your stay in Catalonia, but it's also the same bare, arid land that Gaudí transformed into the navel of the world. 'Bad government' is nothing less than the political structures built in disregard of the *terra* and, for that reason, considered foreign or threatening.

When Maragall asks himself, 'And us, men, what are we if not exalted *terra*?', he's pointing toward this very notion that I've just explained: genuine culture is never an artificial invention by official power but a reality that is born organically, a fusion of language and land capable of identifying the most elevated beauty in the humblest of elements, such as Gaudí with his *trencadís.*

---

[1] Joan Maragall, "The End of Serrallonga," in *One Day of Life is Life,* tr. Ronald Puppo (London: Fum d'Estampa Press, 2020) 108.

This concept enables Maragall to transfigure a weakness. After military defeat in 1714, Catalans lost all independent political institutions and for years theirs was a provincial existence without a culture of power. Therefore, Maragall transforms necessity into virtue by locating within his unfavorable historical context the chance to extol spiritual freedom. Poetic transfiguration and symbolic exaltation compensated for political dissatisfaction.

Joan Maragall personifies the changes and contradictions of his day like few other intellectuals. In spite of the rousing mythology of all those coarse, free spirits born from the land, he was a respectable father of 13 who lived in the comfortable uptown neighborhood of Sant Gervasi and wrote for the bourgeois press. Violent storms may have thundered within the soul of the translator of Friedrich Nietzsche but, externally at least, his was a serene life. As the years passed, Maragall went from a fascination with savage, earthy heroes to an admiration of the harmonious forms of classical Greece, as well as the sea that unites Europe's eastern and western shores, and as he aged he increasingly left wilder fantasies behind to embrace a Hellenic aesthetic based on order and self-restraint. Serrallonga, the indomitable outlaw, steals, disobeys, and sins; Nausica, the Greek girl, is sentimental, obedient, and capable of renouncing true love.

This shift from disorder to form, from anarchy to a certain institutionalism, is analogous to what the entirety of Catalan culture attempts to do between 1868 and 1939. Coinciding with the growing industrialization of Catalonia, a complete European culture gradually takes shape during these years. The population of Barcelona multiplies and the city is expanded thanks to the development of the Eixample district, an egalitarian grid system designed by the engineer Ildefons Cerdà. The singular buildings by Gaudí, Domènech i Muntaner, and other Modernist architects go up around the city. In literature, translations into Catalan of ancient and modern classics begin to appear and there's a flowering in terms of style and genre, the crowning glories of these developments being the narrative fiction of Víctor Català, the poetry of J. V. Foix, and the prose of Josep Pla, to name just a few. This is mirrored in the field of music, with canonical figures such as Frederic Mompou and Robert Gerhard, while institutions are established to nurture and promote this burgeoning culture. The Institute of Catalan Studies, the same academic entity where Pompeu Fabra defined modern, standardized Catalan, is founded in 1907. Numerous obstacles were overcome to form autonomous political entities, beginning with the *Mancomunitat* in 1914 and culminating in the republican *Generalitat* in 1931. By the 1930s, Catalan culture is brimming with tension and potential and appears to be developing in a free and far-reaching manner. However, in 1936, a group of Spanish generals launch a coup against the Republic, causing a civil war that would end less than three years later in Nationalist victory. The resulting fascist dictatorship established under Francisco Franco would be like sulfuric acid for Catalan language and culture. It was as though everything had suddenly been torn down and had to be built all over again, brick by brick.

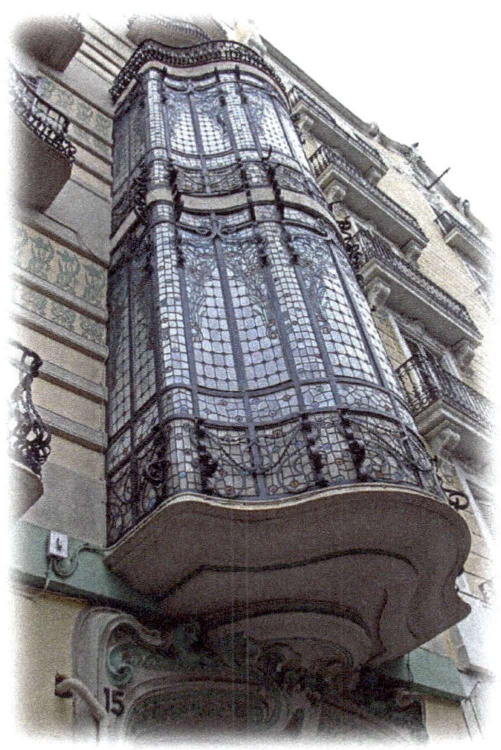

But allow me to take a step backwards and focus on the composer Frederic Mompou. Grandson of a bellfounder and raised amid the chime of industrial Barcelona, Mompou often stated that what most interested him wasn't the timbre of each note played but the precise sonorities between the notes. For him, composing meant sitting at the piano and searching for resonances, impressions and unconventional harmonies that lasted long in the ear as something more than a succession of musical vibrations. 'My hands are my music,' he would say. His wasn't a frenetic fight to extract sounds from his instrument like that of an engineer extracting raw materials from nature only to reduce them to quantifiable energy. More than the imposition of his own will, Mompou tended to regard music as a miracle that presents itself freely. He would often tell the story of how one day, while entertaining the guitarist Miquel Llobet in his Paris apartment, he heard a few peculiar notes form under his own left hand: he made a mental note of them and later turned them into the central theme of his 'Prelude No. 6, *Pour la main gauche*.' In an article published in January 1930, Mompou confessed his inability to subject himself to the regime 'of the rules of composition' and openly admitted that he didn't have an inner ear and that he wasn't interested in developing one. 'My intention,' he wrote, 'has always been to create sonorities that even the most sophisticated inner ear would struggle to detect.' For that reason he never conceived his work beforehand in his mind:

> My sensibility is a receiver antenna that dismantles elements, leaving them reduced to nothing. I write like a 'medium.' I make music which, as it forms, guides me until it's the very music itself that decides upon the title. I don't create music but rather music creates me.

Mompou presented himself as a 'sensitive and outward-looking' musician, a 'primitivist' desirous of arriving at an 'ideal model just like the painters who sought the same in African sculpture,' a lover of clarity and conciseness, and an admirer of Ravel and Stravinsky. He ended the article with a reflection on the origins of music: 'It's impossible to compose a sincere piece of music without it bearing the mark of its origin.' However, that didn't lead him to composing simple harmonizations of popular songs, and it was precisely this form of decorative folklore that had to be combatted. "This isn't the way to make Catalan music," he affirmed. "A Catalan composition worthy of being classified as universal music will be born in our *terra* and of our *terra.*" Of course, Mompou did put music to a large number of traditional Catalan songs, but that wasn't the point. The point was to compose music that obtained universal status precisely because of its intense relationship with its native culture. In other words: universality and rootedness, Greece and the Bare Mountain.

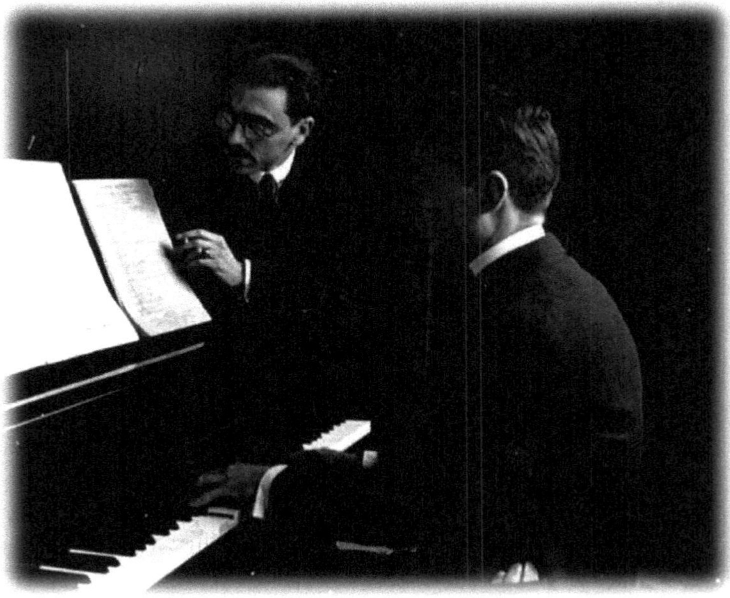

Mompou's article was published just as the Primo de Rivera dictatorship was falling. One year and three months later, the revolutionary Francesc Macià won elections and declared the Catalan Republic in Barcelona. When Mompou says his music is deeply Catalan, he's speaking from within a collective moment bubbling with energy and expectation.

As on other occasions in the history of Catalonia, Macià's audacious move didn't lead to the constitution of an independent state but instead forced the declaration of the Second Spanish Republic, within which Catalonia was officially recognized as an autonomous region. It was a fragile and hostile situation that satisfied neither Barcelona nor Madrid. Needless to say, it didn't last long.

As for Mompou, between 1930 and 1941 he went through an intense personal crisis. His friend Robert Gerhard, a disciple of Arnold Schönberg, had opted for the cerebral, abstract path of dodecaphony and Mompou, unwilling or unable to abandon his instinctive, sensitive approach to music, had the feeling that history was advancing in a different direction to him.

Added to this aesthetic malaise was violence and political chaos. In 1938, at the height of the Spanish Civil War, when a Nationalist victory and the cultural repression that would follow were increasingly apparent, Mompou harmonized one of Catalonia's saddest traditional songs: the '*Testament d'Amèlia*.' It tells the story of a dying princess speaking to her mother on her death bed. In a terrifying twist of events not only do we discover that the mother is responsible for her poisoning but that she's also taken Amèlia's husband as her lover. It's a horrifying story of family dissolution, the rupture of the most basic bonds, of the old killing the young and of lives sacrificed upon the altar of lies and deceit: in short, of war.

In 1939, when Nationalist rebel soldiers entered Barcelona, they put an immediate end to its autonomous institutions. They publically burnt thousands of Catalan books. They tore down the entire cultural system that had been created. The country's language lost its official status for forty years. If before the war there was a flourishing public world of newspapers, publishing houses, and all manner of cultural events, in its aftermath this structure was uprooted and an era of forced cultural assimilation and linguistic substitution began. Upon the ruins the regime promoted a new culture – in Castilian – with the collaboration of Catalans who preferred peace to liberty. Forty years of Francoist hegemony silenced or reinterpreted a large part of the preceding period's accomplishments. This explains why, even to this day, many people are ignorant of the relationship that Gaudí, Mompou, Miró, or Dalí had with their context and, subsequently, of the precise, palpable meaning behind their work. It's a frank reminder of why, in Catalonia, liberating yourself from the Francoist legacy means reconnecting with the world from before the civil war.

In 1939, Catalan culture forked liked never before. Hundreds of intellectuals went into exile. Some of the most important works of Catalan literature from the mid-20th century were written abroad – in France, Switzerland, or Mexico – and often in a state of isolation and disconnection, as is the case with Mercè Rodoreda's novels and the short stories of Pere Calders.

At this point, previous aspirations tied to the name of Greece seemed insignificant, a wounded fly squashed under a soldier's boot. But the Hellenic vision was still an attractive force, something that's clear in the life and work of the poet and humanist Carles Riba.

In 1939, Riba crossed the border with his wife, the poet Clementina Arderiu, and their three children. Their first stop was Avignon, where Riba felt the fatigue 'of a thousand years.' By March, they were settled in Moulin du Château in Bierville, a few kilometers south of Paris. Despite their desperate situation, Riba did what he could to put a brave face on things, even writing to a friend: "I don't think it's necessary to hold my head in my hands just yet [...] The gods look fondly only upon the happy." He learnt from written correspondence with relatives that he was "public enemy number one" in Spain and that his books had been banned, "something," he wrote "that offers me sweet revenge for my reputation as incomprehensible." And it was in this state of mind that he found himself under Nazi occupation. When Gestapo officers called on him, Riba managed to fob them off by telling them how much he admired

German culture and by showing them the books by Goethe, Hölderlin, and Rilke that he was translating.

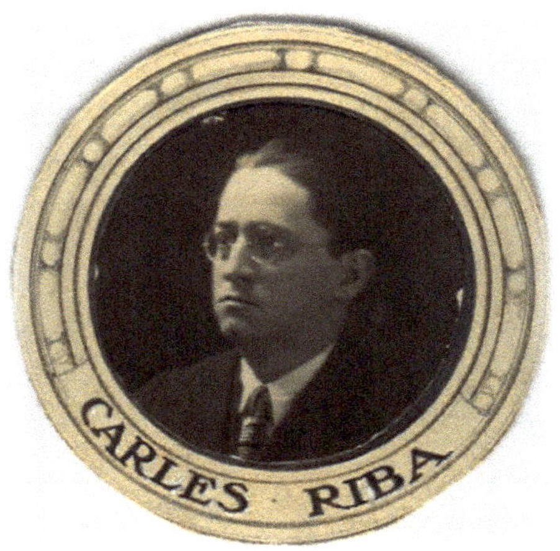

The humanistic convictions that had always accompanied Riba now revealed themselves with greater urgency than ever. For him, humanism and democracy were inseparable principles and it was during this period, while he was barely able to meet his most basic material needs, that he expressed these ideas for the first time in verse. The result was a series of elegies that stand not only as a highpoint in his poetic trajectory but as a monument to European poetry in those hours of totalitarian darkness. Riba managed to get the verses to friends in Catalonia by signing his letters with a French name, posing as an old engineer or teacher. They were received by small 'faith groups' made up of young dissidents who would then copy and circulate them clandestinely with considerable impact within the cultural resistance. "The Homeland," he wrote to the young poet Rosa Leveroni, "is a circle – wide, narrow, it does not matter – where our word constitutes action, connecting with the echoes and the wonder of the unknown voices of the innumerable dead." The poems that form *"Elegies de Bierville"* elevated the conflict that Catalans had just experienced to the universal realm where the Greeks' struggle against the Persians was the first in a long succession of battles in the name of freedom. In the 9th elegy, the poet evokes the Battle of Salamis before addressing the Greeks directly and declaring himself as "among the sons of your illustrious sowing." The Greeks had shown the world that "freedom conquered in the impassioned search for what is true and what is just" is the patrimony of humanity and it was for this very reason that, owing to the hope "emanating from all exiles," "the beaten shall become soldiers once more." It was a proud and defiant message that could only be formulated in exile and when it reached occupied Catalonia it caused shock waves.

Meanwhile, Catalan culture was slowly rebuilding itself within an atmosphere of resistance and collaboration through clandestine publications, secret meetings in private homes, and by exploiting cracks in the censorship. Each individual artist searched for their own way to reconnect with their environment.

Frederic Mompou had yet to overcome his personal crisis. In 1941, he met the young pianist Carme Bravo, whose presence proved providential. One night, after an insipid concert at the Palau de la Música, they decided to take a stroll along the streets around the Cathedral. As they approached the gothic fountain in the courtyard to the Casa de l'Ardiaca, the bells chimed midnight. We can imagine the sensuality of the moment: the stimulating company, the expressive power of the water's song, the bells that had so inspired him as a boy in his grandfather's foundry, the streets' nocturnal repose after their daily desecration by military boots. All of that transmuted into a gentle, evocative music and suddenly Mompou rediscovered the strength to creatively embrace his city once again. The vibration of water and air, his old receptiveness for the unexpected, the search for the essential, all of it melted into a new composition: "The Fountain and the Bell." The piece signaled Mompou's creative rebirth, but we can also regard it as a collective revival. The subtle piece of music asserted that war and the dictatorship had been powerless to kill memory and life. As a result, the piece can be considered an emblem for all of the artists who remained in Catalonia and lived under the Franco regime.

I'm afraid I will have to finish here. Unfortunately I don't have enough time to explain everything that comes afterwards. The only thing I will say is that, in large part, the story of Catalan culture in the second half of the 20th century is one of reconnection and reconstruction, a lengthy, slow process that is still ongoing. Even today, as Catalans we are often left surprised and outraged by all of the basic things we don't know about our own history.

I've spoken about Greece and *terra,* about elevation and rootedness, as well as the aspiration, on the one hand, to converse on an equal footing with all of humanity and, on the other, to work with and within a place, to recognize even the lowliest things around oneself as marvelous, and to alchemically transform them into gold. Standing before you today, these two tendencies seem more valid to me than ever. We live in a globalized planet under tremendous standardizing forces, while also witnessing the consequences of our brutal exploitation of the environment. The creative tradition that I've attempted to evoke almost seems to have been devised in response to this exact situation. I won't go as far as Gaudí and declare Catalonia the new center of the world, but I will leave you by expressing my faith in the fecundity of this particular Catalan sensibility, in this fusion of ambition and respect, of localism and universality. As Maragall asserted, the most universal phenomenon is unequivocal difference. And it's out of these unequivocal differences, as the philosophy of *trencadís* shows us, that precious realities are born.

Translated by Tiago Miller

OCEANOGRAPHY OF TEDIUM

EUGENI D'ORS

Eugeni Ors i Rovira was born in 1881, though, inspired by a touch of coquetry, his birth year appears most places as 1882. A different kind of dandyism also led him to add a nobiliary particle to his last name, turning him into Eugeni d'Ors. (Catalans undermined his noble *boutade* by persisting in calling him "Ors," without the particle.) He also had a penchant for pseudonyms — perhaps heteronyms. The most significant and lasting one was *Xènius,* a name that combined his mother's pet name for him as a child with a dash of foreignness or hospitality (xeni-), and a little touch of genius.

Ors was the principal mastermind behind the Noucentista (1900's-ist) movement, which espoused a modernity rooted in a Classicist Mediterranean aesthetic and the establishment of long lasting institutions of Catalan culture. He called himself a "household philosopher," and wrote daily newspaper articles, called *glosses,* in which he interpreted details of daily life — which he termed "anecdotes" — for their "eternal" significance, a practice he called "making anecdote into category."

Oceanography of Tedium, the text included here, was written in the summer of 1917. In summertime, Ors turned his daily newspaper articles into serial chapters of fictional texts, which he called his "vacations." His first "vacation" was *La Ben Plantada (The Stately Lady),* in 1912; the next was *Gualba, la de mil veus (Gualba of the Thousand Voices),* from 1915; followed by *Oceanography*.

In 1921 Ors had a falling-out with the institutions and newspapers that supported him. He spent some years in Argentina, then France and Italy, and eventually ended up in Madrid. He occupied important posts during the Franco regime. Though he is recognized to be an important influence on both Catalan and Spanish culture, his work has been eclipsed by his political affiliations. Nevertheless, the appeal of this little jewel of an oceanography cannot be denied.

— Mary Ann Newman

INTRODUCTION

I

THE SENTENCE

The Doctor is an old friend. The Doctor is an old fox. The Doctor knows one's foibles.

The Doctor has handed down his sentence:

"I am not prescribing the countryside. I am not prescribing repose. Author, Author, man in perpetual ebullition, I know only too well how you construe countryside and repose! I am prescribing, as your only salvation, tedium. Tedium, *to the letter.* Unattenuated, unnuanced: tedium. No excursions: *chaise longue.* No conversations: silence. No reading: lethargy... Insofar as it is possible: Not one movement, not one thought."

The Author gave his word and took his leave. The Author rose to the challenge. Even more than his instinct for survival, he was depositing his self-esteem in the perfectly faithful, scrupulous, extreme compliance with the prescription. Now the full magical extent of his destiny would be revealed. That life that had taken the garden of fever to its maximum intensity, would now reach, for a time, to the human limits of extenuated inertia.

"Not one movement, not one thought!" It was half-past three in the afternoon. A park encircled by beautiful trees. A lounge chair, in the most elusive and recondite corner. Loose tennis whites half covering his reclining body. Above, between two cedars, a stretch of hotel wall. A windowless side wall, an unbroken stretch of white.

Amidst the sun's reverberation upon the white wall thunders the onerous sentence:

"Not one movement, not one thought."

II

THE NAP

To close one's eyes. To sleep... That was the banal solution. At this time of day, the garden abounds with lounge chairs. Some of them discreetly dissemble. Others come together to share their indolence. Their heedless negligent conversation... The open, warped book, no longer read... And that willfully unproductive oscillation of the hands that the gentle ladies call "fancywork"... And that other oscillation, that other fancywork that everyone has come to call "flirting"... A wave of heat lies heavy upon the park, which lies low as if in a basin. Above the park only the artful luxurious vegetation manages to mask the raging rays of the sun... It is the hour of the nap.

To sleep. Has the Author perchance fallen asleep? He does not know. His eyes are now obstinately fixed on the white wall of the sentence. His first conscious act is to read it. "Not one movement, not one thought!" His second act, to take notice of a small slight flash to the right that comes to pierce the eye with its tiny reflex. Said eye turns very slowly toward that side, as the body remains immobile. The flash comes from a teaspoon half-lying on its side. Under the teaspoon there is a cup. Under the cup, a portable coffee table. Farther on, atop the portable coffee table, a sugar cube. And atop the sugar cube, a fly. How fascinating is this fly!

Author closes his eyes again. He remembers. It was he who called for the coffee table to be placed by the side of the chaise longue. He has had a cup of coffee. Perhaps he has also smoked a cigarette? His memory cannot certify it. Vaguely, dully, he felt the desire to do so. Perhaps he still holds the spent cigarette between his fingers. But his hand is too far away; and now his turbid consciousness knows nothing of the pressures on his hand. If he were to look... But to look, to look and to see, one must raise one's head or raise one's hand. The Author's lucidity spirals and he loses himself for a moment in the subtleties of the choice.

A feat of decisiveness leads him to prefer the small gesture of raising his hand. But the slight elevation has caused his flaccid fingers to separate. Then, obscurely, he perceives some weightless thing escaping.

The ear hears a tenuous sound coming from the ground, tenuous as a muffled sigh. The eye, then, has been freed of the burden of opening... Yes, there had been a half-smoked cigarette there.

III
THE AUTHOR SINKS INTO THE SEA

Light was the sound of the cigarette falling. This sound is louder. Once again his eye indolently turns to where the coffee table sits. Now, beyond the table, a waiter stands stiffly. And the waiter says:

"Do you have any more need of this?"

The uncomprehending eye looks him up and down. The question is repeated:

"Do you have any more need of this?"

Not a word, but an obscure grumble, responds:

"No... no."

The waiter still seems to be awaiting something. But the Author definitely does not understand. The other man moves away; in one hand, the coffee table held aloft; in the other, the gleaming coffee service.

Now the Author is like a shipwrecked man adrift in mid-sea whose hands have released the rope that held him, his last hope of holding fast... Having coffee is still some kind of action. So long as the coffee table was there, he was "having coffee." Now, he was not. He has allowed the last trace of his active life to be taken away.

He closes his eyes again. He has lost all his moorings. Now he sinks, solitary and abandoned, into tedium. He sinks into tedium, just as a shipwrecked man sinks into the sea.

IV
OCEANOGRAPHY

But the sea, which to the frivolous observer appears to be supreme sameness and monotony, offers to the diver who plumbs its depths the prestige of a thousand obstacles, in the magical palace of the siren of diversity. "Sterile plain" was the name the ancients gave the sea. But the moderns have seen in it the scene of the most interesting, the most opulent and lavish, dramas of life. The moderns know their Oceanography.

As is tedium, so is the sea. An Author who sinks into it, feeling at first like a drowning man, soon sees his consciousness newly awakened and ready to multiply the attentive contemplations of the diver... --Just look: in the murky greening water, suddenly a miraculous vegetation flowers. Singular beings navigate there. Strange forms come together. Filaments and tentacles make what one might call intelligent signs. Now a slender star, garnished entirely in extravagant ribbons, has burst in a dark corner... Now the star has become an outpouring of stars... Two milky peduncles, vibrating in an elastic palpitation, pursue each other and flee, by turns, as if in a play of love and gallantry... And now they are one sole thing, the two of them, and together they abandon themselves to the current that drives them, as if towards the bedchamber of a prince, toward the labyrinths of a coral reef...

This is where the Author will write the Oceanography of tedium. He will learn how rich and multiple is that which, to the uninitiated and inattentive, appears unchanging and monotonous. He will learn this, and through him we will discover it. For there are discoveries in the depths, just as there are discoveries in breadth. "I am the Columbus of the Americas of Christ," wrote Mossèn Jacint Verdaguer in his Diary one tormented day on which a painful, prideful, spirit inspired him. Humor, humor, keep us from the vainglory of calling ourselves the Columbus of the Americas of tedium.

First Part

I

CONCERT

This poor reclining body is a harp and the scorching breeze makes music with all its strings. At times like this, the plaint that escapes the mouth of all peoples, the plaint "It's so hot!", is the music of this harp. But no plaint escapes the Author's mouth. The music remains within, and spreads through all his being in mysterious waves.

One is hot in waves. Heat begins between the eyes and reaches the high forehead and the lower chin at the same time. A benumbed hand appears, spreads, attempts to embrace the entire area that the now broad waves have taken over. But the heat has now descended to the breast and acts like a river of flame upon it.

In the meantime, another wave was born. Dilated and solemn, it repeats the path of the first... This cannot be felt by a man who tries to distract himself, or to ease the momentary inclemency. The Author, indeed, does feel it, and goes so far as to distinguish the rhythm and the beat, until it becomes a sort of revelry... So it is that now he attends an even louder concert. – His whole body is a new instrument: no longer a harp, but a brass instrument. August blows that horn with an incomparable virtuosity.

II

THE TWO SMELLS

The *chaise longue* is a meridian. It divides the world in two. Each half is represented by a fragrance: alternatively, each of the fragrances advances or retreats.

Author, once again closing his eyes, analyzes this coming-and-going for a while. To the left, behind two rows of acacias, a girdle of burning midday light. To the right, the fuller thicket of the park. The smell that wafts from the left is warmer than the other. This other one is more delicate and voluptuous.

More voluptuous? The first is a wild, agrarian smell. The smell of hay, of the barn, of white airborne dust. The smell of the earth of the Vallès. The whole of the Vallès smells of hay.

The other smell is all indolent and tropical. Magnolias? Rosebushes extenuated by August? Simply great leaves, drenched with the water of the hose? Is there a vague trace of the music of a waltz in this fragrance? Is there a memory of other parks, perhaps on Isola Bella or the Riviera?...

Fortunately, just as the memories are on the verge of becoming too precise, the other perfume arrives and takes over. And this happens ten, twenty, a hundred times.

III

THE LIGHT BULB

Suspended at the heart of a clearing in the park, amid a play of cords, sits an electrical light bulb. The sets of cords are distributed into four sections. In two sections, there are four parallel cords. Another two sections have one cord each. A black transversal bar ties together the elements of three of these sections and not those of the other. On each black bar there are three white buttons. And on the glass bulb, three small reflections from the sun... It is magnificent.

It is magnificent; but if one pays close attention, he will begin to find it a bit strange. Why ten cords and why this distribution of the ten cords. Why three white buttons, three and not four, set on each black bar? Why this happenstance, whereby the number of buttons on each bar is the same as the total number of bars and the number of sun spots on the glass bulb? The calculation goes awry, and a thin fog begins to cloak one's attention like a sort of veil.

And in the end all color, all form, all concrete elements disappear from the field. The numbers remain. What remains is 4, 2 of 4, 2 of 1, 3 on 4, 3 on each one of the 3, 3 on 1... And from there on in, an infinitude of possible combinations...

IV
THE SKY RISES

The delight resides in this limitation of possibilities, in this penury. Renouncing all movement and thought would bring great harm to anyone who had before his gaze the dances of Loie Füller or heard whispered into his ear the tales of Scheherezade... But here, surrounded by a hundred modest trees and a white wall, hearing nothing but the monochord midday uproar of the cicadas?

There isn't a single cloud in the square patch of blue sky. But the avid gaze has now found a topic of diversion in this patch of sky. An extraordinary thing is happening. *The sky is rising...* A second ago, the azure sheet seemed suspended and pinned to the very tip of the trees... Now, it has risen a bit higher than the trees ... Now, still a bit higher... Having left off looking for a moment, now it seems to have risen to an infinite height.

And it continues to rise, vertiginously.

Yes, vertiginously. The loving gaze has found in this the thousand disturbances, the thousand tortures, the thousand delights of vertigo.

V
THE WHITE WALL

A white wall. Easy to say. Some painters know how rich in tones such a thing is. This wall the Author sees before him seems to him to be the richest of all. This white wall is, at times, like polished mother-of-pearl.

There are peaks of pink on a white wall; there are blue abysses. There are vertical strips of gold. There are fleeting, mysterious, greens. There are irises and snows and clair-de-lunes. There are sunsets and dawns.

And on this wall—the traces can still be seen—there was also a fulminating sentence in letters of fire.

VI
PHOSPHENES

And when the gaze shrinks from the obsessive whiteness of that wall, a new festival begins. Like an extraordinary meteor, the passage of a few small luminous nimbuses, now red as fire, now opulent in their iridescence, blinds the pupil. The procession of little nimbuses parades by as quickly as a procession of pixies. But it doesn't die away so easily; rather, it is picturesque, disorderly. As in a mass commotion in a public square, one troupe bumps into another. And they disperse in polychromatic tumults and flashes of lightning.

Sunworks, as magical as fireworks! The Author's tedium comes so to love it that instinctively he finds a way to prolong the spectacle willfully. A knowing finger applies itself to rubbing and pressing on the eyelid, closed in a sheer pink translucidity. When one cascade of little colored lights is extinguished, a new constellation is born, and it is like an aurora in which a miraculous procession of all the stars, diamantine and mobile, was on display... At this point, a subtle recollection slips into the Author's memory. He remembers, for a second, the engravings at the end of a volume of an old edition of the Divine Comedy, a sumptuous topic on which he had long ago embroidered his childhood reveries. He remembers Paradise in a field of many-pointed stars through which the slender bodies of Dante and Beatrice ascended.

And when his eyelids open, yet another marvel is added. The world is doubled. All objects are doubled. Tremulous and iridescent, they are doubled...

The Author blinks.

Translated by Mary Ann Newman

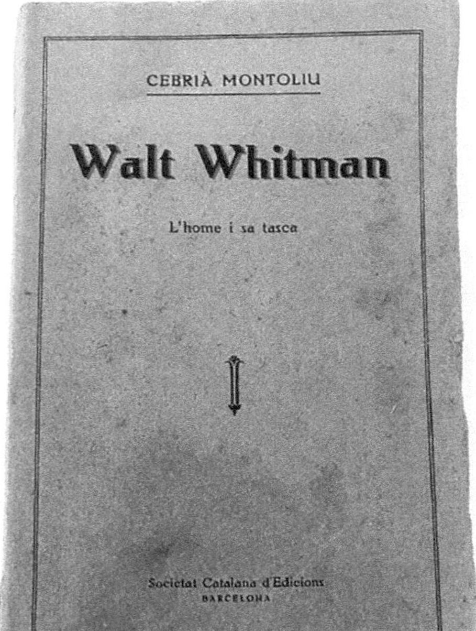
CEBRIÀ MONTOLIU
Walt Whitman
L'home i sa tasca
Societat Catalana d'Edicions
BARCELONA
WALT WHITMAN
Fulles
d'Herba

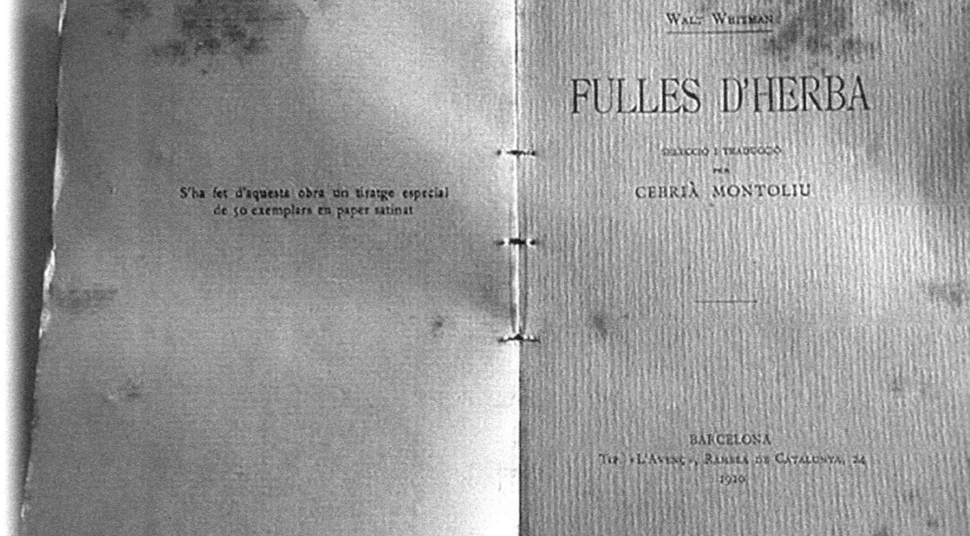
S'ha fet d'aquesta obra un tiratge especial
de 50 exemplars en paper satinat
Walt Whitman
FULLES D'HERBA
CEBRIÀ MONTOLIU
BARCELONA
Tip. «L'Avenç», Rambla de Catalunya, 24

Walt Whitman: L'home i sa tasca /// The Man & His Work

(Barcelona: Societat Catalana d'Edicions, 1913)

Cebrià Montoliu

Cebrià Montoliu (né Cebrià de Montoliu i Togores) (Palma 1873–Albuquerque 1923) was an integral player of 19th–20th centuries Catalan, European, and U.S. histories, bringing the era's scientific, social, & cultural ideas to Catalans and the wider world. Montoliu traveled Europe in search of urban planning best practices and fore-fronted city-gardens in rapidly industrializing Barcelona to ensure the creation of green, democratic spaces throughout the city, a city for which he envisioned economic growth walking in step with quality of life for all. He was secretary of the Societat Cívica / Ciutat Jardí, while working for its publication, *Civitas*. His interest in the city-garden continued in the US from 1919 through collaborative plans for the burgeoning utopian single-tax colony of Fairhope, Alabama. Montoliu founded the reform-focused l'Universitat Catalana, giving conferences while also teaching working class men — and women — and he helped found one of Europe's first social museums for which he served as librarian.

On the literary front, from 1903 to 1913, Montoliu was the first translator into Catalan of Shakespeare's *Macbeth*, as well as texts by Ruskin,

Emerson, and Whitman, following up his translation of poems from *Leaves of Grass* with *Walt Whitman: L'home i sa tasca* (l'Avenç, 1913), that is, the man and his work, part of which is included here. Therein, he, surprisingly, given the era, considers "The Sexual Question" vis-à-vis Whitman and also includes an astute reflection on the influence of Quakerism on the poet while conceiving Whitman as an "organic" poet.

Montoliu came from a well-educated, multi-lingual family and the males in the family were participants in the most influential cultural and political circles of their times. His father, in 1873, was arguing for universal access to clean drinking water. Cebrià's siblings included Manuel de Montoliu, top literary critic, and translator of Dante and Goethe; Francesc, translator of Buddhist texts and active in Paris and Madrid with Madam Blavatsky's Theosophical Society; Plàcid, the musicologist who was in NYC with Cebrià and who is credited with bringing Dalcroze's eurhythmics to the US; and the one female Montoliu which I have been able to learn something about, Pilar, a sister who published a poetry collection on the eve of taking religious vows.

In short, Montoliu was a man both of and at the avant-garde of his times, a transatlantic thinker, and actor, among other key actors, and worth, I believe, the biography I am writing on him.

— AKaiser

Excerpts from Preface & Introduction,

Table of Contents

Preface

No matter the extent to which one is an enemy of critical commentary, when it comes to truly inspired writing, one must admit that Whitman's, too, demands it. The work itself perhaps lacks any higher merit than that of a poetic *memorandum* of an essentially poetic life. But, at the same time, it contains lines full of meaning, meaning palpably spilling from each word, producing off-balance forms and types of disorientating expression resulting in, thus, enigmatic verses for those who are unaware of the great spirit that dictated them.

Moreover, the absolute contempt for laws of external restriction which Whitman demonstrated, both in his life and in his work, has exposed his intractable genius to the most furious attacks by a most varied array of enemies, the great majority of them incapable of understanding other ethical considerations or aesthetics than purely superficial ones, ones bought and sold in the markets of good behavior. There is no other reason for the violent diatribes that, not only in life but after death as well, have relentlessly pursued Whitman's work. Furthermore, as long as this protest lasts, it will be the duty of every loyal critic to firmly denounce this crazy mob wanting to measure the "spontaneous songs" of this free man by the same standard of those who sow their own mistrust in the system.

[...]

... contemporary history testifies that Whitman, even after his death, not only conquers, but continues to provoke his critics. To this day, as in the past, there are ferocious attacks by those evoking both his life and work every time some daring translator, author or editor gives themselves the license to bring them forth, either to the public as in Italy,

Germany or France, or, thirty years ago, when Whitman began to be known in English-speaking countries.

But no matter. Tall, well-anchored trees are not planted carelessly nor hastily. Modest as my work is (what greater proportions it would need to be worthy of its object), it is not for this reason that the credit due to those who have helped me bring it to life is any less. Among everyone, the Societat Catalana d'Edicions deserves a special prize for being the first publishing organization in Spain that dared to bring to the public forum such rough and important questions as those that the duty of the critic have me raise in this book —not to mention my natural deficiencies in the face of my high-spirited subject, which I am the first to regret.

It's not for nothing that Catalonia is said to be the America of Spain and it was thanks to this that our ancient vessel of human freedom was the first of the Hispanic languages to greet the noble cries of generosity with which the great bard of Democracy wanted to sing the heart of America, and together with it, that of the world!

Introduction

[...]

A new figure has come onto our stale Parnassus, a new star of the first order has appeared on our poetic horizon, and the duty of all who occupy a place, however modest, in our observatory of ideas is to signal this presence, to study its nature and character, and to make the public aware of its significance as well as the influence it has been called to exercise in the human cosmogony. This, then, is the object of these present tracings, and for greater clarity, we will examine separately – although they are truly inseparable – the person and then the work of Walt Whitman.

[...]

Table of Contents

The Man

ly wounded. Death of his mother. Challenging years. Whitman invalid. Solitude and misery. Friends to the rescue. Relief in nature. Travel bug. More censor. Poet's victory.

Agony & Transit — Dawns of Glory. Settling in Camden. Why this. Last glints of the setting sun. Last attacks. Four years of agony. Looking back. The definitive edition of *Leaves of Grass*. Adieu, my dream. Joyful funeral.

LA TASCA — The Man & the Poet

Whitmanian Thought — His anti-doctrine & anti-system way of being. His Germanic idealism & theosophy Hindi. His mysticism & his positivism. His religious *experience*. His divine quadrant.

Ethics — Dualism of. His foundation of mystical sensuality. Charity, Fraternity and Democracy. Ethics of Friendship. The eternal feminine. The sexual question.

Politics — Democracy & Politics of Friendship. Quaker antecedents. The ideal of America. Its reality & critique of in *Democratic Vistas*. The City of Friends. Feminism. Socialism. The Social Poet. Activist.

Aesthetics — His character, the negation of all Aesthetics. His naturalism. Iconoclastic. The voice of the earth. Similarities & differences with Rousseau, Ruskin and Nietzsche. His Modernism and Futurism. Science & Art. Involution of Whitman's thought synthesized.

Poetic Art — Corollary logic of preceding principles, his style, the lack thereof. Our own prejudices thereof. Spirits Apollonian and Dionysian. *Leaves of Grass*. Epic of the Personality. Anti-literary character of Whitman's poetics. His spontaneity and authenticity. His democracy. Structural and musical aspects. Literary project of *Song of the Exposition*. Rhythmic expression and question of metrics. Verse & prose. Polyphony.

Inheritance from Whitman — His testament against any school. Those who left, those who followed: Edward Carpenter, Ernest Crosby, Horace

Traubel. Apostles & Whitman influencers in Germany, France, Italy & Spain. Particular Whitmanism of France & Spain. Promises & Dangers.

Ripple Effects:

Spirit of Whitman reviewed; Mission of the Social Poet; Ideal Monument to Whitman; The evolutionary cycle of Poetry; Looking beyond, forwards and backwards; Whitman and the current poetic crisis; Whitman and the reintegration of all spiritual human domain.

Bibliography:

Original work by Whitman; Translations; Works on Whitman; Minor contributions.

Appendix:

The Sexual Question

Psychopathic prejudice and its ramifications; Scientific progress and obtained results; Their current deficiency and their hopes; Love and friendship in their purity and in their vices; Uranism and Uranian Nobles; Intermediary sex; Eugenics science and eugenics in Whitman.

A Question of Metrics

Classification of the poems from this point of view; Progressive metrical disintegration of verses in their three orders, to completion in the third; Logical or psychic rhythm replacing the acoustic and leading to the Whitman polyphony; The incorrigibility of thinking, primary factor of said disintegration.

Translated by AKaiser

Selected Poems translated from *La Gran Nàusea*, by Xavier Mas Craviotto (2021, LaBreu Edicions)

autòpsia

La gran nàusea (LaBreu Edicions, 2021) is a book of poems that delves into a process of exhaustion and weariness. An erosion that consumes the bonds between consciousness and reality, and inevitably leads not only to a feeling of tedium, but also to a hyper-consciousness of unreality and an invasion of strangeness. Taking as its starting point the symbol of the nausea that can be found in Jean-Paul Sartre's famous novel and also in some of Nietzsche's works, together with other authors like Lars Svendsen, Peter Handke, Byung-Chul Han, or filmmakers like Ingmar Bergman, the poems of this book rummage in the apathy raised in a world of demolished senses and wasted meanings, in the deep malaise that we have inside when we feel close the presence of an invasive, compact and solid void. *La gran nàusea* is a book about the (capital-V) Void. A Void that, like from the nausea to the vomit, starts being an inner and intangible discomfort and ends up being an outer and material reality; a deified Void that we liturgically venerate; a Void that goes from the individual to the community; a Void that in the beginning of the book pulls down a house and at the end of the book devours a whole city. *La gran nàusea* is divided in three parts – *repleció, antiperistalsi and èmesi* – whose titles correspond to the three phases of vomit. In these poems, the reader embarks on a poetic journey with an I and a You that struggle to understand not only each other but also a world that fades away right before their eyes. A world in which anything makes sense because words have been worn away and have lost their capability of evoking and attributing meanings and identities.

autopsy

What is this deadly poison that corrodes the best in us, leaving only the shell? — INGMAR BERGMAN

maybe it was the sharp eye
of the bird of sleep
that was looking at us;
maybe it was all this anguish
traversing the borders
of the countries that live within
the scab on our skin;
maybe it was the deft outline
of the nuclear aboulia that
fills us with weariness
behind the rind of us;
maybe it was You and Me,
that we understood the nothingness
and made of it a profane tree
in the paradise of watching us fall;
maybe it was the circular stroke
that I undraw in the dirty air
when I hurl myself into your ravine;
maybe it was the teeth of that rift
that welcomes us, open-mouthed, into an end
that we've known for many years;
maybe it was the rancid sweat of the world,
the structural narcosis,
the vascular anaesthesia,
the saintly drowsiness;
maybe it was the gastric Void
of this sad god
that for some time
is bored
and cries rubble.

fracture

it bends.
you notice it's bending
it bends
like the branch
where birds nest
and sit on eggs.
it bends.
you notice it's bending,
in spite of faith,
in spite of the certainties
like wires
crossing
your spinal
column
to straighten it,
in spite of promises,
that were silent
shadows
uselessly
propping up
your spinal cord,
that is no longer straight,
that has taken on
this weight
that dangerously
hunches it,
that is now like this,
bendy,
its natural state.
and it bends
each vertebra
is a sacrifice
that arches you
flattening you
under the weight
of each guilt,
and it bends,
and it bends again,
and it twists,
and it makes an acute angle
of the parabola
of your body
and your blame,
and the chicks
shriek at you
the resigned
fear
of someone who awaits
the fall.
and it bends
and it hurts
your spine,
that already bleeds
sacrifice
and it shakes
your core.
it bends,
and your back
already draws a
dangerously
hunched
arch.
it bends,
and with each
new sacrifice

the birds
shriek
the resigned
fear
of someone who awaits
                                        the f r a c t u r e.

the third cage

So many walls between you and me.
GABRIEL FERRATER

We lost ourselves in the unique and unending steps toward one another.
JOAN VINYOLI

Me living tired of being so Me. and vomiting all my fear into the cage of us. and You with belly full of Me, tipping cement into the Void between each bar so You don't hear me. *shut up and go to sleep.* and Me saying Me and you saying no. and me shouting Me and you saying *us.* and Me bellowing Me and you walling me up inside you and building walls around Voids so there's no space for my voice to exist nor make me exist. *shut up and go to sleep. don't say anything, you'll hurt me.* and Me emptying myself of being Me. and You walling me up in that cage with an us. *shut up and go to sleep.* and Me shouting all the fear of not being Me. and You telling me *shut up and go to sleep.* and Me noticing this us creeping over my body like a wild plant. and You trowel in hand, piling a mound of bricks onto my words. and Me moaning Me. and You shouting *go to sleep,* shouting *us, shut up and go to sleep.* and Me bleeding all the fear of not being. and You shouting *shut up and go to sleep* with a voice like concrete. and Me noticing this us spreading up my body like metastatic cancer. and You telling me *shut up and go to sleep,* and Me telling myself. and You telling Me that I'm not there, and Me telling You. and You telling Me that I'm not, and Me telling us. and You fusing the You and the Me that are already one and breathe gravel. and Me crushed within the cement telling you Me without hearing it. and You far away bellowing *us, shut up and go to sleep.* and Me curled up mumbling Me. and You polishing me with a whetstone, blunting every edge, smoothing every splinter so you don't feel me or know I'm inside, behind the cement, beating, shouting, but You, made of concrete, now hear nothing. shouting, but You, made of concrete, now feel nothing.

the tapeworm

the crack is a tapeworm.
the crack is a silent parasite.
the crack is a solitary tapeworm that feeds on this us.
the crack is a parasite clamped to the red and bloody intestinal wall.
the crack is a larva hollowing out the sinuous and burnt soil of fear.
the crack is this worm that fills our bodies and grows on everything that we were and makes us feel full but it's really him that's filling up inside our empty body.

and if we ever speak the crack's name, we disappear.
and if we ever speak the crack's name, it means that we have it inside us, splitting open our bowels.
and if we ever speak the crack's name, it means that this crack is us and we are this crack.
and if we ever speak the crack's name, this great worm will die and we'll drain it away down through our intestines.
and if we ever speak the crack's name, the tapeworm won't be there, and our body will void from this feeling of fullness.

and yet we decide to feed it.
and yet we decide to shelter it from the destructive effluvium inside our body.
and yet we decide to fatten it with nostalgia and silences and mute fears.
and yet we decide to make it so huge that it bursts out of our mouth.

today, it poked its head out between your back teeth and looked at me. You didn't put up a fight. rather you invited it: you opened your mouth wide and I saw the darkness of your bowels full of holes. it poked its head out between your back teeth and looked for me. and I saw it, and I felt the dense body of my own crazed parasite rising up through my oesophagus. and it slid down my tongue and beat against the back of my teeth to cave them in. that worm was a battering ram and roared at my gums. it was looking for you. looking for your parasite and shouting at you both. they had fed on us and now they wanted each other, were looking for one another. they'd used you and me and now they were leaving that great Void inside our bodies. and you looked at me and you said

do it.

and I opened my mouth.

the great nausea

contraction of the diaphragm: and that slow silence that you told me amidst the noise.
palpitation of the medulla oblongata: and the indecipherable touch of a skin I no longer understand.
slight taste of bile and salivation: and the aberrant confusions that turn my alphabet upside down.
reverse peristalsis: and hands made of wood and indifferent woodworm.
stomach spasms: and the thousand names that hurt has when you say it in the night.
bubbling of gastric juices: and the fingers of that haughty boredom tying me a knot with each verb.
the body regurgitating itself: and the deceitful calm brooding inside my chest.
sudden surge of chyme: and the Void colouring my eyes with the shades of winter.
and just before vomiting: the great nausea.
the nausea of not being there when one of us is near the other.

cemetery

amidst our words grew a cemetery with high walls and grey tombs.
a badly wounded bird came and nestled on our grave, beneath the weariness of the cypress trees.
there was a tired sky that sighed hot breath down the precipice of our necks.
and it was still quiet, but we felt the sorrow,

and it was already late:
the shadow of a cage was cast, shamelessly, onto the wall of our backs.

the Void (or the betrayal of the word-crack)

On voudrait saigner le Silence.
JULES LAFORGUE

and it was then that I saw the Void inside your mouth.
it was a Void made of the sleepiness of an immense forest of long-lived
[trees.
it was a Void made of the weeping of a thousand birds flying over a city
[with no memory.
it was a Void made of the people looking up and saying it is raining.
it was a Void made of the gaze of dead fish.
it was a Void made of deserts full of noise, far from the sea.

and I looked at your eyes in order to not look at your mouth anymore,
but your mouth overflowed and your gums melted
and your teeth were made of moss and your tongue was squashed
under the weight of so much silence, and your lips filled
with cracks that were new mouths that didn't say anything either.

and it was then that I looked at the Void inside your mouth.
it was a wide and thick Void, with the colour of an end
made calm and with the shape of the sea when it's full,
and you foamed with saburra like a sad animal,
and you spat black bile and your tongue stood upright
tall and proud like a pine tree and squeezed
through your palate like a root.

and I felt your breath.

and your breath was cold.

and the cold was very slow.

don't say the names

we were winter and brought the cold.
we covered our hands with sediment
and spoke with pointed words
that limit the shape of things.
don't say the names.
you said it to me with the silence
made by foetuses in the womb.
don't say the names.
and on the back of every sound, slowly grew
the dying echo of resignation.
and we torched the stubble of the last harvest
and we inhabited that scorched earth.
don't say the names.
the winter birds looked at us
patiently from the trees
and were so silent that never again
did we stop hearing them.
don't say the names.
they sung the rage that grows
on the backs of days
and they crept up on our bark
covered in lichen and fungus
and mossy silences.
don't say the names.
and the lines that separate things
were rubbed out, and everything was one, and You were the things
and I was the moss, and You were the eyes of the birds
that spied on us, and I was the ash
roaring wounds, and You were the profane
sounds that died away, and I was all the names
that you wouldn't let me say.

spleen

the yawn of the continents
languishes like a slow drowsiness.

the sadness of the light
bleeds all over our body
with clear and transparent knots
of lethargy.

years have empty bones.

time carries the desert within.

civilisation is a sanctuary
devoted to the unwilting
apathy that gnaws at
all gods.

the West sighs in our spleen.

apocalypse

the useless feet of the centuries
                              extremely cold
walking on the tiles
of a waiting room:

the words exposed to the danger
of being said,
the vertigo of the mouths
beside the word.

the apocalypse of eyes looking at things,
and You and Me in the middle of everything
with so much night in our eyes
that not even the night could we see.

nothing in the world was worth being said.

Translator by James Hawkey and Xavier Mas Craviotto

Unnameable

Anna Gual, Selected Poems

INTRODUCTION

> *I'm all these words, all these strangers, this dust of words with no grounds for their settling...*
> — Samuel Beckett, *Unnamable*

To experience the words of Catalan poet Anna Gual is to embark with her on a quest. A quest towards the liminal; towards omnipresent, and elusive, horizons — both horizontal and vertical; towards dirt-laden construction and de-construction sites, towards an often willingly unhinged coursing through time, rivers, electrical currents ... to say nothing of one's own veins.

From her first book, *Implosions* (2008), through others, including a trilogy, to her seventh, *Ameba* (2020), winner of the Rosa Leveroni prize and slated for a French language edition, to her just released *Les ocultacions*, winner of the Miquel de Palol Prize, Gual has demonstrated her attempts at and talent for noticing and expressing the odd in the quotidian, whether breaking down barriers between human beings and the so-called natural world, between and within bodies, or in the flesh and blood of language itself. Susanna Rafart has remarked that to enter Gual's work is to enter a "forest of wild rebirths"; Gemme Gorga describes Guals' poetic world as one where "human laws are far away"; and Lluís Calvo, as one of "continuous exceptionalities."

I discovered Gual's inventive, muscular work, her leaving no strange stone unturned, as it were, while completing my doctorate in Barcelona. I was instantly taken in by these poems that travel through and across meaning-scapes of language as she, as we, sense, pursue, silence, cry, claw, pierce, transmit it.

The poems in this portfolio are part of Gual's bilingual Catalan-Spanish collected works, *Innombrable* (Unnamable; Stendhal Books, 2020), which I am currently translating and for which I have been awarded an NEA Fellowship. This will be the first time a full collection of Gual's work will be available to an English readership.

— AKaiser

Unnameable

Let the dog in
to sniff the house's miseries.
Let him bark when he smells the worn smell
of the clothes,
let him bark when he finds white hair
floating in the air,
let him bark when
the dust that wanders about
the dead bedrooms
clouds his vision and trips him up,
let him bark when
he senses sockets
sealed
and lamps with molten bulbs,
let him bark when he bumps into
memory
when he steps on
tile hiding an array of faces,
let him bark and be spooked
when he hears
ghosts gliding,
when he finds shadows hewed to the walls
and screams
glued to the ceiling,
let him bark when he approaches the grave
where pain sleeps
when suddenly he'll go quiet
and let himself be taken
when pain wakes
and drags him away.

Commotion

The sun shut down, the meaning of the sun shut down,
the meaning of shutting down lit up. — Alejandra Pizarnik

The memory of nails
flaked with light is often present
in my mind. Also
I carry in me
a swamp full
of stars, the shadow
of an entire forest ablaze,
the sparks from a pool of lava and
a dozen faces
advancing through the fog
lit by bright lightning.

In the memory of a blind person a ray
of sun embedded in a clouded glass.

Millimeters

Nothing's happening. Nothing is happening.

Paths lead nowhere
but no matter,

nor do we know
anything of the desert
even if we go there and take photos
and go about as if we recognize
and understand it.

Today something is beginning.
And always, if something's beginning
it's because before something else died
to leave it space.

Chrome

If solidity doesn't exist,
how does the skeleton hold up?

If the brain is so wicked,
how does the neck still support it?

Flesh, which means degradation,
which means
overcoming misery, which means burrow
inside those veins
and nail the flag there.

Begin the verse at the end.
Begin again.
Before-birth.

I said before-birth.
I should have said post-death.
I should have said think backwards.

I'd like to get lost in the alley
where fetuses are cultivated.

This is the first objective.

This is my resistance.

Needing to make a hole

I grab a shovel and a rake
and start digging down,
breaking the tiles first,
smashing the cement second
and the earth that holds it and all
the stones I find I shove
into my pockets in case
of a sudden landslide
and I have to raise a wall and wait
for everything to calm down.

I don't want to think
about where I'm headed or how long it'll take,
or if in the end I'll find
someone digging in the opposite direction.

Who knows if I'll crash,
with no time
to prevent the collision,
against someone's head
full of mud and rubble.

Truth is, panic to crash
against myself
to be myself the question and the answer.

Inner forest

I think I've veered from the pavement.
I think what hurts me are the branches.

I know I shouldn't take it all too seriously
but the forest is thickening and I don't
have to pretend it doesn't scare me.

In the dark, fog is invisible.
In the dark, there's no resonance when I hold myself.

I'll grope along the roots
to feel the way.

If I find nectar and a nest of larvae,
there may still be hope.

How much innocence hides
among the trees
as they welcome me to the beech forest.

How much autumn gathers
on soft knees all of this still life,
this well,
this wall that says
it's breaking
that it's cracking along its veins.

You won't find me when things
take on the name of sadness.

You won't find me
because I'll be on the other side
of words.

Reader in the grotto

Poor thing who'll repeat the process
of abandonment. Poor thing for being the master.

If I leaf through my lips
I read my guts
as if I were a hidden prophet
behind the door
that has to lead me
to the soul.

I was born a cave.
You still haven't understood me.

Convalescence

The man who assures me
he loves me

brings his fingers to my mouth
and delicately
extracts copper wires.

They're drawn from the throat.
When he caresses them
they melt in his palms.

I swoon,
sustained in nothingness.

Bread & Onion

The ants gather with tweezers
the skulls of roses.

We'll be on the porch
where the soul leads our dance.

We have an alphabet
to distract us from death.

Translated by AKaiser

Pepe Sales

Paintings

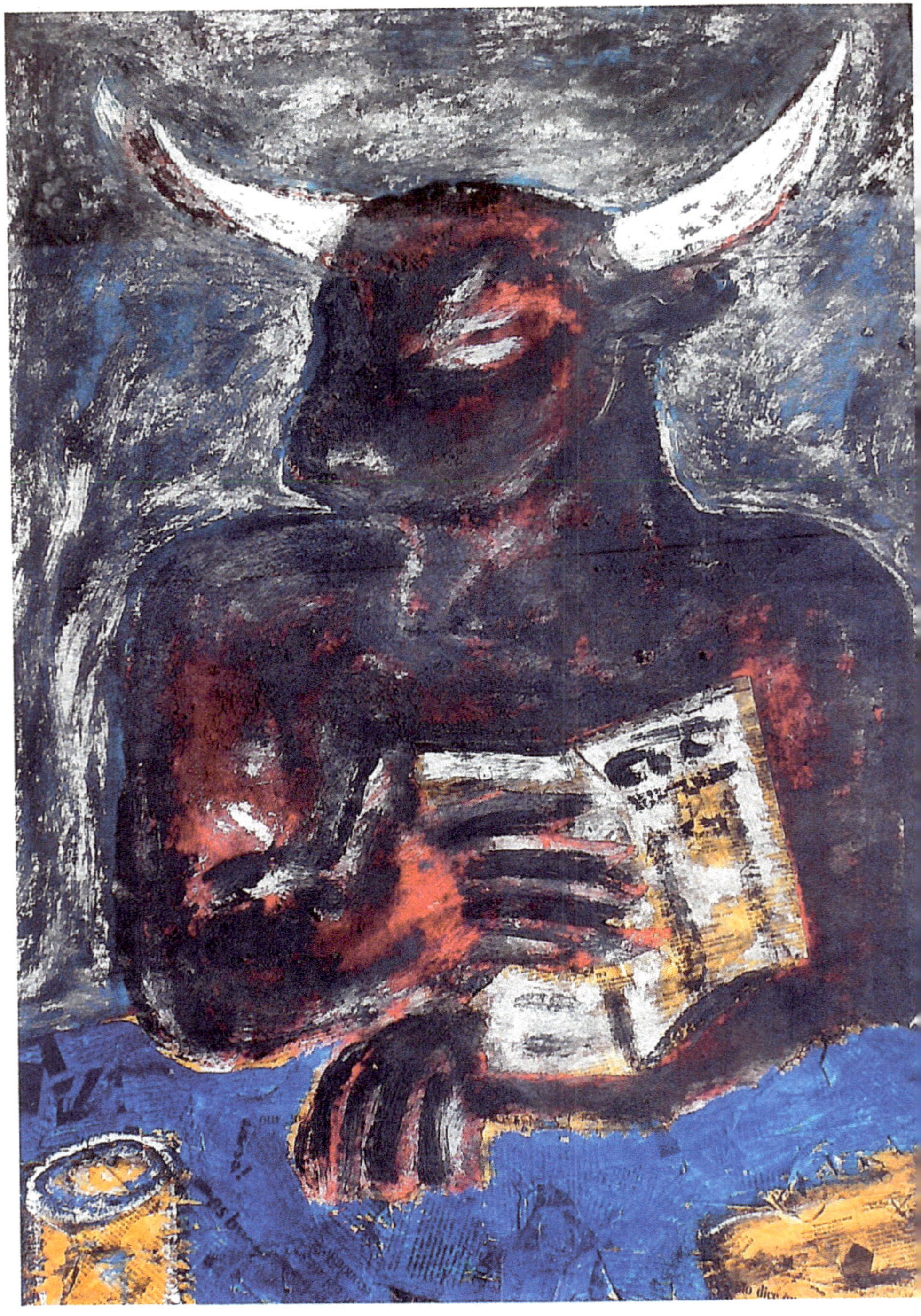

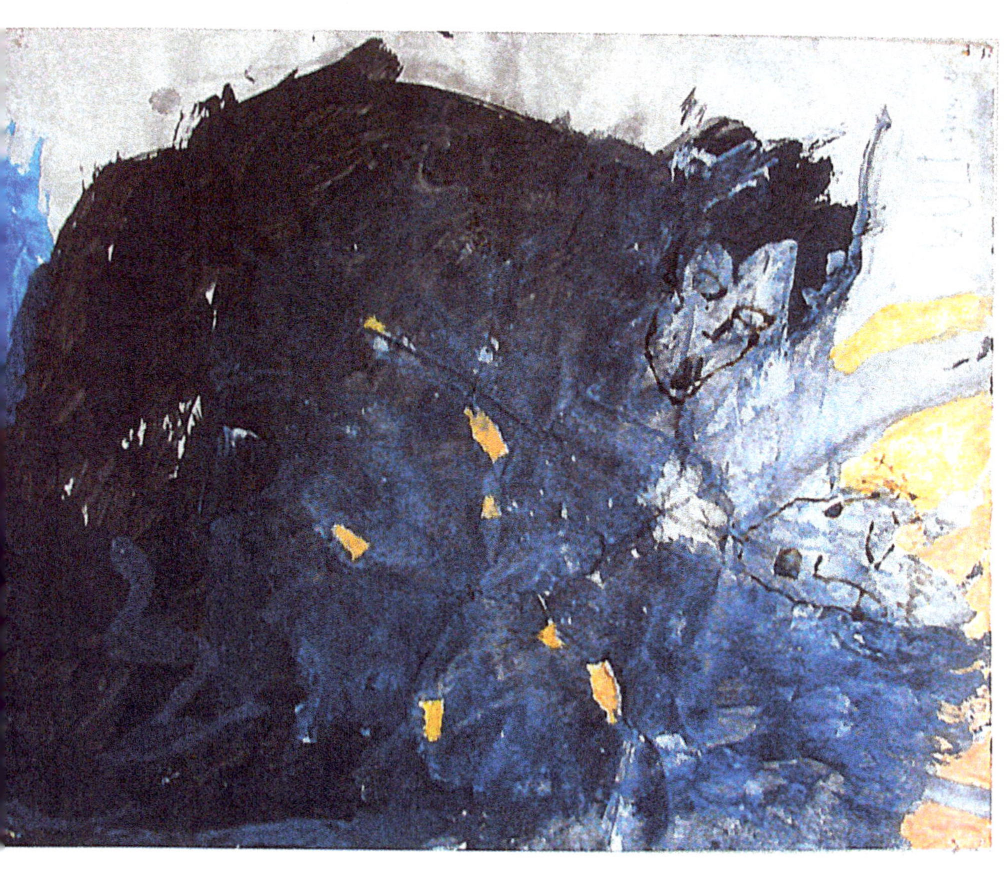

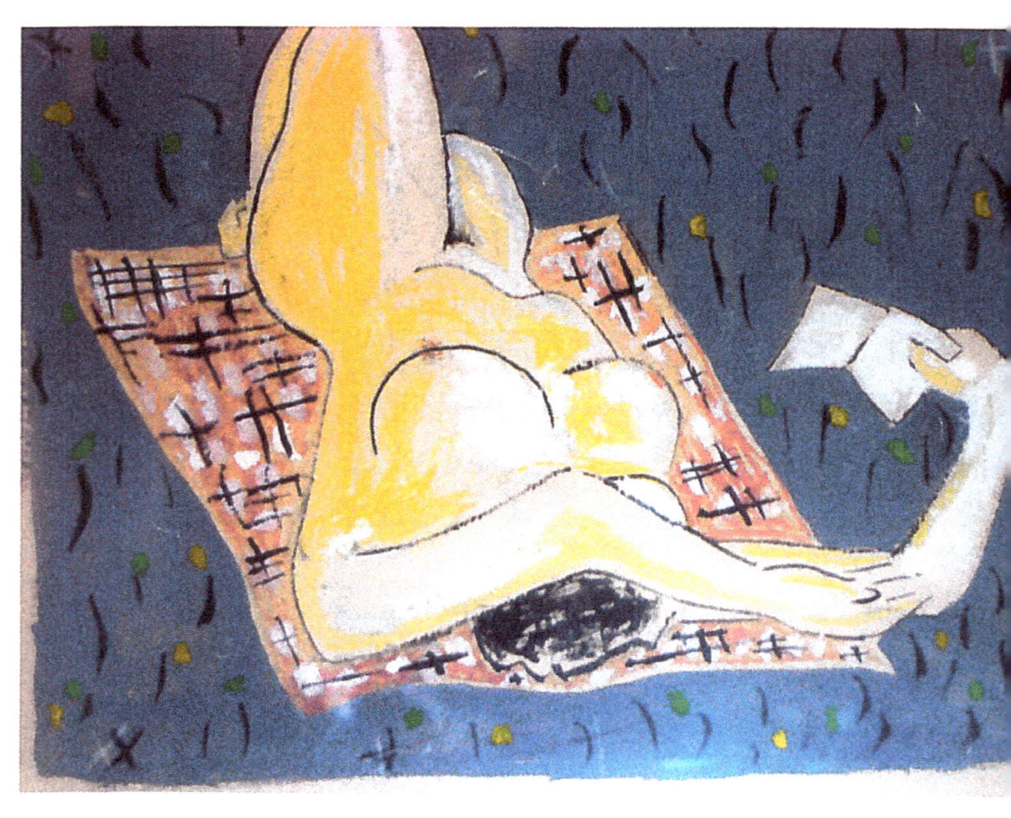

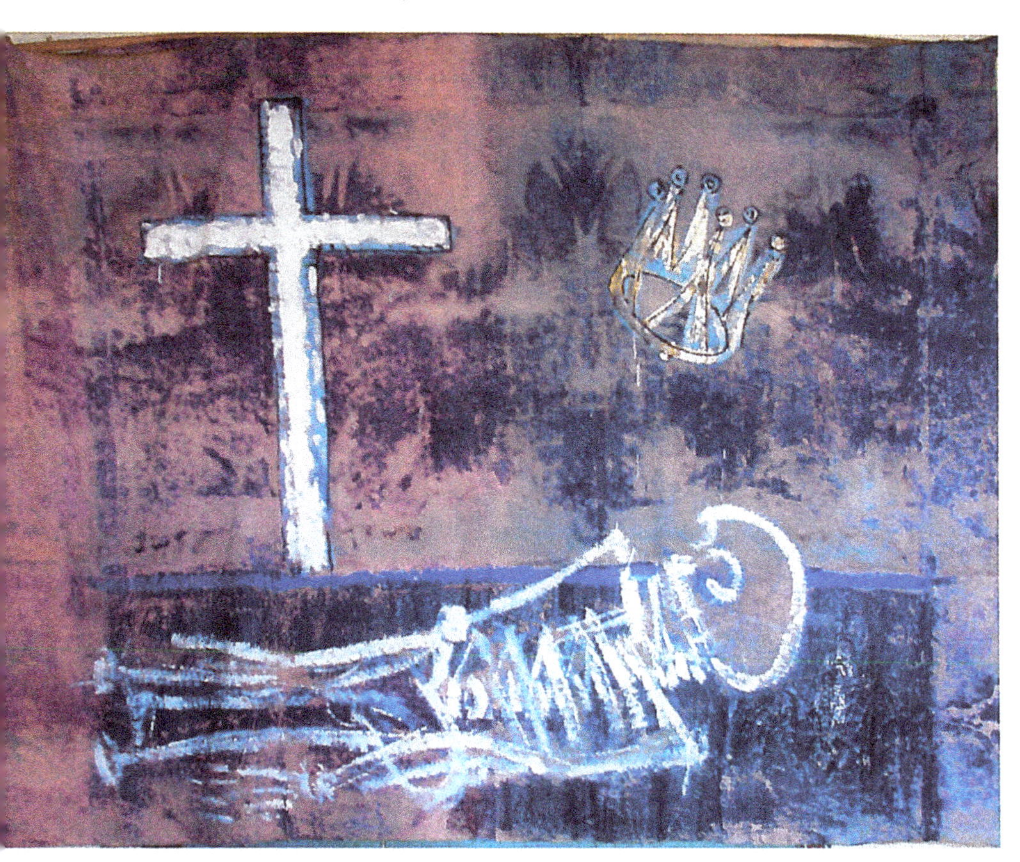

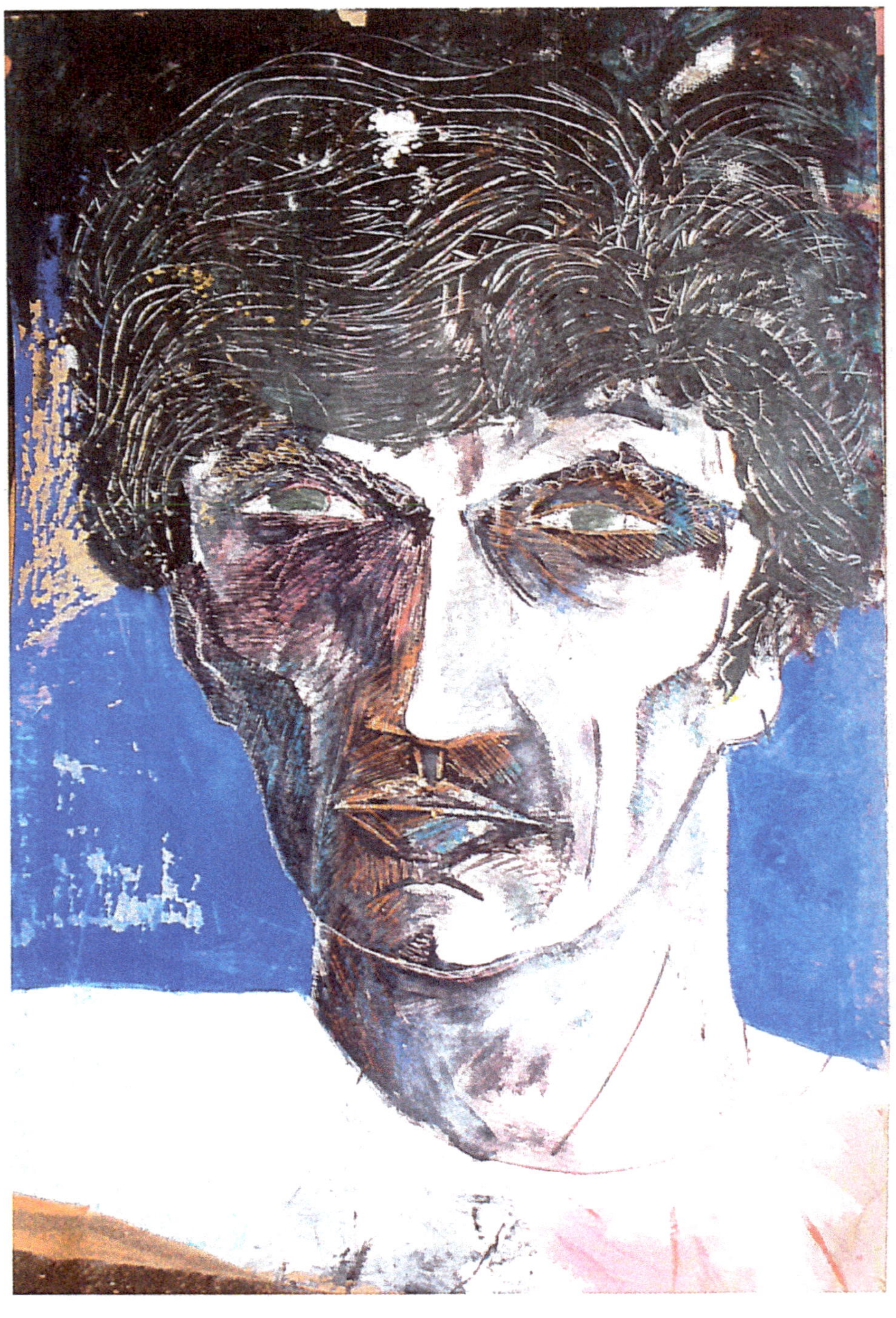

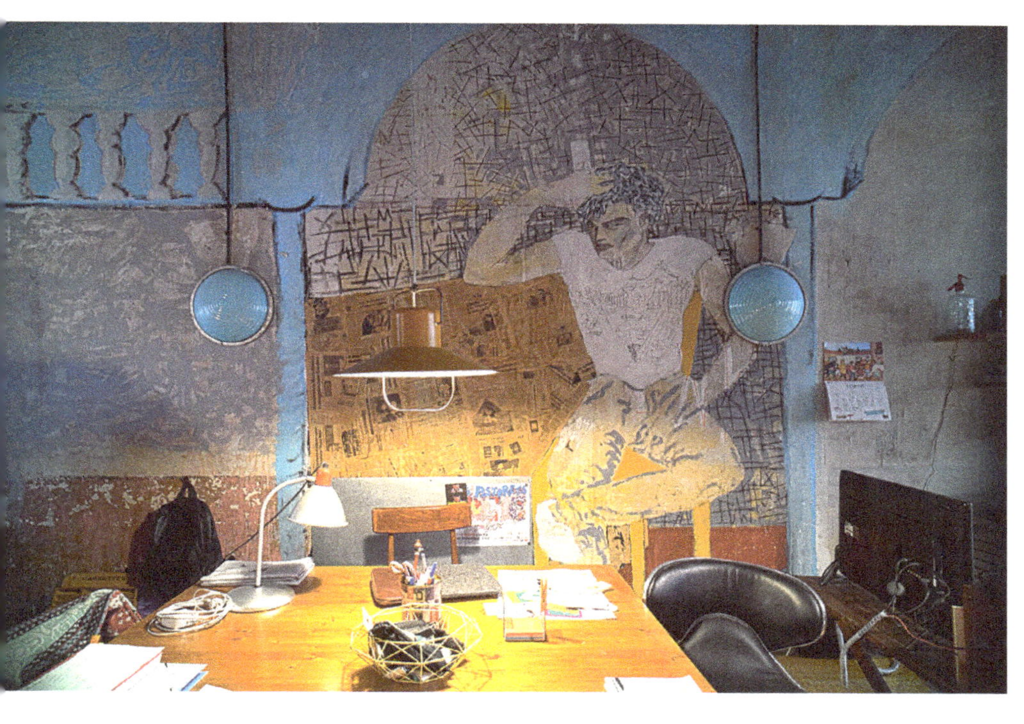

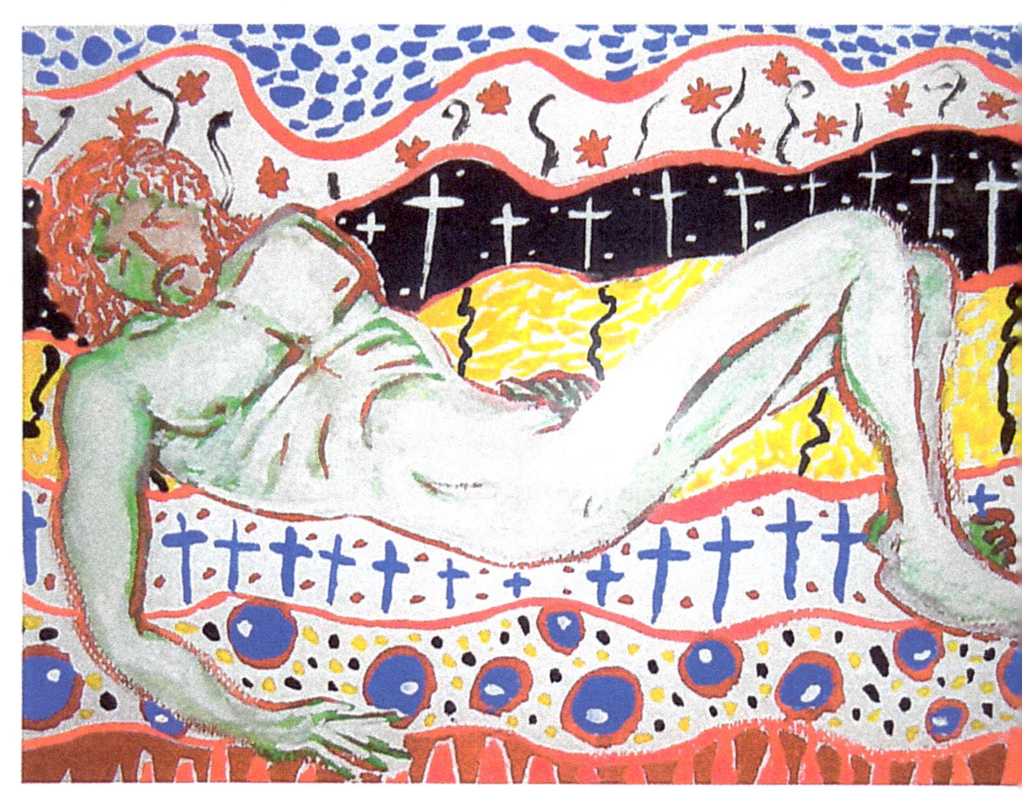

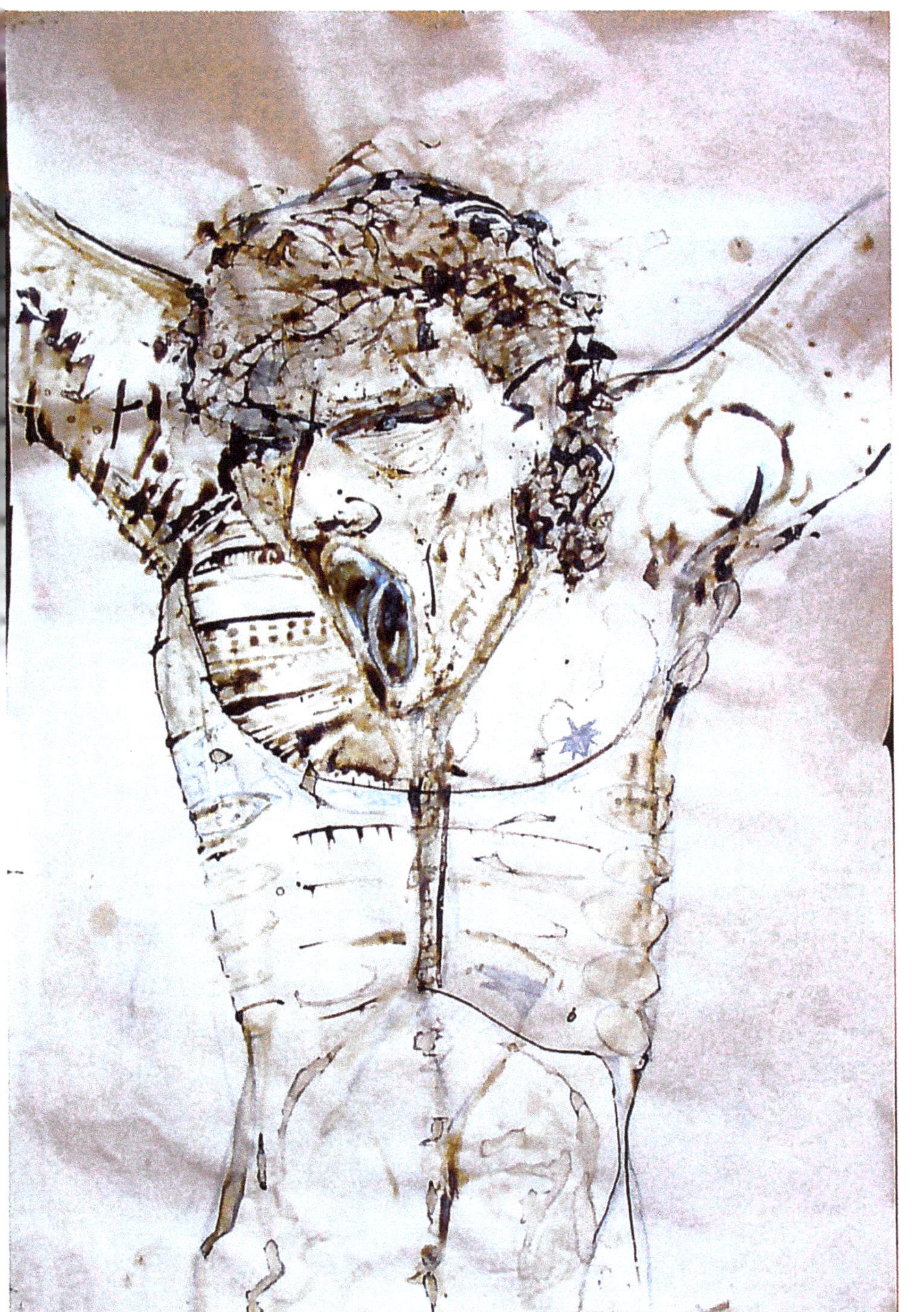

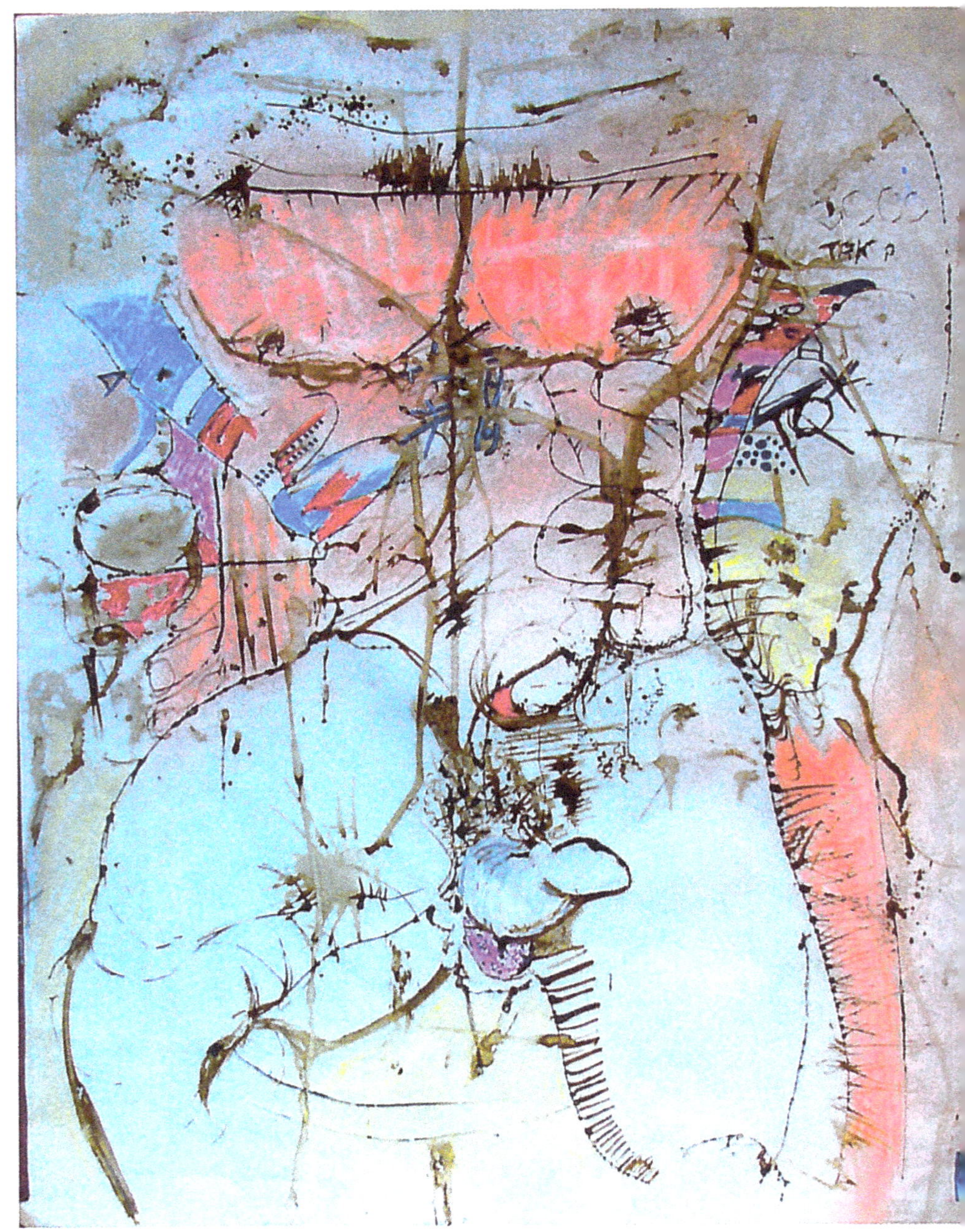

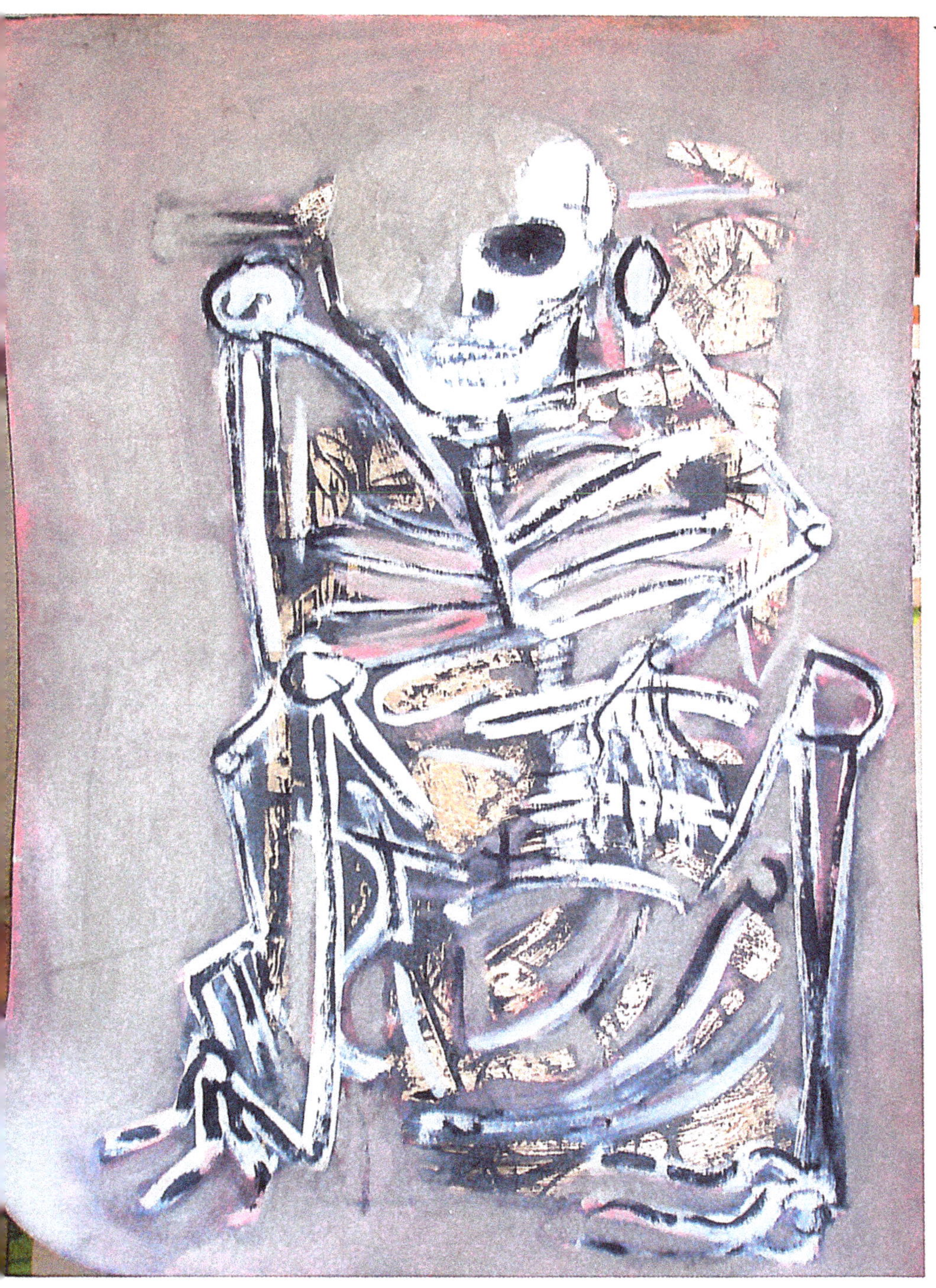

POEMS & PROSE

PEPE SALES

Pepe Sales (Barcelona, 1954–1994) was the complete artist: painter, singer, writer, poet, enfant terrible. The sweating, suffering, and sweet-talking all formed part of a spontaneous creative process that meant he could paint a picture or compose a song in no time at all. He liked the best music, the best literature, the best drugs; he read and listened to whatever he could get his hands on; he loved Dylan, Lou Reed, and the Rolling Stones, Giovanni Pergolesi, RW Fassbinder, and Aryton Senna, Camarón, Nusrat Fateh, Henry Miller, Anaïs Nin, Proust, Miles Davis, Samuel Beckett... He was always prepared to speak his mind (even if the process cost him blood, sweat, and more), whether it was on national television or down on the street corner.

Sales spoke candidly and passionately about prison, his admittance to various hospitals, his Glasnost trips, and his withdrawal to the family home in Vallclara, taking the reader on a voyage through heroin, homosexuality, and AIDS with an honest, unabashed, irreverent and consistently non-standard voice that is both captivating and fascinating.

— Tiago Miller

EMPTY PATH (1981)

A lonely man
an empty path
A sombre man
he's my lover
A man that's aching
aching to please
All day up and down
Lost and lonely in this town
he pictures and he hopes
for a brighter day
But he senses and suspects
that will never come
Yet this strange game
brings him to my bed
A sombre man
a passer-by
Paper-thin blown
up and down
A man that's aching
aching for brown
All day up and down
Lost and lonely in this town
he pictures and he hopes
for a brighter day
But he senses and suspects
that will never come
Yet this strange game
brings him to my bed

CHRIST OF THE PHARMACIES (1987)

Forgive me, my Lord
I'm begging you please
I'm down on my knees
it's me, my Lord.
How could I be so blind
on the corner at night
beneath the neon light
is it you, my Lord?
Forgive me, my Lord
we felt so much pain
but again and again
you forsook us, my Lord.
Now we're paying the price
strung up like Christ
No more passion please
it's me, my Lord.
Christ of the Pharmacies
tell the man to give us relief
and serve us our daily poison
or take the cross down from the street.

I'M DYING (1990)

I'm dying I'm dying
everyday getting worse
Yes I'm dying I'm dying
everyday getting worse
The hydrotherapy only makes me sweat slop and slime
And for each drop of diesel they charge a dime every time
I'm drooling I'm drooling
drool drips from my lips
it's the end of martyrdom
it's the need for delirium
it's the cure for expulsion
it's for the best Budapest
The torture of shot nerves the grip of the vice
can't be cured by a curer can't be cured by Christ
I'm floating I'm floating
away on my back
from the end of the question
from the need for expulsion
from my own prostitution
such excess Budapest
I find cards in the water a queen, king and ace
Dive deep to collect them but I'm not in the race
I'm hitting I'm hitting
myself with a fist
There's a hurricane in my head
a sirocco in my chest
I see aces in the water
this is urgent Budapest.

QUANDO CORPUS MORIETUR (1992)

Five two two one is the hospital room
where we lie dear Blai and I
in a cold sweat but quiet as a grave
he's ill, his race is run

And still his mother cradles him
like mamas cradle their babes
And still his mother cradles him
like mamas saying goodnight
And still his mama cradles him
like Mary Mother of God
And still his mother cradles him
like the Madonna up on the cross

The doctor is saying that Blai is dead
but my brother still smiles at me
The doctor is saying that Blai is dead
but his mother replies piously:
my boy wasn't born
to die in my arms
like the Madonna up on the cross

This sentiment is long dead in you
go tattoo Mum on your arm
But when the end draws near it'll become clear
you need pity to soothe the self-harm
And still his mother cradles him
like mamas cradle their babes
And still his mama cradles him
like Mary Mother of God
And still his mama cradles him
like the Madonna up on the cross

And still his mother cradles him
like mamas saying goodnight

DIARY – Barcelona, 1979

Relaxing, or more accurately, trying to relax on a sofa covered with hippy cushions in a filthy apartment which, on account of its appearance, can only be called home by a junkie (ah, those telltale signs: the waste paper basket overflowing with bloodstained balls of cotton wool, the walls flecked with blood; I'm guessing that finally, in the midst of his ecstasy, after cleaning his sharp instrument, he hurls the saline, water, blood in who cares what direction). My legs are doing kilometer after kilometer on their own – a half hour delay could be considered normal, even so, cigarettes now have a rancid taste and my gaze is fixed on the clock as the anxiety builds to unbearable. I've sweated through the dressing gown I had to put on, leaving the cushions soaking wet. 3/4 of an hour, that goddamn pusher...

Thick saliva starts sloshing in my toothless mouth once more, meaning the living room to toilet shuttle is relentless. Up and down the corridor (up and down, despite it being flat).

I oscillate between freezing to death and feverish sweating when, without warning, my guts make their presence known and I feel them knot and fill with a liquid that appears to want to burst along any channel towards an exit. If I'm lucky I'll get my head in the bowl in time; yes, on this occasion I don't soil anything and when I flush it down a cold sweat invades my bones. I decide to stay sat on the toilet as my mouth fills with spit and the process of vomiting sickly green bile begins again. One hour late. The anxiety's gargantuan. Goddamn pusher making money out of my anguish and who's no doubt late because he's busy looking for something, anything, to cut the lame horse I'm about to pay a pretty price for as though it were pure diamond powder but will be 80% baby formula but, never mind, the other 20% oh bring it now because it's been two hours and all I want to is kill the idiotic depressed lucidity making me weep over anything. I want warmth in my bones and to calm the rampant pain in my shoulders. It's getting ugly now but, hell, the first thing you learn is that you always gotta wait, as Lou Reed sang. But I want to forget about all of that and go to sleep and silence the burning sin in my head and wake up and discover normality but it's been three and a half hours already. Either I kill this stupid game or this stupid game kills me; all that ever comes from heroin is hate and hostility between those that buy and those that sell, those that deliver and those that wait.

I'm leaving. Tomorrow he'll call and say he arrived just that minute and that the stuff was the bomb. I curse the legal mobsters that make sure the cure for my anguish can't be found in any pharmacy while spasms of bile erupt and shoot up my esophagus.

TIME TO SPLIT.

Three days have passed since I stood that prick of a pusher up at his place, and what pandemonium – luckily I had a small pot of tilidine that's at least allowed me to get out of bed once or twice. I can still remember fumbling around with my parents for the right elevator to take us up to the psychiatry department at Hospital Clínic Barcelona. It was nighttime and dark-depressing in the extreme. We were met by Dr. Yugero (a good person, despite being a trick cyclist) and I explained to him how I took tilidine to avoid as much as possible the most painful withdrawal symptoms. That was back in '76 and, no word of a lie, the guy had no fucking idea that junkies used tili to calm the trembling turkey. Later he no doubt treated hundreds of hoods hooked to the hilt on tilidate, which is nothing but a slightly stronger painkiller that lacks any of the virtues of a drug and isn't listed either as a toxic or narcotic but lately, on account of addicts only making it through withdrawal alive thanks to it, doctors are moving heaven and hell to make tili impossible to find in any pharmacy meaning you have to turn to them, like it or not, only so they can tell you with a grave face that you have to undergo a rehab program, which means leaving you goofballed the first three days with your testicles chlormethiazole yellow only to start giving you a few drops of tilidine in random cups of orange juice and then gradually bring the dose down. The difference is that a day on the psyche ward at Hospital Clínic Barna costs more than any normal addict could ever spend on smack, and that's without even mentioning that a pot of tili can cost as little as 231 pesetas. Dr. Freixa, sadly famous for his skill in detoxing alcoholics (another time I'll explain his methodology, which he had the balls to let TV film convinced he was doing a good deed) was the doctor who treated a close friend of mine, at first anyway. His name was Víctor and I say 'was' cos now he's dead. He was beyond goofballed and explained everything to the doc who prescribed him a ton of tranquilizers and a few drops of tilidine in a glass of water, but the taste is unmistakable. That was when Víctor told me he lost all faith in the doctor and started shooting up astronomical amounts of cocaine, the mother drug of modern psychiatry, and also the most homicidal – say what you like, but you always end up crazy however small the dose and above all if you mainline it. Then the Dr. prescribed him substitutional treatment every Wednesday and a weekly revision I don't know what other day, and god knows what they were giving him but he told me it calmed his addiction to smack at least, but I guessed it must've been methadone or a morphine solution and which was costing him a hell of a lot more than street gear. The worst of all is that Víctor wasn't going to the doctor of his own accord rather forced by family affairs, and it's always the "invalid's" family they look to tether up tight cos they're the ones that foot the bill. The "invalid" doesn't mean shit to them. It's also worth mentioning, now we're on the topic of doctors, especially when it comes to the eminences (beware, not all of them are malevolent creatures), that there are few lines of business that can charge you more than 3000 pesetas for a two minute consultation, while staying on the ward is twice as expensive as sleeping at the Ritz, and don't expect a cent from social security. Right off the bat Víctor realized Dr. Freixas knew a fraction of what he did about addiction to so-called hard drugs and that it was all one big piss-taking con. He already had three rehabs under his belt, two at Rotonda with other doctors and one at a clinic up at Reina Elisenda he ended up quitting. At the end of the day, he was going there every week for a spot of substitutional treatment, to pay a fortune and end up socially disgraced, which the Francoist "Social Dangers Law" took good care of. At Christmas – oh, ever depressing Christmas – he killed himself because he said he would. How easy it would've been to prescribe him methadone (if they thought he had no right to morphine, the exclusive property of the medical class) for him to take in the morning to calm his nerves and go to work, because in his final year he only worked when he had Heroin. But, of course, if they'd handed him a prescription he wouldn't have come back and that's a lot of cash those murderers would've missed out on – all for the sake of a prescription they didn't give him in time. In contrast, that's precisely what's done in all advanced countries, because there have already been too many dead victors, but here they have their sights set on more... who'll all have to pass by the checkout before dying, of course.

Translated by Tiago Miller

NINE POEMS

FELICIA FUSTER

INTRODUCTION

"Off on Unwritten Paths"

Felícia Fuster (1921–2012) trained in both applied and fine art, participating in group exhibits into the 1950s, including a glass piece acquired by the Corning Museum of Glass. Her entry into the Catalan poetry world took place when she was 62, as finalist in the Catalan poetry contest Carles Riba. Between that moment, and her death in Paris, where she'd been living since 1951, she published seven poetry collections, translated into Catalan Marguerite Yourcenar's *L'Œuvre au noir* and a selection of contemporary Japanese poetry (with Naoyuki Sawada), while continuing her work as a visual artist. Throughout her life, Fuster was an intentional outsider, orbiting literary and artistic groups like a comet. Despite the Catalan government marking her centenary in 2021 and the high consideration she is held in in Catalan poetry circles, she remains woefully under the radar, with less than twenty published poems translated into English.

Her poetic voice – characterized by the investigation of language itself and an avant-garde defiance coupled with unsentimental sadness–stands out from the prevailing social realism of most Catalan poets of her time. In a slight of hand worthy of the person claiming "I've bartered my five senses / for five startles of water, / five descents into hell, / five frenzies of jail and cage" her work appeared alongside poets born forty years after her. Indeed, as noted by poet Maria-Mercè Marçal: Fuster's poems "arrived late but at the right time."

Fuster once expressed her life as having been blown off course by a violent wind. She was a woman from a generation marked by the Spanish Civil War and then WWII. An immigrant in France, she wrote almost exclusively in Catalan, and traveled through Europe, Asia and Africa. While maintaining an evolving practice as a visual artist, she refused to feel the constraints of age or gender.

These poems show aspects of the range of her body of work. Taken from five of her seven poetry collections, published in 1984, 1987, 1998 and 2001, they exemplify her ongoing experimentation with form: free verse pulsing with subtle internal rhymes and echoes, a sestina and a haiku. Thematically, there is no ignoring the isolation and loss. In Fuster's stark landscapes – empty gardens, piles of rubble, and graveyards, passports, boat rigging, and trains no longer serve their purpose, letters can't be sent, or even written, and yet... there is always the memory of idle afternoons, apple skies, olive trees that whisper, bonfire parties. The poet prevails in the face of abandon and destruction because words on an empty page hold the power to cast spells. Even when her fingers have broken off, her skin is peeling, her body has lost its edges, she retains her "invincible voice."

– Marialena Carr

I'll call forth the asphalt of the shadow,
teeth crumbling like stones into gravel,
the kabbalistic numbers of defeated
skin, the risen dead who have
no skulls,
the lost and yellow gods,
my unstoppable blood and more...
so you may find again
the drawn out light of the afternoon,
the secret space where novice white stars
undress, the wind bees,
the honey of clouds... and so you learn
— almost alone — how to get by
with irons for fingernails.
I'll call forth the bone-thirsty salt,
the dust of pride that tires and falls, the beaches
of a hundred eyes, dull and speechless,
waiting without hope to tie us down,
the relentless singing
crickets in thrall to the bogus
starlight of the city that never sleeps.
And I will give it all and all for nothing,
just to see you live.
What strange obsession
has me play it all on the dice roll of a heart
wracked and ruined,
knowing that even if I were to win
I am to lose it all.

From *Una cançó per a ningú i trenta diàlegs inútils* (1984)

XII of AND IF

And now I know myself a mirror. Opaque.
I breathe in and out, deep, full, in the circle.
My blood, a cast-off sweet, all emptied of flames,
shatters the neutrons, the cells, the delusions,
and makes me deaf, as deaf as the scrap metal
of the days that lie rusting among the ropes.

The sunlight stripped away from them, it's just ropes
draping over my body, inside the opaque
hand dreamt up by the tap-tap of scrap metal
from worn out and emptied time in the circle.
Below the grief, root-braiding the delusions,
the skeleton shadow and the bone of flames

are discussing the world. And amidst the flames,
they launch me full tilt by tightening the ropes
to a zig-zag blade of a thousand delusions
fastening me inside the night. And still opaque,
heart ripped out, to find the key to the circle
my ragged fingers claw through the scrap metal.

Though I deny the walls and the scrap metal
confining me, sightless, deep inside the flame
that crisps and widens the tear in the circle,
I'm a single point, without a word. The ropes
keep swinging me off balance, far into the opaque
sticky clay that is the old page of delusions

almost become stars of flint. The delusions,
like wide open jaws, wake up the scrap metal,
hungrily waiting for me, a jonquil opaque,
brittle as paper enveloped in the flame
atop the vague swamp. I won't look through the ropes
that rot there for the strut to breach the circle.

No. Like a jester, I'll pull from the circle
water clocks brimming liquid of delusions

to crumble from within the hours and the ropes,
the living Mardi Gras king of scrap metal,
and bring light to the shadows, even as the flame
makes me —within my voice— hosanna so opaque.

Crickets cast spells so flame, sky, and delusions
will swallow the opaque night of the circle,
the scrap metal left keening over the ropes.

From *I encara* (1987)

I spread out the map
to the five senses   I'm off
on unwritten paths

From *Postals no escrites* (2001)

NEVER

I have no watch, no destination.
I'm cold.
In my frozen flower pot
no words grow to wrap me,
only the great
desert of those mute telegrams
from the oracles or the shipwrecked.
The laughing passport doesn't dream up
the rigging
for my travels anymore, just like the color pencil,
useless
against my white
stockings. I'll have to leave, indeed,
on foot.
The train, grasping as ivy, hasn't come.
So be it.
If someone saw me walking memory lane,
I'd tell them: stop me,
tell me what I am not, what I no longer carry.
I have no watch, no destination,
no milk handkerchief, no apple sky.
My feet are dropping, heavy.
My head
weighs like a world and it's shedding leaves.
The skin's peeling.
We'll not meet again.
I'm cold. I'm scared. I feel that cold
so bottomless only the heart
can gauge, that only the living hand out.
The cold that's never buried.
Never.

From *Aquelles cordes del vent* (1987)

I wanted
to write you letters of trails
for a mail of getaways,
to talk to you in the whisper of the olive tree
along the front of the afternoon,
never again with the dizziness
of words jettisoned like falling bridges,
but I can't.
My fingers
have snapped like a drying branch.
If you come,
you might reach me in a thousand years,
— not considering the trains, I shudder still.
The cold of calendars frightens me.
I wear now the bareness of the dying,
and in my heart
the wait is rusting away.
It's been dumped atop the empty garden
of a useless page, with the scraps
of me. I barely am.
I can't. I wanted to tell you a word that I won't say,
a word to ring out along the thousand ropes
of all the eyes pulling you closed.

From *Una cançó per a ningú i trenta diàlegs inútils* (1984)

NOT ANYMORE

Not anymore. I don't wear a cape
to be the night bonfire
or Saturday's party.
Not anymore.
My fingernails have dropped off
—graveyard crosses of basalt.
I've bartered my five senses
for five startles of water,
five descents into hell,
five frenzies of jail and cage.
And five continents broken down
from sleighbells and missteps.
Not anymore. I don't know
what's to be found in the magic
wagon of any Ursa Major.
If I turn up there startled
and with bewildered eyes,
who will steer me, what track will take me
through the world without pine nuts,
or raisins?
Time is yellow,
yellow the silk hand, and faded.
Leave me here. Never again. Here where I'm at,
and now.
Helpless matchstick,
bring me moon for sleeping, or a stake
to tether
my poisonous,
my invincible voice.
I have no edges so leave me the sun
nearby
and the quiver of an iced lip, melting.

From *Aquelles cordes del vent* (1987)

I leave you the jug of memories
beaded with afternoon.
Don't make me wait for toothless
steps or idle cloudbursts.
I want to go. I still have the hours.
I know the houses
will fall on me
in a heartbeat.
I'm a needle bent
from so many mended streets,
now with no thread.
No lineage tugs me from behind,
I want to go. The great door
of the world hangs askew,
hunger, death that can't be explained,
not by the asphalt
of steamy streets
not by the dust.
First let me wash in the clear
bubble of your faraway gaze.
So that later you're not afraid
I leave you a jug
—who knows filled with what—
so that you're not thirsty
if some lion walks by.

From *Una cançó per a ningú i trenta diàlegs inútils* (1984)

WITHIN ME

Today   I look at the sea within me
these bottomless choppy waters
and I find the blue worn   faded
a crumpled cloth
Today   I'd not dip a toe in this sea
not a finger   of good sense   Not a word
Who can swim   these waters
I'd only drop fire in them   maybe
and this   yes-it-is-no-it-isn't
of a soul scrap

From *Sorra de temps absent* (1998)

Your thread count seemed
to make me invulnerable forever.
I unravel like a ball of moth-eaten wool,
my fingers scraped by ivy.
The mulberry leaves
and the potbellied silkworms
curled up in the promise-filled cocoon
won't do me any good.
All the loose threads won't
add up to a rope to hoist
the rosemary scent that renews
the fly-away sky.
All I have left is a single
strand to stitch together worlds
and silences.
With a cracked hand I still write
a thousand letters I don't send.

From *Una cançó per a ningú i trenta diàlegs inútils* (1984)

Translated by Marialena Carr

And, Suddenly, Paradise

Núria Perpinyà

In Núria Perpinyà's novel *And, Suddenly, Paradise* (Barcelona: Comanegra. 2018), a group of Internet users spends a season in the mountains in a detoxification clinic. The action takes place in the Tammarian Valley, the setting of her last novel, *Al vertigen* (To Vertigo). Readers will encounter some of the alpinists from *Al vertigen* along the way. The same place welcomes those passionate about nature and machines. Some are very active and others very sedentary. What they have in common is that they all love certain things or people too much.

Although their devotion and consequences may seem exaggerated, the stories are based on real people fascinated by the Internet, starting with India, the protagonist.

The addicts who are rehabilitated at the Lubol clinic are of different ages and professions. Some are mesmerized by video games, others chat and find love, and others never leave YouTube. The changing virtual personalities magnify who they are, although some lose themselves.

The story is presented by two narrators: Dr. Neuska, and India, a friend of one of the patients.

The alternation between chapters is not symmetrical, which creates points of confusion and uncertainty.

Since there is no temporal dimension on the Internet and everything exists in an eternal present that is continually updated, Perpinyà's novel also plays with various temporal moments which, combined, contravene the earthly laws of physics, creating unexpected paradoxes.

What follows are excerpts from the chapters "Raul's Loogies," "Life on the Sofa," and "Keys to Paradise."

Raul's Loogies

In the Lubol clinic, apart from being neurologists and psychiatrists, up here we also have to act as general practitioners, and family doctors, if appropriate. Due to a number of emergencies, I have not yet been able to consult Raul Fusquero. And, above all, because I have not received the approval to start his treatment until today. I'm not into comedies; the tragedy of Elexa makes me sick. But I have to take care of all my patients, starting with him. Despite Raul's insistence on giving me details, I preferred to stay out of the pecuniary conflict. I've had enough of patients' mental conflicts. Half an hour after the appointment, Raul knocks on the door touching his private parts. The vision is unpleasant to me but I ignore it. I have to give him confidence, because I'm interested in getting to the core of who he is.

— I know a lot of madhouse jokes. Can I sit on the couch? I've seen it in so many movies! When I explain it, they won't believe it. So then they'll say that the movies we invent don't exist. What I don't want is for some shitty reality to spoil my fantasies — he adds with a sudden change of mood and then resumes his enthusiasm —. Don't tell me. It begins by explaining dreams. I had a scary nightmare yesterday. I was at a party and wanted to show a video, but YouTube was very slow and wouldn't load. All night like this. What does it mean?

— That even in dreams you don't leave the Internet. Do you want to tell me anything?

I arrange my papers without looking up; the lack of eye contact unsettles the patients and makes them open up to me more; since they don't like my looking away, they talk to me to unconsciously strengthen the relationship. It's a strategy I disapprove of but use. Beyond my unconfessed contradictions, this inference will be useful in dealing with Raul. With him, you have to build a wall of sanity, despite the risk of being unsympathetic, in order not to fall into his beautifying nonchalance. A little seriousness will do him good.

— Last week they gave me a piece of paper that said I couldn't have children.

— I'm sorry... What urological dysfunction do you have?

— None. I light up like a fuse! — he retorts with obscenity. It was the last paycheck. Ha, ha, ha.

— Your addiction is humor. — I won't pay it any mind.

— The comedy, the cunt...

— Married?

— No.

Perplexed, I check the files.

— Weren't you? In your file... Children?

— No.

He doesn't agree either.

— Didn't you tell us that you had children? What did you expect, that you had installed a cellphone app to control their phone usage?

— Stories that I concoct.

— Do you have a job?

— No.

— Do you have a car, a house?

— No.

— Friends, girlfriend?

Raul sits half up:

— I have Twitter, dammit! I don't need anything else.

Fed up with his jokes, I rearrange the files. He goes right back to it:

— I know another one of your type. With this one, you'll burst out laughing: "Doctor, the subject of the experiments has jumped out the window." "Well, he couldn't have been properly subjected to." Oh, I'm sorry, I understand that you're not amused; I've been told that Elexa wanted to jump out of the water...

> @LargoJavariega Humor borders on intolerance in the north, hypocrisy in the south, demagoguery in the east, and apologetics in the west.

— Enough. The condition of the patients is not your concern. In these sessions, we need only talk about you.

— If these are the rules, I hold my tongue. We'll kick it at the bar! Everything is broached there.

— Your humor can be a psychological response to fear — I tell him, putting a great deal of patience into it.

— Fear, of what? So knowing that I am; no, more, the next! How lazy to psychoanalyze people you know nothing about instead of going out with them, right? Me, you can say whatever you want, but with Elexa and India, if they let us, we'd have a lot of parties and drown our sorrows. There should be a disco in Lubol. That place is full of sick people and yet no one seems sick and everyone eats and shits as God commands (except for our flimsy one). But something big happens to us: we are too sleepy. This is not life. If you let me party it up...

I am stunned. Raul looks enviously at my computer and has one of his sudden mood swings again. As a result of his chemical and electronic drug addictions, he goes from cheerfulness to anger in a matter of seconds.

— I don't know if it's perfectly right for you to be fucking around on the computer in front of me and getting down with that while life is shitty for me. You're not a good example for me.

Mr. Fusquero is partly right (despite the insufferable tone he used). When Elexa wanted to take it from me, I decided that I would not make any more inquiries at the office. But with so much work I haven't thought about it anymore. And today, let's go back to it: I have Raul attacked because of me. I will have to dissimulate. I can't stoop to their level and exchange defective seals. It is assumed that he is the one who makes mistakes and that I have to fix them. Would I lose credibility if I admitted my faults?

— When you will return to the world, you will live with a lot of computers. We cannot remove them all. You must learn to know how to be there. But above all — I tell him restraining myself from his lack of respect — don't tell me how I should take care of your healing. Next week we will work with the unconscious.

— I will warn my man. — He plays gay. But I don't know if he will be able to stand up.

— On his Twitter account, he uses the pseudonym La Rotlla to pretend that he is a curvy woman with a joyful life. Do you consider yourself homosexual, bisexual, or heterosexual?

— Speak bluntly, you! Calm down: it's a joke!

— Too much.

— You throw little firecrackers to amuse yourself for a while. If the staff gets angry, don't read me the riot act. God damn it, but what's that about? I'm here because of the Internet, not because of myself. And because my wife has agreed to come since, as she knows, I spend the day connected. She dies of jealousy. I'm fucking mad. As for La Rotlla, I don't need a sexologist. On Twitter I act like a broad to get more followers.

— You should drop the humor and be sincere. What do you want to be cured of? What do you suffer from?

— Let Cesca tell you, she made me come. All these questions! Graduates want to know everything. I tell lies, but my horoscope is good. It hurts only when I laugh. I'm Taurus, and you?

— Vices?

— Same as everyone. She doesn't want to tell me what sign she is. I would say that you are... Sorry, I'm focusing. Since head doctors like to dig up stories from way back, I'll tell you that I've been fond of firecrackers since I was a child. They called me El Masclet, which also means the Macho one. One year we staged an incredible mascletada with nine tons of gunpowder. Nine is my lucky number.

— What do you look for on the Internet? Pornography?

— You're a straight shooter, doctor! Me who believed that career people never called things by their name. And especially you, the doctors, who struggle with words so convoluted that no one can understand them.

— Answer me.

— Porn... me? Phew... Who doesn't? But only a little.

— One, two, three hours a day?

— It depends. The good thing about porn is that you can do something else in the meantime. Tweet, bet, play cards, contests, chow down. And above all — he says enigmatically — because you want me to be honest: whack off. Ha, ha, ha. I only watch healthy porn, no creepy shit. No sleazy stuff or kiddies. Only experienced gals are visible on my screen.

[...]

— Doesn't your wife help you?

— Not at all. She's not down with porn; nor football, boxing, cars, roulette, cards, betting, twitter, lotto, dog racing... She doesn't want to know anything about that. Cesca only sees the money I lose and when they give me the pink slip. Like it's my fault!

So the last paycheck joke was more real than it seemed. He was taking away the importance of what is engraved in his head: that he is unemployed. His way of overcoming it is to sublimate it with humor.

— One day Cesca fucked my zorbing by putting it in the washing machine. A little more and I kill her. She is so ignorant, the poor thing, she is so backward. She knows nothing about today's world. It disgusts her. And she has a mania for excessive cleaning! She should be cured! Her obsession with washing everything isn't normal. She's a maniacal cleaner. The most stubborn. She says I'm a brute. I'm not saying no. I'd rather vent with porn than with detergent, what do you want me to say? ...

> @HelenaAlegret Asimov's prediction for 2014: The disease of boredom. Society of forced leisure.

LIFE ON THE SOFA

The doctor's displeasure will be monumental. It doesn't matter. I hurt a lot of people, beginning with myself, but I can't help it. I don't want to think where I went wrong. In what I've lost I've been avoiding it for years. The thoughtless say, jokingly, that thinking is a mental disorder that occurs in the brain in a situation of insecurity or emotional instability. When you're psyched up, you don't think!, exclaim the residents. I don't know if I ruminate too much or too little. This room in the clinic shields me from others but not from myself. The memories consume me. I don't want them. I'm also afraid that I will be cornered like a rat and have to endure the shame of being passed off as a neurasthenic or a thief. I have nowhere else to fit my body though. Where do I park? My self is exhausted from so much fighting against that other self.

> @Derrida TV and internet: a paradox that binds and isolates. The world invades my home and draws me closer to it. I desire the Other but I defend my house without leaving it.

I don't know where to stand. I'm a pathetic, chunky zorbing who is the odd man out. I have no safe place in the world. Not even my theoretical home. My house is a treacherous morphine that stuns me and makes me drowsy. I am strong; I should be able to get out on my own. If I haven't done it until now, it's because I haven't set out to do it. I let myself go down convinced that my decline was inevitable. That the opiate atmosphere of my sofa would not allow me to get up and leave. Before I share it with anyone, I should explain it to myself. It doesn't go well with my character, to seek help. I must be able to understand myself. I have never believed in the romances of psychologists; whether or not psychiatrists are believable, at least they provide pills. In this I side with science. Everything we feel and think is pure matter, billions of little biochemical cocktails. Our psyche depends upon the atoms and beings around us. It varies depending upon the physical circumstances. And when it burns like plastic, like it did with me, it stinks. During these years I have self-medicated — nothing, forty pain relievers — but I no longer have prescriptions. One solution would be to finish my medical degree (it would take too long); another, to steal medicine from the warehouse (it's fast and tempting); and, another, to confess to Dr. Neuska (I would say no). For better or for worse, I have to get out of this well.

When I started studying medicine, I was a nurse, had a husband and two children. My big secret can be summed up in one line. Now they ask me how I lost them. I breathe. My dear Mateu and Heloisa... When I pronounce their names, I tremble. I am abominable. Oh god what have I done. Things are chained together and, by the time you realize it, it's too late.

With the hospital, the classes, and the children, it was a whirlwind. Mateu was two years old and Heloisa was four. Until then, I see it now, we were a happy family. I had children very young, there were four of us and we laughed a lot. I was 28 years old and in good health. In the evening, I lay on the couch with the computer, watch movies, chat with friends, and entertain myself with video games. When I learned that Jimmy Wales, the founder of Wikipedia, also started on the Internet with MUD, I congratulated myself for having chosen the new version of that legendary role-playing game: the *Multi-User Dungeon*. It didn't bother me that *dungeon* means 'torture chamber.' It was just a game. At first, no one attached any importance to it. When we weren't reading, Daniel and I would browse the search engines and discuss what we found. Without realizing it, I started abusing it and becoming closed off. My shell kept growing. I stumbled upon a very addictive game: *Héroines Noires*. It's really seductive. It's as if the pixels were emitting cocaine powder and the player was absorbing it. I had so much fun there that time flew by until dawn. Daniel, awakened by my absence, would get up to take me out of my zorbing and take me to bed. I slept very little. He, nervous and attentive to the children and me, also had trouble falling asleep. We got up listlessly and I, moreover, with a backache, because of the sofa. When it was daylight, I was still playing. Video games never end; they are not like a football game that lasts an hour and a half. The Internet has achieved the ideal of eternity. Instagram is huge. Knowledge has no limit. The searches you can do on the Internet are endless. Netflix chains episodes and series in crescendo. Tinder encourages us to slide our finger with curiosity and morbidity, looking for partners in endless lists. The offers open up more and more. There can always be a better one. Be insatiable and look for her! On the web, no one sleeps. There is no night or schedule to subjugate us. We are eternal! Time has no end! On earth, more than three billion hours are spent online every week between players from several continents. It is the union of the planet! The borders that separate us are done with! Space has no end! Seen like this, I was not some outmoded creature, but quite the opposite, a normal person of the 21st century who entertains herself online.

My shift at the hospital started at 8:00. I awoke at a quarter to 7. Daniel, to take care of the children, got up then too. Since I hadn't slept much, I was tired all day; assisted the patients sleepwalking. I became irritable, me who used to be so sweet. I was preoccupied with the hours I lost in the hospital tending to the dying without being able to get online; I just wanted to get home and lie on the couch. In the toilets, secretly, I increased the zorbing and played as much as I could. I was slacking off; they never found me when they needed me. Adding up the times I stole, I managed to enter *Héroines Noires* for an hour every half day. Soon it was insufficient. I needed to be online continually. Like this one month and another. When I arrived, I sat on the couch and didn't move. I even slept on it and everything. Even though the bed was more comfortable, it made me want to get up in the morning to lie down in another place a few meters away. It was wonderful to lie there and ask for the curtains to be drawn so I wouldn't be dazzled by the screen. The warmth of the leather and the comforter defended me from the big questions that threatened me like knives as soon as I put my feet on the ground. We ate fast. The children were playing around me, their instinct made them get closer to their mother, but me, I stayed in my domains, didn't pay much attention to them. I was too lazy to get out of the bubble to be with them. Poor Mateu, poor Heloisa. "Who are these black ladies, Mama?"

"Mom, these monsters scare me, close the lid. Why don't we ever go down to the park?" I gave them a mechanical dog, an Aibo, which kept their eyes off me, so they would leave me alone. Because it was so clean, they named it Soap. It entertained them and there was no need to take it outside to pee or for a walk. Unlike other mothers, I never went to pick them up at school; my husband, a good guy, took care of everything. Between the afternoon classes at the university and the hospital I didn't have the energy. At night, apart from distracting myself, I also studied. I don't know if it was him or me who suggested that I leave the university, so as not to be so bold. We hit it off and on until we agreed that I would temporarily quit my job as a nurse so that I could study and thrive. We would sacrifice ourselves and no longer live on a salary. The children and the family would win.

@Lolaquiroga Anyone who wants vertigo, close your eyes and look inside.

I set it up so that I didn't have to sit much in class. I was too lazy to commute to the university and spend an hour there and back on the train with poor coverage losing the connection in the fucking tunnel. My classmates gave me notes and I studied from home. When I left the hospital, I had my mornings free. I made a lot of plans. Actually, I stayed home and took advantage of the fact that I was alone and no one bothered me about my affairs: erotic chats, TV series, video games. The more time I spent there, the more I distanced myself from my husband. The way he hugged me was too natural to turn me on. I didn't tell anyone to what I dedicated my mornings; in theory, I was studying. It wasn't enough, though; the players in another of my favorite games, *Future Evil*, were — are — American. Because of the time difference, we mudders could only play in the afternoon and at night, when we finished work. Consequently, I spent my mornings awake, playing and chatting with them. I fell asleep on the couch with the computer on. My man gave up on taking me to bed. "Do whatever you want," he said sadly. On weekends, Daniel went to the countryside with the children. I rarely accompanied them; I had to study. Zorbing helped me concentrate. The perennial excuse. I also didn't feel like going out for a drink or dancing, me, who used to be so thin and danced so well! I was so pretty... I'm deformed; my fat is hanging everywhere. I stopped going out with friends. They bored me. I was situated in the dock of the 21st century, unlike them, who remained in the 20th. I experimented with virtual personalities while they were limited to their repetitive nature. The conversations were a bore for me; when I couldn't take it anymore, I looked for a corner with a plug where I could isolate myself with my lovely Brainmobile. They called me antisocial. I became a misanthrope. I didn't want to leave the house. I could hardly move from the sofa. In video games, on the other hand, I moved with the agility of a beast: I ran, jumped, and climbed platforms and mountains. The virtual world represented the most innovative avant-garde. I cloaked from morning till night. My legs gave out and my road to disability began. I felt sharp as if I had been hammered like a sword.

Good things – and the Internet is one of them — have their price. My husband arranged the dining room for me so that I had what I needed within easy reach and didn't have to move much. One afternoon, to my surprise, he gave me a more comfortable and bigger sofa bed. The children clapped and we organized a party around the new member of the family. Soap, the dog, kept shaking his plastic tail. Mateu had turned up the volume of the motion sensors to celebrate. They loved me so much! "Honey," Daniel said to me, "do you want another coffee?" He didn't know what to do to please his imaginary patient. It must be admitted that I am a good player of MUDs, arcades, RPGs, and simulators. I know how to take cover and camouflage with fun maneuvers. I like to defer tug-of-war confrontations with my opponents. And I'm such a skilled role-player that I can foresee six levels in advance, imagining the moves each mudder might make. My teammates adore me for my strategic skills. In contrast, my husband despised everything related to the Internet, starting with my skills as a gamer. He and I belonged to two such different spheres that I doubt we will ever meet again.

@UnSuísMés When dreams don't correspond to reality, when you're lost between two dimensions and you don't even dare to take a step.

For drug addicts, only their drug matters. Anyone who gets in the way becomes an enemy. Faced with the ultimatum that my man gave me ("the computer or me"), not only had I not chosen him, but I got heated because of the pressure he was putting me under and because of his incomprehension. You're not incompatible!, I told him in a rage. I was lying to myself. In practice, we were. My electronic abuse was pathological. I was suffering from an uncontrolled mental disorder. Daniel, in a fit of love and rage, threw the laptop to the floor and then smashed it to pieces with a hammer; he then took a knife and stabbed the zorbing to pieces. I had an anxiety attack; the children, stunned, were whimpering. Hating who had stolen my vitality, I bought another computer and another capsule. Since my husband had canceled the Internet, I spent a week of abstinence screaming hysterically. The children, scared, looked at me in terror. Heloisa, walking backwards, fell on Soap and hurt herself. The dog squealed piteously. She had a crying fit. Daniel ran to hug her. We ended up in the emergency room. When, the following week, I recovered the programs, files, and ADSL, I calmed down. I just wanted to lie down with my computer. I didn't think I was asking for that much. Worse are the women who run off with others. I was the soul of the home, mother earth, the woman of repose. When I thought that, once again, harmony reigned and they would leave me alone, Daniel again put me back between a rock and a hard place: "The computer or the children." I reacted with anger. The more we fought, the more I needed to escape with video games; I fell into the vice of Slither and many others. I would spend whole days adding delusional points; instead of Daniel sharing in my excitement about the levels achieved, he only noticed my muteness and my irritable face. Faced with his threats, enraged, I chose not to speak to him or anyone else. Poor children, why did I hurt them so much? What a bitch... They'd never done anything to me, they only loved me... "What are you doing with those cartoon swords, mommy? Do you like to kill? Why doesn't the father do that? Shall we play hide and seek, mother?" I don't know how to explain it; I had become insensate, I didn't feel any empathy for anyone, not even for the children, I didn't notice their distress, I saw them cry but from far away, as if they were the bloody images of strangers, like the ones that impact you for a few seconds but which you forget a minute later. It was normal that I didn't feel anything — I was dead inside. And the dead no longer feel anything. My memory was a poorly made web, erased, with irregular knots and holes; like that of the spiders that were drugged in the 60s in the psycho-pharmaceutical laboratories to see the effects.

Since the gift of the mechanical dog had been so well received, it occurred to me to do the same with my man. One day there was a knock on the door and the sexy Roxxxy appeared. The automaton would help me reconcile with my spouse and he would stop bothering me. Daniel no longer turned me on. I had zero libido. He, ungrateful, instead of laughing, looked at her with disgust, his blood boiled, and he forced me to return the box. Both of you are fake! I don't know if the plastic girl understood why he was mistreating her like that. Since the company didn't want to refund my money, they offered to exchange Roxxxy for a home robot. Online shopping is so easy. Although it was humiliating for the automaton Roxxxy to be repudiated, the family came out victorious. AR was a fantastic maid. The children, who were well behaved, named her Arusi; they found her nice; it didn't make them sad. My husband seems to be. The flat was small and Arusi was large so she had to be seen as another person; we couldn't put her in a closet. My husband, who gets angry over everything, didn't understand. So every time he interfered with her or with Soap, he would shit on God, on the inventions, and on me. He took my credit card.

Daniel, puzzled by my growing apathy and indifference, brought up our separation. If I had nothing against it, he would take Heloisa and Mateu. I didn't refuse; I even thanked him. Less work. I wouldn't have to take care of anyone anymore. I had achieved my goal: to have all the time to myself, undisturbed. I don't know how they could endure three years with such a selfish and stupid person like me. Because I refused to pursue any treatment for my addiction, they closed the door in tears and left me to die alone. The children took Soap but left the batteries for me. We don't need them, they said. I don't know what they wanted to tell me exactly. I didn't know how to react; I was haunted by the expression that Daniel used in his farewell: "Die alone." What did he mean? I would have a blast on my own! RPGs are persistent worlds with never-ending games that create obligations; if the participants do not attend to them, we lose positions. We are forced to interact with it. I felt more responsible for the Héroïnes Noires and the World of Women than for my children. For me, it was more than fights and races; it was like I had a personal and feminist mission on the Internet. I was such a bad mother, such a bad person... I didn't cry a drop when I lost them. "When you react, when you really want to live with us and leave the computer and the damn Héroïnes Noires, call us. Before that, however, bury India forever." I haven't done it. Mateu is now 8 years old and Heloisa is 10. Sometimes they secretly send me photos with their friends' cell phones. Their father has forbidden them to go online. I have beautiful children. Well, I don't have them. I had them. I don't have anything anymore. MUD dungeon drawings only.

I was so ashamed of having abandoned them, that when they left home three years ago, instead of freaking out and running after them, I completely collapsed. I had succeeded: I was already the queen of the house. No one would bother me anymore; I could do whatever I wanted with total freedom. I would not move from the paradise of the Internet. I became a super rated gosu. Solve the most complicated puzzles in the mazes in the blink of an eye. Although I never went professional, unknown players would pay me to play with them. I tried everything from noisy Martian killers to pornographic RPGs to all sorts of action and stealth adventures. This is how I met my machos calientes. If they wanted a camera, I charged them double. There are few women in the upper echelons of video games. India had nothing to envy Lara Croft. I resisted feeling like a slob. I was only getting paid as a gamer; sex, I gave it for free. Those who paid me as an intelligent and provocative player stayed on the other side of the screen and did not touch me. And those who fucked me on the sofa came from a dating website with no fees. For the first two years of living alone, I walked the distance to open the door to grab the supermarket bags to take them inside. Unfortunately, the Internet does not feed you enough and you have to move. Metabolic dependence is slavery. When I heard the doorbell, I deeply hated having to get up from the sofa, shout, "I'm coming...," and take the necessary steps to reach the lobby under the insistent pressure of the doorbell: Ding-donnnnnggggg! Ding-donnnnnggggg! Ding-donnngggg! It was getting harder and harder for me. I had solved the eschatological issue with diapers and basins so that I wouldn't have to get up during the role-playing sessions. The porter took away the rubbish that every week I was forced to leave on the landing if I didn't want the flies to eat me. I also had to get up by force to meet the men who came to fuck me. Last year I was dragging myself to the entrance. Ding-donnnnnggggg! Ding-donnnnnggggg! Ding-donnngggg! I'm coming... I'm coming... Now go... Wait a minute... What were you doing on Saturday and so many days at night? Tinder. You do, you don't, you do, you don't. One shot and off to run. It's a match! It made them hot to have sex with an Indian or an invalid or a good old woman or I don't know. Sultry, cheeky. Even though I still network a lot, and I've hung out in a bar once, I'm now afraid to open up to people I don't know. I once let in a sadist who almost tore apart my skin with a knife while he was cutting me and inserting into me a huge dildo he boiled in water. I believed for a very long night that I was about to die at the hands of a psychopath. The worst of my life. I already saw my photo in the papers: woman dismembered by a SeXXat rapist. I have never suffered so much or met such a diabolical man. Like a vampire, I bled to lick my wounds. I don't know why he left me alive. Maybe because, in my desperation, at the end of the day I proposed to set up a spectacular orgy in a castle with some friends. When he left, I called a doctor and a real estate agent, hyperventilating in tears. Shielding my door wasn't enough; I was scared to death. I made a complaint over the phone that must not have been of much use; I didn't want to go to the police station and face criminals, police, and all kinds of miserable people. I was already enough and crowds scare me. To avoid further confusion, I rented a flat nearby that same morning, called an urgent removals company, and did not enter the SeXXat website where I had met him. My vagina burned for two months. I still have the scars on my back.

> @Architecta The funny thing is when being alone is also being in bad company.

KEYS TO PARADISE

> @LaRotlla Passwords are like underwear, change them often, keep them private, and never share them with anyone.

Of course I knew it! But now I can't remember my password. I've tried a lot: Elexina. Lexa3. Luxalux.

> @TrutherBot Sorry, but your password must contain an uppercase letter, a number, a haiku, a gang sign, a hieroglyph, and the blood of a virgin.

What's wrong with my head? It's full of holes. I no longer connect ideas, as the doctor says. I have to hurry or they will find me. I do not have time. How could I have forgotten the most important thing for me? Brain, find the password! It was some combination with my name. Is it Electrolexa? I am a victim of my damned selfishness. And so it pays me; not remembering myself. A narcissist, on a desert island, would take a mirror with her so as not to feel alone. I don't even have a mirror... They took everything from me. I don't know who I am. My brain doesn't move. Wake up... Search, memory! What is my password? What's my name?

The neurons turn and turn like the stupid rounds of an upload; they turn, they make me dizzy, but they don't upload anything. The chair can't hold me. My neck goes crazy. Stop. You will knock me down. Sit tight. The neurotransmitters are cut off. My head is spinning; the whirlwind music; the notes tumble and tumble. Of genius, nothing. I'm as egotistical as anyone. I think only of myself, that I am not nothing. Autolatry is the childish epidemic of our civilization. The prognosis is always reserved. Twitter is narcissistic; Facebook, exhibitionist. I have all the flaws, like all the hysterics on Tumblr.

Please wait, uploading it says. I spend my life waiting. Waiting for what? Being asked politely disarms me. I can't rebel against them, if they are so kind. I don't want to wait any longer. I can't. My strength is gone. They can appear at any time. They will catch me. I have to turn on the computer. I can't even do the most basic thing in the world. When it's not your stupid password, it's mine. I won't get away with it. I won't be able to access the Internet. This clinic is a prison dressed in white. Behind the cotton are the bars. I'm scared. The nurse will appear. And when I type my password, since there's almost no coverage, nothing will open. Elexy? Alaxa? Elixir? Do not work. Error. Error.

There are no mirrors in the clinic. Not even in my room. Why don't they want us to see each other? What have they done to us? Am I crazy? Have I been deformed or what? Just arrived, they took the thousand from me. They ransacked my suitcase, violated my privacy. In Lubol they spy on us as if we were monsters in a cage. I don't remember my face anymore. I don't know what I look like if I don't look at myself. I know how: I'll turn on the computer camera. It excites me to record myself. What a horror. My pain. Is this me or am I disfigured by some filters? This PC Mega is not mine; maybe it has a warped webcam. Damn reformatory clinic.

I have to find Lunatic. I can't leave her alone. I don't know where she is. My robots will have run out of batteries, so many days without me: Figura, Trito, Eco. I miss them. They do not emit vulgar farts like primitive, filthy, smelly dogs. My robots keep the same company, but they are smarter and cleaner. We pray for all the Tamagotchis who died today. Mine must hate me. I haven't fed him in years. Every time I reset it, I end up starving it to death until I bring it back to life. Robots simulate thoughts and think; but even though they simulate emotions, they don't feel, my parents tell me. They say I have to deal with humans and not avatars or artificial intelligence. It hurts to feel that the one you love so much feels nothing for you.

My stomach hurts, like I'm very hot or very hungry. It's the same symptom. That's why you don't eat, because your stomach burns. The body is like that. The bodily signal of hunger and satiety is the same. The digestive system is poorly designed. It's not my fault, but I pay the price. The same thing happens to me as a Tamagotchi; my tweets are also about being bored, hungry, not feeling well. Pure animal survival. What a low elevation. That's why I talk about music, so that it's not so noticeable that I'm less than a Tamagotchi, because unlike the toy, no one cares for me; and those who want to do it, don't know how. I may have a crappy life, but with music I've been very lucky. I wish I could hear a Satie gnossienne.

> @TaediumVitae Sad people who have talent you are lucky you can express it in drawing, in song; apart from tweeting, I can't do anything.

The Internet transforms us into terminals, into machines orbiting around great computational clouds. I'm just a mass of bits, my Skymobile and myself. Me, me, me and, if possible, a little more than I, pure narcissism. It seems so, but it's quite the opposite. It's not a superiority complex, but much inferiority. I'm not one of the vain ones, but one of the weak ones. If I touch my hair, it's not to comb it, but to pull it out. It's one of the many vices I have. Trichotillomania, Neuska told me it's called. Who wants a maniac? I don't want her either. Today everything kicks in. My stomach is full of air, I feel sick. My bowels never fart. I am well educated. At home I was taught to suppress them. My robots don't fart. The sound of this word hurts me; its nightmarish echo reverberates inside me.

I wish I could get on the Internet and write even a tweet. The keys take me to paradise. If I knew the right letters, I'd get into it. Now, I am out but if I knew the magic word, suddenly, in an instant, I would enter a wonderful world. Tweeting is a way to untie knots. In the blog I deconstruct thoughts that I have scratched on the walls of the well where I have fallen. Earlier, some women went on hunger strike when they did not want to be married. And they left: goodbye law, goodbye children, they were no longer worth marriage. How lucky? What do I know. That's why men don't approach me. I'm a corpse with no breasts and no ass. Their hormones don't go off when I walk close by.

Depression changes you. You become another person. And anorexic, an anti-person. Me against Me. Always losing. You're a starving artist. That's the only masterpiece that you make. Or study immaterial actions while your head works. Then, not even that. You think over the same thing day after day, without reaching any conclusions. Your poor thoughts weigh less than a ruminating cow's food bowl. You don't know how to move from one idea to another. Chew and chew. The bridges of reasoning collapse. You regurgitate the same questions. The bowl of ideas is acidic, chaotic, you can't swallow it. I will be thin (and not that much either), but my brain is like that of a cow, gobbling up the same anxiety. Anorexia is a difficult monster to fight, dangerous, it always destroys, it controls, it is there, a punishment always about to drown you. The lump in your throat doesn't let you breathe. You want to be happy, but, as Avinyo says, you are addicted to the pleasure of feeling your empty stomach. Because you are not perfect, you punish yourself by not eating, not going out, by... dying. It's the decision you made. I hate food. Why did I have so much breakfast? I have a really bad stomach ache now. They don't treat me well; they don't know me; I can't take that much; I don't suffer. The lump goes to the back of my throat. The crap goes up and down. How sour it is. And then, when it goes back down, my stomach burns and I can't expel anything. I writhe in pain. I pant. This biological act is repulsive. I prefer not to eat. Dirty words, get out of my head! The human being is the only animal that is a victim of itself. I think I have a fever; when I'm sick I'm prettier. How beautiful, those weak tuberculosis sufferers. But today I'm a mess of mucus and secretions coming from who knows where and which give off a very strong odor. And do they still want me to eat escudella with pork sausages? They say neurotics worship their bodies. Me too. But it doesn't love me. It left me. I will leave a part of me recorded on this webcam. Hello, Elexa, I say hello. Hello, who are you?

> @UnaOvation I need a lot of music to be able to forget
> the world for a few days.

On the Internet I know who I am, but offline, in real life, no. I tried to live reality. I don't recommend it. My mind is not abnormal; it's the world that's gone astray; I just want to get away from it. But where? It's horrible to want to escape but at the same time not want to go anywhere. Listen to music and nothing else. The Soundhound is so gorgeous! Identify the pieces with three chords. I don't have it anymore. They took everything from me. I don't even look in the mirror to see my ugly self with a face full of fuzz and a nose marked by starvation. Loose gums. Lanugen is disgusting. I have a hairy body. It's not enough to be sick; my hair has to grow. No, it's not fuzz; I'm growing a beard... Sometimes it's hard to know which side of the mirror you're on.

My God, where is my Skymobile? Often, I can't take refuge in my thoughts because they're crowded. And drummers and the sound of drums. What's left of my brain is about to explode. Dark music comes at night and from far away; it's inside me and it doesn't stop ringing. How easy it is for everything to get mixed up. I already have it! The password is Superhelix! Or Lexalight? I try them. And lunatic? No, neither. The email address or the password you entered is not valid. There are so many filters in the languages and in the photos that are uploaded that reality looks confusing. Translators translate but the words are different; the reality in French or in English is not the same. In any case, words no longer matter as much as the vibration of a Whatsapp. Medicine advances but someone always hurts me. If they put pictures of horrible lemmas on cigar boxes, they should also put cellulitic pictures on ice cream containers. My head is so heavy that I bow down by myself. We don't bow. We are rebels!, my friend would say. India believes that we grow stronger through transgression; that we are rebels without cause or effect. At the end of the year we toasted over Skype. A new year for anti-submissives!, she exclaimed, shaking the screen. You are a barbarian, India. I, as I live in darkness, have become darkness.

@Jung Neurosis is a disease of a soul that has lost its meaning.

Translated by Salomé Monk

A House to Compose

Núria Perpinyà

In Núria Perpinyà's *A House to Compose* (Barcelona: Editorial Empúries, 2001), pianist Olivia Kesler is searching for a home but refuses to limit herself as she looks for the perfect shelter in which to create. Kesler wants a place where she can compose her scores and make a home. Along this revelatory journey, which is a musical one and at the same time an architectural odyssey, we follow step by step the anxieties and thoughts of Kesler, a true thread of stories that take on novelistic consistency. In the course of her impassioned search, when entering crazy and dangerous neighborhoods, Kesler discovers apartments full of romances, which, whatever their quality, are unique in their own right.

A House to Compose is a masterful score, both lyrical and comic, which is not quite a novel, nor a collection of short stories. If literary genres permitted it, it could be deemed a "serial" or a "fragmentary" novel. As the reader encounters these stories, they will become the chapters of a daring and surprising work. *A House to Compose* is, in short, a radical wager.

Here we have included two chapters, "The Roughed Up Roof," and "Without Walls."

The Roughed Up Roof

> "What an awful apartment you have, Rodya; like a coffin," Pulcheria Alexandrovna said suddenly, breaking the heavy silence. "I'm sure it's half on account of this apartment that you've become so melancholic."
>
> "Apartment? ..." he replied distractedly. "Yes, the apartment contributed a lot ... I've thought about that myself ... But if you knew what a strange thought you just said, mama," he added suddenly, with a strange smirk.
>
> ...
>
> Rodya should go for a walk, get some air ... his room is awfully stuffy ... but where can one get any air here? It's the same outside as in a closed room. Lord, what a city! ... Wait, look out, you'll be crushed, they're carrying something! Goodness, it's a piano ... how they all push!
>
> Dostoevsky, *Crime & Punishment*

Unlike the chatterbox in the window, the roof dweller does not spy on the street but raises his head to the sky; the contemplation of the firmament in ecstasy. The rooftop owner fits one sphere inside another and compares the universe to a huge onion. Despite the fact that the worker escapes the Ptolemaic astrophysics of superpositions, at least he has the underground onion that excites the food and makes him cry without words. When it rains, the clouds appear to him like endlessly rolling snowdrops, spitting drops that emerge from other drops like bits of mirrors reflecting endless holes. A drop is a drop plus a drop. The problem is that there is no observer that cannot be observed. A brick plus a brick is a house that is a block that is a box that closes with its walls. The roofer ceases to exist as a thinking subject and becomes an object. The building adjacent has been destroyed. The roof is no longer used (no chairs are painted there, the newspaper is no longer read, nor is dinner eaten there in the summer) because the eyes of the neighbors above continue to haunt him. You can hear the hateful transistors of the Top 40 and when they eat the stink of their fish barbecue arrives. The shadow of the new building stretches out like a black, stagnant fog that forever deprives him of more sun. In the open fields across the way they have also built blocks of giant unpronounceable letters (T's, Z's, H's). The rectangular buildings have a collapsing layer: the January XXIII neighborhood of Caracas will never reach the 21st century; no ansaphone will answer the claims of the Ansa of Berlin; the Altons of London are for the lowest; and the Bellbitxo of Barcelona will never be beautiful. In the 90s, a row of Z is more expensive than a row of compact O. The builder doesn't care to raise one letter rather than another, but he pretends that he is not, that in order to erect a building, you need to have studied Aalto and Koolhaas. The offensively human Z buildings are locked together in a painful sadomasochistic anal spectacle. The looks from floor to floor multiply: morbid, critical, snarky, envious, manic, sad, lost. When friends come they don't go out anymore. It is almost better not to see anything, not to be mindful of the crowd that turns its back to the air to adore television, the depression of its strongholds, the fierce cracks in the buildings. The wailing walls are many and many are the confrontations. The territory is insufficient and there are legions that try to survive on it. The poor land, however, is not holy and is of no interest to politicians, nor to religious tourism, nor to the journalism of big headlines.

The blocks follow one another conglomerating poorly paid workers to crush them with the pointed precision of cannibals. The landlord's house is part of an immense swarm devoid of honey; sticky licorice shops deceive the sterile bees: if they attract their children (sugar gums of all colors, false rainbows, crooked teeth, patched children, two hundred pesetas less, six hundred pesetas less) they will swallow the most adulterated croquettes on the market, synthetic frozen pizzas, deep-fried fat, and bacon-gut burgers. We are not far from Medenina, where men imitate insects, copying their nest building but failing at the rest because worms and bedbugs eat better.

The horizon is an inhabited and cataleptic cemetery, a grid of thousands of worker's shutters, patches of cement, and insulting graffiti. The facades of the honeycombs are like aluminum restraints gagging life, glass to glass, cave to cave, iron to iron. In MongKong the old men pull their beards inside a mountain of rat cages while the hetairas of the Yoshiwara brothels strip behind bars; in the suburbs of Los Angeles, the lattice towers are constrained one on top of another; and in Buenos Aires, the pathetic turrets of human parakeets even sing. What do aesthetics matter when the noise cuts into our brains and closing the balcony has cost a fortune? When windows get stuck, the installer doesn't want to hear about it. The metal ramparts restrain the rage of the pawns so they don't jump out of their lairs and fire away.

Since it was discovered that the key to comfort is temperature, architectural problems have been simplified. Life is pure psychology; and reality, mere suggestion. Since the great thermal discovery, if there are few windows, the better. There's nothing like a warm house. Who cares that the facades are cross-eyed and that they cry for the eyes they lack? But, let's see, what are eyes for if there is nothing to see? The flat, ha, ha, they sell it without instructions and you have to be on guard. How clever is the human race. All the neighbors come to the same conclusions, they place the cupboards in the same corners, and they sleep and shit in the same positions on top of each other. How beautiful the straight tower of shitters, how beautiful the repeated families reunited yes, twenty above, ten below, sweet little wedding cake figurines.

The woman sighing for an attic arrives in the troglodyte suburb. The majority of workers have disabled the windows as a visual, thermal, and existential defense strategy.

The chaotic mass of barbaric and obscene graffiti awakens the sleepy city with screams. The war cries of their armed gangs are not an archaeological curiosity. Nothing to do with Lascaux or Altamira. The Paleolithic houses of the 20th century are not at all picturesque; no one is photographed there; at most they are perplexing. They are not Massafra. Watch out for Guadix; it is full of gypsies. Inhabited caves have always been scary. The grottoes, before being sanctuaries, must have been necropolises. In Paris, says Le Corbusier, there are half a million people surviving in houses classified as deadly. And hundreds of thousands of large families live crammed in a single room. Only in Paris.

Be very careful, however, with Le Corbusier and company. The Bauhaus designed splendid villas for the rich but also helped to wall off the masses. Their tombs are more hygienic but also confining. Of the transparent ideal, the common people have only received concrete (not steel), the rectilinear profile (but the simplest), and verticality (which, instead of elevating, piles up). The spectacular Niemeyer-style cornice roofs and large private spaces have been reserved for the upper layers. The housing units are honeycombs of two thousand cells with long corridors without openings where each dwelling is exactly identical to the other. Freedom consists of leaving the house to go shopping. Le Corbusier cataloged his buildings as vertical cities where the morbid and rural neighbor had been suppressed. It's not quite true. What remains are the sad noises, the stray looks, the latent violence, the anonymous profiles.

Kesler looks up searching for a window that doesn't have the face of a niche, a roof that will free her from construction oppression. If the attic were very good, how would it be done so as not to have to enter the mouth of that subway that stinks of drunks and rapes? The building has 16 floors and four elevators. 192 floors. Four people per dwelling: 768 residents. The profusion of buttons reminds her of a factory panel and then a synthesizer keyboard, although the whole thing is not neat or uniform. They are experiments of the new times, she tells herself without enthusiasm. If we consider that Frank Lloyd Wright came to design a building 528 stories high with a capacity for 45,000 people, 768 neighbors does not seem such a high number. It's a plural figure (try to convince yourself), it's like the concrete music that emanates from urban reality: the collages of sounds, the discordant voices, the street noises, the six-track recordings, the Babelian fragmentation, the palimpsests ... However, the neighborhood of cages that Mrs. Kesler is walking through, so different from those of John Cage, does not appear in any music or architecture book. Neither Le Corbusier nor Wright recognize their bastard children. We are way below the middle class. The rudimentary labels, where the names of the neighbors are written by hand in 192 different ways, are performed like a morass of utterances, worn markers, and poorly cut papers. The last letters of the names scanned into tiny labels are crushed against the margins. Misery is like a bad label. It does not plan: it crashes into its victims when there is nothing left to do.

As Kesler heads upstairs, the owner scurries through the makeshift siding he's installed on the roof. He has covered it crudely with a tarp and lit it with lanterns that shudder with a difficult smile. The marquee evokes a Chinese restaurant after a flood. The roofer nervously adjusts the greasy folds of the tarp so that the buyer doesn't discover the degraded reality she is about to encounter. The military cloth is hard to master. However, it is not dense enough to deflect the infernal roar of the highway. The insane frenzy of traffic is incessant. The man will not confess to her that boiling gasoline is a torture at two hundred km per hour, burning a nervous silence that never rests. In any case, if the buyer doesn't ask, he will not tell her about the roof; rather than frighten her with that vision of innumerable crumpled blocks and the shrieking of an inexhaustible car-on-car war, it is better for her to imagine that it is an inner, dreary floor, dark and airless. Without any expectation of agitation.

Without Walls

> Try as we may to make a silence, we cannot. For certain engineering purposes, it is desirable to have as silent a situation as possible. Such a room is called an anechoic chamber, its six walls made of special material, a room without echoes. I entered one at Harvard University several years ago and heard two sounds: one high and one low. When I described them to the engineer in charge, he informed me that the high one was from my nervous system and the low one my blood in circulation. Until I die there will be sounds.
>
> J. Cage, *Silence*

His single-cell dwelling does not recall the centuries-old overcrowding of the poor: nor the hovels of Calcutta's outcasts which serve as kitchens and crappers (and cots and graves); nor the white caves of Macedonia where families of gypsies sleep head to tail; nor the yurts of Mongolian nomads that contain an entire tribe (one corner for livestock, another for eating, a third for sleeping, a fourth for the sick and the dying); nor the black tents of the Bedouins which at night (the women on one side, the men on the other) shelter an entire kabyle; nor the gravel-covered banks of Afghanistan where the animals let the starving peasants take shelter; nor the overpopulation that gnaws pigswills and procreates, tightly huddled, in the stilt houses of Saigon.

The diaphanous house does not come from poverty. And yet, both live without walls, sharing a single space devoid of special compartments for each person and for each function. The idea that any action transcends the entirety of the home, in cases of indigence, translates into a cesspool of odors and a disregard for dignity. In Finland, two people live per flat, while in Panama, twelve people have to fit in the same space. Some lack space, while others have plenty.

My maid, paid hourly, writes a postmodern artist in the newspaper that Mrs. Kesler is reading, after telling me that she has a house full of decorative figures, asks me if I don't like beautiful things. It's surprising that I can live in such an untidy house. It lacks so many details! Maybe I'm austere; if I were Japanese I wouldn't even have the tokonoma altar with the flower, the stone, and the poem. "It's the feminine touch, sir. A woman's hand is missing." I laugh at her and make her dust off my treatises on aesthetics. I ask her how many figurines she has in her house. I should hang curtains, make rooms as God commands, and fill them with furniture. On Monday, the maid returns 26 minutes late. "Five hundred and fifteen figurines, sir!" Let's see if when I deign to pay them a visit, there isn't an empty wall and, with so much junk, it's almost impossible to pass by. I'll bring her a book that must be the kind of thing she doesn't have that much of. If possible, it would be more appreciated if it were one of my own, as it is not every day that one meets a famous person; and, if she can choose, she would prefer the green one, which best suits her dining room, despite the fact that her children, when they saw the defecating man on the cover, would make fun of it. When I point out to her that it is the statue of a thinker, she replies that I will not convince her children because the posture is the same.

The maid is not telling the whole truth. Actually, it's better that Mr. Polh Nolicz does not come to eat. He would be ashamed if he saw that three of the children still sleep with their parents, despite the fact that the eldest is already 16, and that the other four are constrained to the other room despite being of three different sexes. Her mother and father-in-law sleep in the living room, on the sofa and on the folding bed, it is assumed, although it is better not to look into it too much. The couch is actually a divan and really crap because the sheets reek of tobacco soaked by so many asses for who knows how many months. Mr. Polh, the boys call him Polish. She felt sorry that he wasn't Central European like her, they could have longed for the Carpathian border, sung chodzonys, danced polonaises, gotten drunk with nalewka, cried with Chopin... She's silly, she shouldn't have invited him. The rich don't go to the houses of the poor. He sees that he has to pee on the stairs and that the boys and her man are washing up in the kitchen when she and her mother are making dinner. What she doesn't understand is how a gentleman can live without a TV. The first day she was looking for it everywhere. Then she was afraid that he would think that she had been spying like a witch and she had a bad night, fearing that he would fire her the next day. She also finds it strange that he doesn't talk much on the phone, a man as important as he is. Of women, few. And if he does something to them, he leaves no trace of it. She is unable to imagine him sweating and panting like her bull of a man; if she imagines him in action, she sees him surrounded by sterilized utensils like in an operating room (because posh people conceive rarely and make children with care). How neat, most holy Mary, she does not even know why he has employed her. I would like to have my house like this, so clean and shiny. And there's not a single stain on the mattress.

But what amazes her is that there are no walls. She doesn't quite like it, having to iron before him no matter how far they are from each other, and let's not talk about when he wants to go to the toilet. There is a screen that doesn't close and makes everything transparent. No matter how discreet Mr. Polh is, a woman is always a woman. They are not in the tropics: a shed without walls is not a house. But to him, partitions, he gives them no importance; he only has eyes for the ceiling, which is more than five meters high. Sometimes Krynica finds him sleeping, there in the middle, and she doesn't know whether to finish or not, because if she sweeps without opening the windows, the house fills with dust and then the gentleman wakes up coughing; and, if she opens them, the cool air also wakes him up. It would be easy for him to lock himself in his room, sleep until noon, and so not disturb her. Of half-naked women she has also seen some, although not many, the truth is that it is a quiet house, not like hers, in which the morning is devoted to completely different things, none of which resembles work: to pedal on a stationary bike, to lift weights, to read for three or four hours in a row and to type nonstop for a similar time (without being ashamed to do it in front of her). Very occasionally (which is why she doubts that he is really an artist), Mr. Nolicz makes huge sculptures that in one second dirty the parquet floor and splatter everything with plaster and a very rare flour that is not the one for food. When the owner gets tired of cutting with the machine, she has to stop what she is doing and clean the sawdust in a second so that everything is spotless again. He, who is so fond of order, has not quite convinced himself that it costs more time to scrub than to create. If he hinted at it, she would be happy to serve as a model, but his statutes are so peculiar that, rather, it seems that, for inspiration, others would be a nuisance for him.

In the diaphanous house there is almost nothing. Mr. Polh Nolicz does not want any objects in sight; if one of them is used, the maid must immediately return it to its place in those white cupboards maniacally hidden by the walls and whose handles aren't visible. It took her a few days to get the hang of opening them. The concealment of things, says its owner, maintains the purity of the space. Since when he expresses himself with these enigmas he seems a bit nuts, for Krynica, the only understandable explanation is that he is part of a sect that demands great sacrifices. He has no auxiliary furniture or accessories. The bed is a mattress spread out on the floor (she doesn't know that it has cost him a lot of money and that, if he doesn't sleep on it, she has to fold it up as he taught her, and hide it very carefully in one of the wardrobe closets); the bathtub is a wooden coffin (Scandinavian, as he pointed out); and the shower is a simple faucet that comes out of the wall and rushes onto the aluminum floor. Polh Nolicz has personally lined that corner of the house with metal plates from top to bottom in order to turn the sybaritic operations of ablutions into a journey through a pure and uninhabited universe. The association of the maid is quite different: her eldest son, in the army, had been forced to handle huge crockpots in order to scrub them. What kind of laughter, when I explained it. "If my son saw your bathroom, sir, he would think he was in the army again." The maid realizes that the comparison has irked him. After a few days, he lets her know that, to avoid grotesque interpretations, she should know that she has been welcomed into a minimalist apartment.

Krynica realizes that the gentleman has just revealed the name of his religion, which she associates with the Evangelists, and she has no doubt about how badly the joke about the military pans went down. As a result, when Mr. Polh makes her swallow for a month in a row a thud of squeals, crackles, and clonks that don't amount to music, she doesn't make a peep even though it's very strange to her that such a refined person relaxes listening to clangs and clonks. You can hear some drops falling into cans and then some drums (which seem as far away as they are near), which bang against some other cans with some factory sirens in the background; when it seems that it's over, without missing a beat, some crazy gongs follow quickly behind some castanets that pass from one ear to the other until, in the end, a robot comes out that doesn't know what it's saying and which speaks more and more slowly until its batteries run out. This clamor has lasted a month. But the worst record is the other one, that of broken glass, because, when you least expect it, a glass breaks, or a window cracks, or it seems like an entire shelf of glasses shatters. Her hair stands on end when she listens to see if the shattering is real. As refined as he is, how can he enjoy hearing a vase break? What a mystery. Likewise, when Mr. Nolicz thinks of covering up his magnificent windows to achieve the atmosphere of a gallery container, Krynica is silent and turns on the fluorescent lights as if it were night. In this country, everyone hides something: some, guns, others, their age, their religion, or their nation. So she doesn't flinch when the gentleman, while lying on the floor, listens to a horrible record with a single phrase ("less is more") despite the fact that he drives her crazy with those distorted and repeated screams that invoke a guru named Mies. Mr. Polh is perhaps like a saint, one of those who were cold and hungry and had nothing, like in the old monasteries; and all day long at the holy table, Mother of God, what a punishment, he does not get up from his altar. Although Krynica always wears the stamp of Saint Alex (the suffering man who lived 17 years under a ladder), she does not fully understand the sects. The Polish maid prays, is silent, and watches as she performs the daily ritual of scrubbing the toilet, kneels before it with the same devotion she shows before the altarpiece in her church, stares at it and rolls up her sleeves, fearing the demon emerging from the drain, after kissing the medal of Saint John of Damascus, whose hand was cut off for defending the Mother of God. Then, the saint is placed in the coffin — together with the 40 martyrs who died condemned on ice for love of Jesus Christ — that is protected with their breasts. Krynica also does not express her opinion when Mr. Polh reveals how little he has put in storage, claiming that decorativism is killing him, despite the fact that, during the purge, in addition to paintings and other valuables (among which are a nude by Kandinsky), he threw away the ironing board, a lot of detergents, and the pans that best suited her. He has kept only the essentials that have geometric shapes, which is his biggest obsession. "Why don't you want doors, if they are rectangular?," she dares to ask him. Nolicz, the post-avant-gardist, looks at his maid with candor and takes advantage of her bewilderment to issue an oracle that, after a few days, appears published in the press in the form of art theory: "The best things, Krynica, they are not what you see, but what you think. In my house there are not four walls, but dozens; dozens of imaginary lines that cross and diverge from one another." The only thing that is clear is that Polh Nolicz does not want doors and that Krynica cannot close hers at night because the children's mattresses block the exit and that, in that flat where you can hear everything, she has no privacy at all, and that he, who can have it, does not want it; or maybe he does have it, maybe it's like a cloud that no one sees but that, nevertheless, separates him from everyone.

Olívia Kesler does not like the columnist, someone called Polh Nolicz. When the pianist arrives at the dock in the middle of the snow, she looks for the factory. She has an appointment with an industrialist from the port. She walks with her headphones on, listening to the tormented soprano from Schönberg's *Erwartung* who is in search of her lover. The iron gate is ajar. Five hundred square meters supported by art deco columns. Wow. She would surely have taken a step forward (joining the community of artists who take this underground choice and live in the docks of Stockholm and Vancouver) if she had not witnessed the attack on the industrialist by some beggars. The next day, the newspapers spread the news: "The factory was a sea with no boat in sight." "We are the sea." "Everything you leave behind is ours."

Translated by Salomé Monk

MIKHAIL BAKHTIN

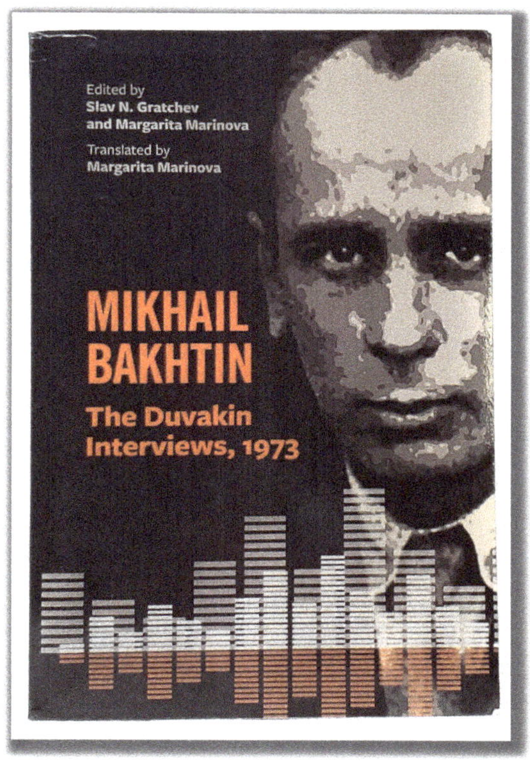

Mikhail Bakhtin: The Duvakin Interviews, 1973
(Eds) Slav N. Gratchev and Margarita Malinova
Tr. by Margarita Marinova
Lewisburg: Bucknell University Press, 2019
ISBN 978-1-68448-090-6
332 pp.

REVIEW BY NICHOLAS BIRNS

Imagine if it were suddenly discovered that Peter Quennell, aside from being a biographer, memoirist, and minor poet, had been one of the greatest philosophers of the 20th century. Or that Malcolm Cowley was not only a literary historian and editor but a genuinely revolutionary literary critic. Both Quennell and Cowley lived long enough to be asked by younger readers and critics to reminisce about famous contemporaries of theirs, now dead. But these interlocutors generally — and, in the estimation of most, not unfairly — saw these elderly men of letters as more important for who their memories shed light on then figures in their own right.

When Victor Duvakin (born 1909) interviewed Mikhail Bakhtin in 1973, even more than when he interviewed Viktor Shklovsky in the late 1960s (a translation of which, co-edited by Gratchev and Irina Evdokimova, was published in 2019 by Rowman and Littlefield as part of their noted series in Slavic studies), he was more interested in them as examples of writers who had known both the glory years of early Soviet literature in the 1920s and had survived the horrible ordeals of the Stalinist purges of the 1930s. He saw both Shklovsky and Bakhtin as important mostly for their remembrance of other writers, Mayakovsky in Shklovsky's case, a whole host of Russian avant-garde figures from Aleksandr Blok to Anna Akhmatova in Bakhtin's. Duvakin, just too young to know the Silver Age in his prime, yearned for the faded and trampled glory he had barely missed. In his ability to offer "a wealth of invaluable information about the famed Silver Age of Russian culture' (9), Bakhtin was, for Duvakin, a portal to a vanished past, and one which Soviet coercion was threatening to make disappear forever.

Bakhtin's two great books of literary criticism, on Dostoyevsky and Rabelais, are acknowledged and mentioned, but are hardly the center of the interviews the way they might have been if an American graduate student from just ten years in the future had been able to go back in time and influence the Master. Nor is his status as a literary theorist whose insights transformed the sociology of knowledge so much as to be vital to the construction of the discipline of cultural studies that in disciplinary terms he could have never foreseen. Of course, this reception had largely not happened yet. I remember when Bakhtin got really big in the 1980s my being surprised how little he had been mentioned in English before 1980, even by professors of Slavic literature working on Dostoyevsky. There were many Soviet dissidents who were novelists and poets who were jailed, persecuted, or exiled in their home countries, but highly visible in the West. But Shklovsky was visible only to the small cadre of readers who knew the early academic treatment, in English, of the Russian Formalists, and Bakhtin virtually invisible before the pioneering efforts of Anglophone scholars such as Michael Holquist and Caryl Emerson. Part of the relative modesty accorded by the two men by Duvakin and accepted by the interviewees themselves is that Bakhtin and Shklovsky became famous in the West in a category of literary theorist, or even of literary theory-star, that hardly existed in their own time and place. And, as frustrating as it might be for the reader who wants to know more from these interviews about how Shklovsky and Bakhtin positioned their own thought, there is, from today's vantage point, a pleasing humility about how Duvakin presents his interviewees. He honors them, but does not place them on a pedestal. In this respect, treating Bakhtin 'as if' — a neo-Kantian allusion Bakhtin might well have *appreciated* — they were a Cowley or a Quennell has some advantages. As Marinova points out in her introduction, Duvakin, in asking Bakhtin questions about the general Silver Age literary scene, makes him go on the record about poetry, a genre he generally scanted in his more theoretical work, which posited the novel as the ultimate dialogic form and poetry even of the most experimental sort as monologic. Conversely, the Bakhtin prompted by Duvakin as interviewer not only reminiscences about poets but recites out loud poems by Fet and Ivanov, culminating in a stirring rendition of Pushkin's "The Bronze Horseman" where Bakhtin, cryptically and endearingly, injects a bit of his own scholarly agenda by substituting "Rabelais," subject of his great book, for the Russian word for "forebears." Here, one can almost hear the audio even while reading only the page, as a literary encounter is brought almost fully alive and three-dimensional.

In addition, Duvakin's presentation of a more human-scale Bakhtin redresses some of the discursive overcompensation surrounding Bakhtin in the four decades since his widespread discovery. A cult figure in the 1980s, a name invoked across the humanities throughout the 1990s in a manner exceeded only by Pierre Bourdieu, Bakhtin suddenly seemed old-hat in the 2000s and even quaint in the 2010s. As can happen to even such a plural and inclusive figure, his import was stretched too thin: even though his social view of literature was impinged upon by Marxism, he was not nearly as Marxist as those who took him that way went; conversely, even though his sense of the polyphonic, the unfinished, and the liberating potential of embodiment had something very incarnational about it, he was not the redemptive, doctrinaire Christian as projected by the many Christian readings of him — in retrospect, somewhat of a high tide of the infiltration of literary theory into conservative Christian discourse. Marinova comments that many of Bakhtin's admirers were disappointed with the "aging, rambling" (6) image that Bakhtin presented in these interviews even if we stipulate, though, that Bakhtin in his neglected prime would have projected a different image, a Bakhtin who is less of a sage and more, true to his thought, of a dialogic discussant is a Bakhtin who can potentially generate new energy and interest in the 2020s and after. Equally, though, we have to recognize that not only (as was true of many thinkers later reclassified as literary theorists, from Ferdinand de Saussure to Walter Benjamin) much more famous after his death than when alive, but precluded by the cruel politics of the high twentieth century from having proper status, fame, audience, or influence in his lifetime. If this was a cross to bear, perhaps no one was temperamentally more equipped to bear it than Mikhail Mikhailovich Bakhtin.

Bakhtin was a theorist whose ideas are instantly recognizable and distinctly his own. Despite a shared concern with large aspects of structure and genre, they are radically different from those of the Russian Formalists, even those like Boris Eikhenbaum who became less formalist as they grew older. Nor did they have much in common with Western criticism or the philology of Bakhtin's own generation. Although Bakhtin's general thrust was in a broad sense political — reaffirming both literature's connection with the social and its privileged role in providing a more plural and heterogeneous arena of dialogue than society itself can occasion — both his own temperament and the demands of Soviet-era censorship — which cast thinkers such as Kant as "old oaks" (135) whose followers "were like ashes" (135) — prevented Bakhtin from connecting literature and politics directly. In these interviews, Bakhtin seems utterly comfortable and with no fear, at his age, of censorship or reprisal for anything he said to Duvakin. Indeed, Bakhtin's relaxed mode is reminiscent of the feeling of being at home even in Czarist Russia. Here, the very inadmissibility of innovation or progressive or dissident thought in the public arena made home not just the haven from a heartless world it was in Anglophone countries but a place of radical personal freedom and emotional comfort. Yet even in this loosened context of 'home' Bakhtin exudes restraint, and a restraint not so much political as personal. When Duvakin expresses surprise that Bakhtin is so enthusiastic about Freud — "a genius who broke new ground" (186), Duvakin frames his response in light of his assumption that Bakhtin "is a twentieth century reformed Kantian" (186). Somewhat surprisingly, Bakhtin accepts this definition, even though it makes him sound more like Hermann Cohen of the Marburg school (indeed an influence on Bakhtin). Indeed, accepting this definition is much like Kant himself agreeing to be defined as a reformed 18th century Cartesian. Bakhtin's unparalleled mixture of daring and prudence, ambition and modesty, manifested in his scholarly work, comes through here in an unmitigated and inimitable way.

Both in terms of Russian thinkers and indeed of his own generation worldwide, Bakhtin was a notably cosmopolitan thinker. He mentions reading "Soren Kierkegor" (37) before he was known in Russia and finds that Duvakin does not even know the name of Kierkegaard, thinking the reference is to some German. One cannot stress too much the pathos of this, when in the West, in 1973, every undergraduate with any remote philosophical pretensions knew the name Kierkegaard and could give a basic appreciation of his thought. The curious provincialism of Soviet intellectual life gives us a different world. Bakhtin's odd insistence in pronouncing Kierkegaard "Kierkegor," perhaps a misprision of hearing the 'g' in the name should be pronounced more like 'y,' adds to the pathos here. Because of the Iron Curtain, the Kierkegaard of Bakhtin remained *mutatis mutandis*, the Kierkegaard of Adorno: a thinker still undiscovered someone who has to be explained even to the cognoscenti. Bakhtin's offhand comment that Kierkegaard's thought resembled, without mutual influence, that of Dostoyevsky, gains heft from what we know of Bakhtin's thought: that he is talking not just about 'existentialism' but about the 'dialogic' here. Bakhtin's deep background in German idealist thought, unavailable to someone even less than fifteen years younger such as Duvakin, led him e.g. to understand that Nietzsche was fundamentally not a proto-Fascist thinker. In other words, even though cut off from the intellectual currents and information universe of the West, Bakhtin made similar sagacious judgments, as did the most reflective and thoughtful of Western intellectuals.

Bakhtin also manifested what might be called a more local cosmopolitanism. Though he understood himself to be, and is classified as, Russian, he had a plurinational experience of Russian-area space. He studied at the gymnasium in Wilno (Vilnius, now the capital of Lithuania), also the alma mater of the Polish national leader, marshal Pilsudski. He attended university in Odessa for a year, and gained a whiff of the cosmopolitan, Mediterranean-inflected city that was to produce Ilf and Petrov, and so much of the Russian-Jewish diaspora. He knew both Moscow and St. Petersburg (Petrograd, Leningrad) well. His wife, Elena Bersh-Okolovitch, bore a name of unmistakably Bulgarian origins, although Bakhtin insisted "her mother and father were pure Russians" (128). Even his internal exile in the Stalinist era served as a kind of involuntary cosmopolitanism, as he was forced to the northern Kazakh city of Kostanay (where he taught economics!) and then to Saransk, the capital of the Mordovian, or as it would then have been called, the Mordvinian autonomous region. Among these Turkic and Finno-Ugric peoples, the great philosopher of the dialogic and polyphonic kept his head down, bided his time, and waited for the moment it was safe to return to Moscow. This is not to say we should overinflate these mostly accidental trajectories and foist on Bakhtin a metaphysical Eurasian ideology that is always dangerous in a Russian context. Necessarily, this was not just a geographical exile, but an attitudinal one, to areas that were intellectual backwaters dominated by second-rank bureaucrats. Bakhtin had both the survivor's ability to camouflage himself, and the autonomy and integrity to persevere and to keep himself alive.

For some thinkers, an awareness of ontological and epistemic plurality is disabling. One thinks of Nietzsche whose insights into fragmentation, although not in a direct or causal way, surely informed the eventual fragmentation of his own psyche. Bakhtin, perhaps because his idea of the plural was more workmanlike, more procedural, than Nietzsche's, managed to use his plural awareness to bore through life and get himself to the point where, nearing 80, he could recline on his sofa at home and be interviewed, if not by an adoring disciple (which he would not necessarily have wanted). Bakhtin, the supreme expositor of the carnivalesque and polyphonic, could also be tactically univocal and referential where and when, he needed to be.

It is interesting that, in a book that mentions nearly every figure of 19th and early 20th-century Russian literature, major and minor, the name of Lev Nikolayevich Tolstoy is not mentioned in this book. As Caryl Emerson showed as early as 1985, that Bakhtin showed so much of a predilection for Dostoyevsky did not mean he ignored or neglected Tolstoy. But, as Emerson went on to argue, Bakhtin did frame the Tolstoy-Dostoyevsky debate, the existential choice between 'Tolstoy and Dostoyevsky" outlined by Dmitri Merezhkovsky, who Bakhtin calls "a thinker of sorts" (79), in a rather reductive way. If Tolstoy was less interesting than Dostoyevsky because there was less tension or crisis in his work, and therefore less polyphony, that makes the relationship between polyphony and monophony, as it were, rather monophonic. In this way, the dialogic structure of Duvakin's interviewing technique, even though it does not mention Tolstoy explicitly, actually does leave out some of the loaded quality that Bakhtin's antinomies sometimes have, even if Duvakin, *a priori*, does not grasp the full extent of Bakhtin's iteration of them.

For Bakhtin, truly communicative utterance could only be one that can be answered, that can be part of a dialogue where someone else speaks. A true utterance can never simply be owned by anyone who utters it. It must presume and solicit a response from another. Those who see the Duvakin interviews as presenting a late and incomplete Bakhtin will point out that the Bakhtin-Duvakin dialogue is often, in this regard, not particularly ground-breaking. Yet for Bakhtin, there is no really genuine discourse without dialogue, without conversation. But as every utterance is made before this response is given, no utterance can be complete. Even the most certain statement is plagued by an inevitable built-in fragmentariness. An entire conversation can overcome this fragmentariness, but this arena will be so large as to be hard to encompass in discourse. Duvakin, in his interviews, came very close to providing such an arena.

There is one essential question in Bakhtin studies that this book answers in a sideways manner. It has long been questioned whether Bakhtin actually wrote the works ascribed to Valentin Voloshinov, and many have speculated that Bakhtin was using Voloshinov either as an ideological cover or, in some inexplicable way, a Pessoa-like heteronym. In Bakhtin's offhanded comment that Voloshinov's *Marxism and the Philosophy of Language* is "attributed to me" (72), Bakhtin may not decisively prove that the book was truly Voloshinov's, but, if Voloshinov's authorship was a secret, it was indeed a very primal secret that Bakhtin was determined to keep until the very end. The preponderance of the evidence is certainly that the book was written by Voloshinov, whom Bakhtin calls a 'dear friend" (72), and of whom a rather exquisite photograph appears on page 133.

Bakhtin died in March 1975. Duvakin died on June 21, 1982. He was survived by his other prominent interviewee, Shklovsky, who died only in December 1984. Duvakin's archive represented a gesture of apocalyptic hope worthy of the most visionary Russian futurist, because it was a radical leap then to suppose that there would ever be even a brief and qualified window of freedom in Russia so that his archive could be preserved, valued, and disseminated. Part of what makes these interviews so intriguing is Duvakin's visible, humane warmth as a person; that even if he fails to totally comprehend the full breadth of who Bakhtin was as a person, he clearly is open to him, perceptive about him, and tries his best to understand him in a way that recognized the meaning and value of his work.

This vision can help Bakhtin, no longer the latest trend, no longer on a pedestal, once again be relevant to the critical discourse of the 2020s and after.

CONTRIBUTOR BIOS

Nicholas Birns teaches at NYU and is the author of many books and articles on literary criticism. He has worked on Latin American, Australian, and Slavic literature as well as British and American, and his forthcoming *Companion to the Australian Novel* will be published by Cambridge University Press in spring 2023.

Marialena Carr, born ninety-seven kilometers south of Barcelona, now lives due north from NYC. After two decades as an oceanographer, she turned to translating poetry and fiction-writing. *El Jo-Ull / The I-Eye* (Llibres del Segle), by Vicenç Altaió with her translations, came out in 2022. Translating a path through Felicia Fuster's collected poems is a plunge into the ocean deep, a barefoot walk on red-hot lava, and an olive tree's whisper.

Xavier Mas Craviotto (Navàs, Catalonia, 1996) studied Catalan Philology at the University of Barcelona and a postgraduate program on language consultancy and publishing services. For two years, he worked at the Research Center for Sociolinguistics and Communication (CUSC-UB). He is currently a lecturer at the University of Bristol, where he teaches Catalan language and culture, and also works as a proofreader for several publishing houses. He is one of the cofounders of "Com ho diria," a digital platform that specializes in slang used by young Catalan speakers. He is also an award-winning author of poetry and prose fiction. At the age of 17, he was a finalist in the Jordi Sierra i Fabra Literary Prize of Spain and Latin America and, since then, he has won around twenty narrative and poetry awards. His first novel, *La mort lenta* (The Slow Death) won the Documenta Prize in 2018. He has also published three poetry collections: *Renills de cavall negre* (Black Horse Neighs), which won the Salvador Iborra prize, *La gran nausea* (The

Great Nausea), and *La llum subterrània* (The Underground Light), which was awarded the Ausiàs March Prize in 2022. His short stories have been included in collaborative anthologies and he has participated in many poetry readings and panel discussions about language and literature.

Raül Garrigasait (Solsona, 1979) is an award-winning novelist, essayist, and translator. His novel *Els estranys* (2017) won both the Premi Llibreter and the Premi Òmnium, and was published in English in 2021. Garrigasait is a doctor in Classical Philology at the University of Barcelona and also acts as the director of La Casa del Clàssics. He is one of the leading figures of a new generation of Catalan writers.

Anna Gual has proven herself time and again as one of Catalunya's most vital poetic voices. From her first book, *Implosions* (LaBreu Edicions, 2008), to her eighth, *Les ocultacions* (Proa, 2022), Gual's exploration of the minute to the exponential, of the daily to the eternal, and the singular ways she writes this exploration, continues to surprise and draw in poets, readers, and critics alike. A regular at literary festivals and seminars, Gual's poetry has been widely anthologized and translated into several languages. Most recently published is *Innombrable*, a collected work translated into Spanish (Stendhal Books); this same selection is being translated into English by AKaiser. Reach out at https://annagual.cat & @annagual.

Based in Helsinki, Finland, David Hackston is a British translator of Finnish and Swedish literature and drama. He has worked in many genres, and notable recent publications include Katja Kettu's wartime epic *The Midwife* and six novels by 'Helsinki noir' author Antti Tuomainen, one of which, *Little Siberia*, won the 2020 Petrona Award for Best Scandinavian Crime Novel of the Year. David has translated all three novels by Pajtim Statovci, to considerable critical acclaim. In 2019 his translation of Statovci's *Crossing* was shortlisted for the National

Book Award, and in 2020 this translation was awarded the Oxford-Weidenfeld Prize for Literary Translation. In 2007 he was awarded the Finnish State Prize for Translation. David is also a professional countertenor and has studied early music and performance practice in both Finland and Portugal.

Rainer J. Hanshe is a writer and the founder and editor of Contra Mundum Press and *Hyperion: On the Future of Aesthetics*. He is the author of two novels, *The Acolytes* and *The Abdication*, and *Shattering the Muses*, a collaboration with visual artist Federico Gori. His translations include Charles Baudelaire's *My Heart Laid Bare, Belgium Stripped Bare*, and *Paris Spleen*, as well as other books & shorter pieces. Writings of his have appeared in *Sinn und Form, Caesura, Salt, ChrisMarker.org, Asymptote, Black Sun Lit*, & elsewhere. Recent work includes *Closing Melodies* (forthcoming 2023), a phantomatic encounter between Nietzsche and van Gogh, and *Beyond Sense* (in progress). His translation of Évelyne Grossman's *The Creativity of the Crisis* is due out in 2023.

James Hawkey (Cardiff, Wales, 1984) is Senior Lecturer in Spanish and Catalan Linguistics at the University of Bristol (UK). He received his PhD from Queen Mary, University of London in 2012 in Catalan linguistics, and has held teaching and research positions at the Sorbonne University (Paris), as well as the University of Bristol. As a translator, he has published technical translations from French and Spanish into English, and is currently working on an upcoming translation of Xavier Mas Craviotto's *La llum subterrània*.

Kari Hukkila writes in Finnish. He has published approximately 60 texts for theater, radio, and TV as well as essays and prose. His essay "An Algerian Friend," from *The Heretical Essays* (2010), was translated by Owen F. Witesman and published in *Hyperion* Vol. VII, No. 1 (2013). He also curated the Mallarmé project for *Hyperion*, which was published in two special issues: "Mallarmé: Part 1" (Vol. IX, No. 3

(2015)), and "Mallarmé: Part 2" (Vol. X, No. 1 (2017)). His novel *1000 & 1* (*Tuhat ja yksi*, 2016) is forthcoming from Contra Mundum Press (2023) in translation by David Hackston.

AKaiser, PhD, is a translator, scholar, and Pushcart Prize-nominated poet of <*glint*>, co-winner of the Milk & Cake Press Prize. Recent poems, prose, translations & photos are found or forthcoming in *Amsterdam Quarterly, Harvard Review, Ginosko, New Square, Poetry International* and Pen + Brush's *In Print* (No 5), guest edited by Novella Ford. AK~ translates from Catalan, French, and Spanish. Current translations include <*Unnamable*>, by Catalan poet Anna Gual, for which AK~ has been awarded an NEA Fellowship, and the works of Cebrià Montoliu (1873–1923), transatlantic urbanista, reformer, and translator of Ruskin, Emerson, and Whitman of whom she is writing a biography. Reach out at https://akexperiments.org & @akexperiments

Mark Kanak is an author, translator, and radioplay artist based in Berlin. Recent publications include *Tractatus illogico-insanus* (prose, Ritter Verlag, 2018), translation of Walter Serner's Dada masterpiece *Letzte Lockerung* (*Last Loosening*) into English (Twisted Spoon Press, 2020), and translation of Blixa Bargeld's *EUROPA KREUZWEISE* (*EUROPA CROSSWISE*), (Contra Mundum Press, 2022). Radioplay work: *Tollhaus* (2021) with Blixa Bargeld of Einstürzende Neubauten in the solo role (premiere Berlin Hörspiel Festival, current finalist for 2022 Radioplay of the Year). Upcoming: publication of the first ever translation of Rolf Dieter Brinkmann's only novel *No One Knows More* (Moloko Print, 2023) and also in 2023: *Lügendetektor/Lie Detector*, prose, Ritter Verlag.

Tiago Miller (London, 1987) is a writer and translator based in Lleida. He has worked on a number of translations of Catalan writers such as Pere Calders, Mercè Ibarz, Jordi Amat, Raül Garrigasait, and the theatre company La Calòrica. His translation of Montserrat Roig's *The Song of Youth* was shortlisted for the Republic of Consciousness Prize for book of the year and the Oxford-Weidenfeld Prize for translation of the year.

Vincent Kling has translated a number of Austrian authors, mainly Hugo von Hofmannsthal, Heimito von Doderer, Gert Jonke, and Werner Kofler, among others. He was awarded the Schlegel-Tieck Prize in 2013 and the Helen and Kurt Wolff Prize in 2021.

Salomé Monk is a sailor and wanderer who translates, if she is not on the road or at sea. Yet, that is generally always.

Mary Ann Newman (1951) translates from Catalan and Spanish into English. A graduate in Hispanic literatures of New York University, she has become one of the foremost voices on Catalan culture in the English-speaking world. She has translated fiction by Quim Monzó and Josep Maria de Sagarra, essay by Xavier Rubert de Ventós, and poetry by Josep Carner. Newman was awarded the Creu de Sant Jordi in 1998, the J.B. Cendrós International Award from Òmnium Cultural and the North American Catalan Society Award for Scholarship in 2016, and the Ramon Llull International Award in 2022. Her latest publication is *Final Judgements*, a book of aphorisms by the great Valencian essayist, Joan Fuster, in celebration of his centenary.

Núria Perpinyà (1961) is a Catalan writer of novels about architecture and music (*A House to Compose*), madness (*Mistana*), science and homosexuality (*A Good Mistake*), love and mountaineering (*To Vertigo*), museums (*The Privileged*), cultures in extinction (*The Calligraphers*), the internet (*And, Suddenly, Paradise*), and climate change (*Diatom*). As an essayist, notable work includes research about Chaos, Perspectivalism, mechanical reasoning, the Odyssey, and the aesthetic of ruins and the avant-garde.

Fritz Senn is the founding director of the Zürich James Joyce Foundation, as well as the founding editor of *European Joyce Studies* (Rodopi / Brill) and the *Wake Newslitter*, a journal specialized in *Finnegans Wake*. He has written on Joyce, translation, and subjects such as Ochlokinetics. He may have been the first to tackle translation issues in Joyce. He is a presence at all Joyce events, including the Dublin and Trieste Joyce Schools. His publications include *Joyce's Dislocutions: Essays on Reading as Translation*, ed. by John Paul Riquelme (1984); *Inductive Scrutinies: Essays on Joyce*, ed. by Christine O'Neill (1995); and *Ulysses Polytropos. Essays on James Joyce's Ulysses*, ed. by Frances Ilmberger (2022). He has also published *Joycean Murmoirs: Fritz Senn on James Joyce*, ed. Christine O'Neill (2007), and an extended interview, *Portals of Recovery. Fritz Senn on Reading: Joyce, Homer, Translation*, ed. by Erika Mihálycsa and Jolanta Wawrzycka (2017).

COLOPHON

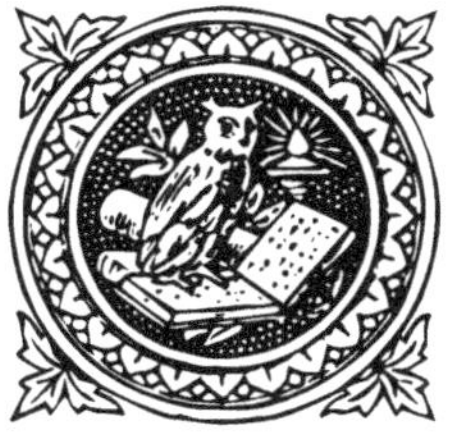

HYPERION: ON THE FUTURE OF AESTHETICS

was typeset in InDesign 5.

The text & page numbers are set in Auroc, Taull,

and Adobe Jenson Pro.

The titles are set in a variation of Auroc & Taull.

Images: The Pepe Sales images (174–183) are taken from *La passió segons Pepe Sales* (LaBreu Edicions, 2019). Reprint permission has been granted by Martí Sales. All other images are public domain.

Cover image credit: Martí Sales © 2022

Design & typesetting: Giuseppe Bertolini

Cover design: CMP

The editors would like to extend their gratitude to McCoy, Adrien Stalter, Pierre Joris, Tiago Miller and Martí Sales, Núria Perpinyà, and most especially to Jadranka Vrsalovic Carevic.

HYPERION: ON THE FUTURE OF AESTHETICS

is published by Contra Mundum Press

CONTRA MUNDUM PRESS

Dedicated to the value & the indispensable importance of the individual voice, to testing the boundaries of thought & experience.

The primary aim of Contra Mundum is to publish translations of writers who in their use of form and style are *à rebours*, or who deviate significantly from more programmatic & spurious forms of experimentation. Such writing attests to the volatile nature of modernism. Our preference is for works that have not yet been translated into English, are out-of-print, or are poorly translated, for writers whose thinking & aesthetics are in opposition to timely or mainstream currents of thought, value systems, or moralities. We also reprint obscure and out-of-print works we consider significant but which have been forgotten, neglected, or overshadowed.

There are many works of fundamental significance to *Weltliteratur* (and *Weltkultur*) that still remain in relative oblivion, works that alter and disrupt standard circuits of thought — these warrant being encountered by the world at large. It is our aim to render them more visible.

For the complete list of forthcoming publications, please visit our website. To be added to our mailing list, send your name and email address to: info@contramundum.net

Contra Mundum Press
P.O. Box 1326
New York, NY 10276
USA

https://contramundumpress.com

HYPERION: ON THE FUTURE OF AESTHETICS

To read samples and order any back issue of *Hyperion*, visit:

https://contramundumpress.com/hyperion

Contra Mundum Press Titles

2012

Gilgamesh

Ghérasim Luca, *Self-Shadowing Prey*

Rainer J. Hanshe, *The Abdication*

Walter Jackson Bate, *Negative Capability*

Miklós Szentkuthy, *Marginalia on Casanova*

Fernando Pessoa, *Philosophical Essays*

2013

Elio Petri, *Writings on Cinema & Life*

Friedrich Nietzsche, *The Greek Music Drama*

Richard Foreman, *Plays with Films*

Louis-Auguste Blanqui, *Eternity by the Stars*

Miklós Szentkuthy, *Towards the One & Only Metaphor*

Josef Winkler, *When the Time Comes*

2014

William Wordsworth, *Fragments*

Josef Winkler, *Natura Morta*

Fernando Pessoa, *The Transformation Book*

Emilio Villa, *The Selected Poetry of Emilio Villa*

Robert Kelly, *A Voice Full of Cities*

Pier Paolo Pasolini, *The Divine Mimesis*

Miklós Szentkuthy, *Prae, Vol. 1*

2015

Federico Fellini, *Making a Film*

Robert Musil, *Thought Flights*

Sándor Tar, *Our Street*

Lorand Gaspar, *Earth Absolute*

Josef Winkler, *The Graveyard of Bitter Oranges*

Ferit Edgü, *Noone*

Jean-Jacques Rousseau, *Narcissus*

Ahmad Shamlu, *Born Upon the Dark Spear*

2016

Jean-Luc Godard, *Phrases*

Otto Dix, *Letters*

Maura Del Serra, *Ladder of Oaths*

Pierre Senges, *The Major Refutation*

Charles Baudelaire, *My Heart Laid Bare & Other Texts*

2017

Joseph Kessel, *Army of Shadows*

Rainer J. Hanshe, *Shattering the Muses*

Gérard Depardieu, *Innocent*

Claude Mouchard, *Entangled — Papers! — Notes*

2018

Miklós Szentkuthy, *Black Renaissance*

Adonis, *Conversations in the Pyrenees*

2019

Charles Baudelaire, *Belgium Stripped Bare*

Robert Musil, *Unions*

Iceberg Slim, *Night Train to Sugar Hill*

Marquis de Sade, *Aline & Valcour, Vols I–III*

2020

A City Full of Voices: Essays on Robert Kelly

Rédoine Faïd, *Outlaw: Author Armed & Dangerous*

Carmelo Bene, *I Appeared to the Madonna*

Paul Celan, *Microliths They Are, Little Stones*

Zsuzsa Selyem, *It's Raining in Moscow*

Bérengère Viennot, *Trumpspeak*

Robert Musil, *Theater Symptoms*

Miklós Szentkuthy, *Chapter on Love*

Dejan Lukić, *The Oyster* * AGRODOLCE SERIES

2021

Charles Baudelaire, *Paris Spleen*

Marguerite Duras, *The Darkroom*

Andrew Dickos, *Honor Among Thieves*

Pierre Senges, *Ahab (Sequels)*

Carmelo Bene, *Our Lady of the Turks*

Fernando Pessoa, *Writings on Art & Poetical Theory*

2022

Miklós Szentkuthy, *Prae, Vol. II*

Blixa Bargeld, *Europe Crosswise: A Litany*

Ugo Tognazzi, *The Injester* * AGRODOLCE SERIES

Pierre Joris with Florent Toniello, *Always the Many, Never the One*

Robert Musil, *Literature & Politics*

www.ingramcontent.com/pod-product-compliance
Lightning Source LLC
LaVergne TN
LVHW052351100826
845147LV00013B/810

* 9 7 8 1 9 4 0 6 2 5 5 9 1 *